I0037638

Investment Terms

Financial Education Is Your Best Investment

Published February 09, 2020

Revision 2.2

Financial Terms Dictionary

Copyright And Trademark Notices

Limits of Liability and Disclaimer of Warranties

The materials in this book are provided "as is" and without warranties of any kind either express or implied. The Author disclaims all warranties, express or implied, including, but not limited to, implied warranties of merchantability and fitness for a particular purpose.

The Author does not warrant that defects will be corrected, or that that the site or the server that makes this eBook available are free of viruses or other harmful components. The Author does not warrant or make any representations regarding the use or the results of the use of the materials in this book in terms of their correctness, accuracy, reliability, or otherwise. Applicable law may not allow the exclusion of implied warranties, so the above exclusion may not apply to you.

Under no circumstances, including, but not limited to, negligence, shall the Author be liable for any special or consequential damages that result from the use of, or the inability to use this eBook, even if the Author or his authorized representative has been advised of the possibility of such damages.

Applicable law may not allow the limitation or exclusion of liability or incidental or consequential damages, so the above limitation or exclusion may not apply to you. In no event shall the Author's total liability to you for all damages, losses, and causes of action (whether in contract, tort, including but not limited to, negligence or otherwise) exceed the amount paid by you, if any, for this eBook.

Facts and information are believed to be accurate at the time they were placed in this book. All data provided in this book is to be used for information purposes only. The information contained within is not intended to provide specific legal, financial or tax advice, or any other advice whatsoever, for any individual or company and should not be relied upon in that regard. The services described are only offered in jurisdictions where they may be legally offered. Information provided is not all-inclusive and is limited to information that is made available and such information should not be relied upon as all-inclusive or accurate.

You are advised to do your own due diligence when it comes to making business decisions and should use caution and seek the advice of qualified professionals. You should check with your accountant, lawyer, or professional advisor, before acting on this or any information. You may not consider any examples, documents, or other content in this eBook or otherwise provided by the Author to be the equivalent of professional advice.

The Author assumes no responsibility for any losses or damages resulting from your use of any link, information, or opportunity contained in this book or within any other information disclosed by the author in any form whatsoever.

About the Author

Thomas Herold is a successful entrepreneur, mediator, author, and personal development coach. He published over 35 books with over 200,000 copies distributed worldwide and the founder of seven online businesses.

For over ten years Thomas Herold has studied the monetary system and has experienced some profound insights on how money and wealth are related. After three years of successful investing in silver, he released 'Building Wealth with Silver - How to Profit From The Biggest Wealth Transfer in History' in 2012. One of the first books that illustrate in a remarkable, simple way the monetary system and its consequences.

He is the founder and CEO of the 'Financial Terms Dictionary' book series and website, which explains in detail and comprehensive form over 1000 financial terms. In his financial book series, he informs in detail and with practical examples all aspects of the financial sector. His educational materials are designed to help people get started with financial education.

In his 2018 released book 'The Money Deception', Mr. Herold provides the most sophisticated insight and shocking details about the current monetary system. Never before has the massive manipulation of money caused so much economic inequality in the world. In spite of these frightening facts, 'The Money Deception' also provides remarkable and simple solutions to create abundance for all people, and it's a must-read if you want to survive the global monetary transformation that's underway right now.

In 2019 he released an entirely new financial book series explaining in detail and with practical examples over 1000 financial terms. The 'Herold Financial IQ Series' contains currently of 16 titles covering every category of the financial market.

His latest book "High Credit Score Secrets" offers the most effective strategies to boost the average credit score from as low as 450 points to over 810. It teaches the tactics to build excellent credit, repair credit, monitor credit and how to guard that good score for a lifetime. It reached bestseller status in 2020 in three categories.

For more information please visit the author's websites:

High Credit Score Secrets - The Smart Raise & Repair Guide to Excellent
Credit
https://highcreditscoresecrets.com

The Money Deception - What Banks & Government Don't Want You to
Know
https://www.moneydeception.com

The Herold Financial IQ Series - Financial Education Is Your Best
Investment
https://www.financial-dictionary.com

The Online Financial Dictionary - Over 1000 Terms Explained
https://www.financial-dictionary.info

Please Leave Your Review on Amazon

This book and the Financial IQ Series are self-published and the author does not have a contract with one of the five largest publishers, which are able to support the author's work with advertising. If you like this book, please consider leaving a solid 4 or 5-star review on Amazon.

Herold Financial IQ Series on Amazon

Table Of Contents

401(k) Plan

401k retirement plans are specific kinds of accounts that the government established to help individuals to plan and save for retirement. Individuals fund these accounts using pre-taxed dollars from payrolls.

People invest money in these accounts into several different types of investments. These include stocks, mutual funds, and bonds. Gains earned in the account include dividends, capital gains, and interest. These gains do not get taxed until the owners withdraw the funds.

The name of the 401k comes from the portion of Internal Revenue Service Code which pertains to it. This vehicle for saving for retirement began in 1981 when an act of Congress created it.

There are a number of benefits to 401k accounts that recommend them to individuals. Five of these include tax benefits, flexibility of investments, employer matching programs, loan abilities, and portability.

The advantageous tax benefits are one of the main reasons that 401k plans are so popular. Money contributed does not become taxable until individuals withdraw it. Similarly gains accrued in the account are also tax-deferred. Over several decades, this makes a significant difference in the amount of money that people can save.

Investments that the IRS allows in these 401k retirement plans provide some flexibility. Those who do not want to take on much risk can choose to put more of their funds into shorter term bonds which are lower risk. Others who are more concerned with developing wealth over the long term can put a larger percentage of the money into equities like stocks and mutual funds. Company stock can also be acquired at a discount with many employers.

A tremendous edge that these 401k retirement plans provide their owners is the employer match feature. A great number of employers match their employees' contributions as a company benefit. This is done on a percentage basis. Newer employees may receive a 25% of contributions match, while employees who have been at a company longer may receive 50% or even 100% matches. Matches are only made on a certain maximum percentage of income that an employee contributes. This is the closest thing to free money a person can obtain at work.

Loan abilities from 401k retirements are a helpful feature for individuals in times of need. When people find themselves needing money with no other place to turn, the government permits them to obtain 401k loans from the plan. The plan administrator has to approve it as well. Loans from 401k plans are not taxed or penalized so long as they are repaid according to the repayment schedule and terms.

There are no restrictions on the uses of such loans. Some employers have minimum amounts that can be borrowed of $1,000 and a maximum number of loans an employee can take at a time. Sometimes employees will have to get their spouse's written consent before the company will issue the loan.

There are limits on the amount of a balance that can be borrowed. This is typically as much as 50% of the vested balance to no more than $50,000. When an employer will not allow an employee to take out a loan against the plan, hardship withdrawals can be requested. These are taxed and also penalized at a 10% rate.

Portability means the 401k retirement plan can go with the employees as they change jobs. Investors have four different choices for their 401k plan when they move to another company. They can choose to leave the plan with the old employer and pay any administration fees for the account staying there. They might instead do a rollover of their account to the new employer's 401k retirement plan.

A third option is to convert the 401k retirement plan into an Individual Retirement Account. Finally they might decide to close the 401k and receive the proceeds in cash. This would mean all money would be subject to taxes and the 10% penalty fee.

403(b) Plan

403(b) plans were created for employees of schools, churches, and tax exempt organizations. Individuals who are eligible may establish and maintain their own 403(b) accounts. Their employers can and often do make contributions to the employees' accounts. Individuals are able to open one of three different types of 403(b)s.

The first is an annuity plan that an insurance company establishes. These types of plans are sometimes called TDAs tax deferred annuities or TSAs tax sheltered annuities. A second plan type is an account which a retirement custodian offers and manages. With these 403(b)s, the account holders may only choose from mutual funds and regulated investment companies that the custodian allows. The final type is a retirement income account. These accounts accept a combination of mutual funds or annuities for the investment choices.

Employers have some control over these accounts. They are able to decide which financial institution will hold the employees' 403(b) accounts. This determines the kind of plan that the employees are able to set up and fund. Employers receive several advantages from choosing to offer a 403(b).

The benefits which they get to offer their employees are worthwhile. This helps to ensure valuable employees stay with the organization. They also enjoy sharing the funding costs between themselves and their employees. Employers may also choose for the 403(b) to only accept employee contributions if they do not wish to participate financially in the account.

Employees also experience several benefits from these types of retirement vehicles. They may contribute tax deferred dollars from their income. They may also contribute taxed dollars to the accounts. In these Roth 403(b)s, all of their earnings accrue tax free for the entire life of the account. Deferred tax payments until retirement typically allow for the employees to pay fewer taxes as they are often in a more advantageous tax bracket at retirement point. Employees may also obtain loans from their 403(b) accounts as they need them.

A variety of non profit organizations may choose to establish such a 403(b) plan for their employees. This includes any 501(c)(3) tax exempt organization, co-op hospital service organizations, public school systems, ministers at churches, Native American public school systems, and (USUHS) Uniformed Services for the University of the Health Sciences.

Such 403(b) plans can obtain a variety of contribution types. Employees may have elective deferral contributions taken out of each paycheck. These are taken out in a pretax dollars arrangement. Employees also have the ability to contribute taxed dollars to the accounts. They have these deducted from their payrolls as well.

Employers may also choose to make contributions which are either discretionary or fixed amounts as they desire. Employees and employers may make contributions to Roth 403(b) accounts. These 403(b) accounts may also receive any combination of the previously mentioned contribution types, which demonstrates their flexibility.

Employees have generous annual contribution limits with these plans. In 2016, they may contribute up to $18,000 (or $24,000 if they are over 50 years old and catching up on contributions for retirement). For 2016, employers may also deposit as much as $53,000 (up to 100% of the employee compensation) as an annual contribution.

Regarding distributions, the rules are comparable to the other types of retirement savings vehicles. Distributions of deferred taxed dollars become taxable like regular income when the employee receives them. If these are taken before the employee turns 59 ½, then the withdrawn dollars are assessed the standard 10% penalty for early withdrawals. There are some exceptions to this penalty for which an employee may qualify. One of these exceptions is if the employee terminates the job even before reaching the age of retirement.

408(k) Plan

The 408(k) Plan is a retirement plan that employers set up to assist their employees in saving money for their post working years. It is named for the section of the IRS code that describes these accounts. Though there are some distinctions, a 408(k) Plan is actually a simpler version of the ever popular 401(k) plan.

These 408(k)'s are intended for smaller companies which employ fewer than 25 staff. Self employed individuals are also able to take advantage of these plans. SEP Simplified Employee Pensions are another name for the 408(k)'s.

These plans are practical and useful for workers because they are able to contribute dollars that have not yet been taxed. In addition to helping them save for retirement, it lowers their net incomes for the tax year in question. This can reduce the tax bracket into which the employees fall. It leads to lower taxes for the individuals who contribute. The deposits do not become taxable as income until the point where the employees take their money back in the form of distributions.

Employers are also able to contribute funds to the account on behalf of the employees and in their names. The employer contributions are similarly tax deductible. Besides providing the employer with a nice benefit to offer their workers, it saves them on their annual company tax bill as well. Though these accounts are set up by employers, they remain in the name of the employees and for their sole benefits.

408(k) plans share many features with their 401(k) cousins. The 408(k)'s are somewhat simpler to understand, set up, and utilize. Both plans have yearly maximum contribution limits. With these plans, the employees also do not pay any taxes for contributions which the employer makes in the account. Both accounts are also tax deferred.

Taxes will only become due when the employee takes distributions at the retirement age starting at 59 and a half. Until that point, none of the money they contribute will be treated like income. There are some limitations and restrictions on these kinds of accounts. They can be utilized by self employed individuals and smaller companies. They may not be set up by larger companies which count more than 25 employees.

Employees can not contribute more than the maximum annual limit to these accounts. If they do, the surplus dollars will be treated as income, taxed, and also penalized by 10%. Money which an employee takes out early before retirement age is also subject to taxes and 10% penalties.

There is an exception to this early withdrawal rule. If an employee feels the financial need, he or she is allowed to take money back without penalties on a loan basis only. 408(k) plans do allow for such loans, provided that they are repaid. The money must be paid back to the account according to a payment schedule set up with the plan administrator. In the even that it is not put back, the loan amount becomes treated as an early withdrawal distribution. In this case, the full tax and 10% penalty amount will apply to the total loan principle.

The maximum contribution amounts to the 408(k) Plans vary by year. The IRS increases the limits from time to time to compensate for projected inflation. When employees reach 50, they are allowed to increase their contributions per year to an IRS allowed larger dollar amount. This is to help them to catch up on any contributions which they may have missed out on over the years.

412(i) Plan

412(i) Plans are pension plans that are classified as qualified defined benefit arrangements. They were established by the IRS for small companies and self employed business owners to have a way to save for their retirement and those of their employees. Employers fund these plans with only fixed annuities or both annuities and permanent life insurance.

For the 412(i) Plans to be qualified and legal, they must meet the standards for these kinds of plans. This includes non discrimination rules and eligibility requirements. All employees of the firm who are over 20 years old must be included if they have worked there for at least a year.

These plans have become more popular with time. This is in part because employers fund them with guaranteed investments. When they contribute fixed annuities, the retirement benefits are figured by utilizing the annuity's guaranteed purchase rate. If life insurance contracts are contributed, benefits are based on the guaranteed cash accumulation of the policies. One advantage this gives the small business owner is the ability to fund contributions in dollar amounts which are larger than the amounts that competing qualified plans allow. The contributions they make are also tax deductible. This reduces the tax burden for the contribution year.

There are several benefits that these plans feature. The monthly benefit for the account holder is guaranteed. They create large income tax deductions for the benefits of the employers. Besides this these plans offer significant death benefits for the account holders. These mean that these 412(i) Plans provide small businesses with an attractive package for obtaining and keeping important talent. They also help the small company's employees who can count on the guaranteed and fixed benefits at retirement.

412(i) Plans are special because they do not have to live up to complicated rules for funding them adequately. There are also no yearly actuarial requirements to certify that the plan is properly funded. The guaranteed parts of the fixed annuities and life insurance vehicles ensure that these defined benefit plans will be solvent. The only requirement to ensure that this happens is for the employer to continuously pay the annual policy or annuity premiums.

The life insurance company provides all of the guarantees that the plan requires. One important feature of these and other defined benefit plans is that they do not always allow account holders to take loans out of the plan. The Pension Protection Act of 2006 set out many of the standards for these plans and also provided an alternative number of 412(e)(3) for them.

If annuity policies yield a greater amount of dividends or interest than is guaranteed, this benefits the employer. The plan rules stipulate that the extra payments credit against upcoming premiums. If the life insurance contract offers dividends, these are also applied against premiums in the future. They do not go to the account holder, but always to reduce the premiums of the 412(i) Plans.

There are important reasons that employers choose to include a contract of life insurance in such 412(i) Plans. They offer fully tax deductible ways of giving the small business owner and employees death benefits. When the beneficiary receives this benefit, the face value minus the cash value (of the policy's death benefit) distributes as a tax free income. This life insurance contained within the plan gives the account holders valuable estate liquidity that it will likely need after they have passed away.

The insurance companies which offer the annuity contract or the insurance policy for the plan do not usually provide administration for the 412(i) Plans. This service is typically supplied by IRS approved third party administrators.

457(b) Plan

A 457(b) plan is a retirement savings vehicle. It derives its name from the Internal Revenue Service code that regulates the plans in its section 457(b). Many times this retirement account name is simply shortened to 457 Plan.

There are many similarities between these 457 Plans and tax deferred, employer provided retirement vehicles including 403(b) and 401(k) plans. All of these retirement vehicles are defined contribution plans. People who participate in these 457 Plans set up payroll deductions so that a portion of their income is put into this investment account that is tax free.

The government established these 457 Plans in 1978. They were set up to be another defined contribution account that would help two particular kinds of employers. They are intended for both government employers and non government employers which are tax exempt as with hospitals and charities.

Despite this fact, a few different rules apply for the government plans as opposed to the non government plans. The principle difference revolves around funding. Government 457 Plans have to be funded by the employer in question. The non government 457 Plans are practically all funded by employees. The vast majority of 457(b) plans that private not for profit companies use they only offer to well paid employees usually in upper level management.

With 457 Plans, there must be both a plan administrator and a plan provider. Each plan provides its own limited choices for investment options which are particular to the plan.

Rollover rules are different for these 457 Plans as well. The non government versions can not be transferred over to qualified retirement plans which include IRA and 401(k)s. Instead they can only be rolled over to other tax exempt 457 Plans. The rules are different with government sponsored employer plans. These may be transferred into another employer's 401(k), 403(b), or 457(b) plan as well as to an IRA account. The new plan must permit account holders to make such transfers.

Withdrawals are easier for government sponsored plans as well. Individuals may do early withdrawals before they reach the 59 ½ year old age of retirement and not have to suffer the 10% early withdrawal penalty. The full withdrawn amount would be taxed as regular income. Employees who are switching jobs may also keep the money where it is assuming the plan permits this.

Rollover rules on 457(b) plans are pretty standard. If funds are dispersed to the account owner, he or she has a maximum of 60 days to finish the rollover process. Beyond this time, the IRS considers this money to have been distributed and to be taxable. Owners are also restricted to doing a single rollover in a calendar year with these retirement vehicles.

The date on which the owners receive their 457 Plan distribution is when the one year rule commences. While the money is in the 60 day process of being rolled over, it may not be invested. Direct rollovers avoid the dangers of the 60 day rule. An account holder never obtains a distribution check (as with indirect rollovers) in this type of transfer. Instead, the plan provider will directly transfer all money to the new IRA or retirement plan.

Investment choices in 457 Plans are more limited than with Self Directed IRAs or Solo 401(k) plans. The plan provider will restrict choices to ones that fit their plan. If they permit them, owners may invest their funds in individual bonds and stocks, fixed or indexed annuities, exchange traded funds, and mutual funds.

Gold bullion can not be purchased by these plans. Paper gold investments such as stocks of gold mining firms, mutual funds containing gold mining companies, or gold ETFs like GLD and mining ETFs may be purchased instead.

Agency Bonds

Agency bonds are those bonds that are actually issued by United States' government sponsored entities. This means that these bonds are not government guaranteed, as they are created by private companies. They are backed up implicitly by the United States government, since these organizations were created to permit some categories of individuals to have the ability to receive lower cost financing, in particular first time home buyers and students.

The biggest, best recognized names in Agency Bond issuers prove to be Sallie Mae, Freddie Mac, and Fannie Mae. These three large companies are different from government agencies in that they are not guaranteed by the United States' government's promise of full faith and credit. Instead, they are all privately held and run companies that are given government charters as a result of their critical activities that carry out government directed policies.

Agency bonds are used to raise money to help these companies offer farm loans, home loans, student loans, and international trade financing. As a result of the government deeming these activities to be significant enough to grant charters, the markets consider that the Federal Government will not permit these chartered firms to go under. This gives their agency bonds the implied government sponsored entity guarantee. As a result of this implicit guarantee, these agency bonds carry ratings and yields that are comparable to government issued debt.

As an example, Private Export Funding Corporation bonds prove to be backed up by actual collateral of United States government securities. Federal Farm Credit Banks' bonds are not, although it is a government sponsored entity. Despite the differences, the yield-to-maturity of the two bonds are 4.753% and 4.760% respectively. These two organizations' debt obligations are nearly priced the same, demonstrating once again the implicit guarantee in the government sponsored entity securities.

The issue of taxation is another important one to consider when you are looking at Agency Bonds. All agency bonds are taxable on Federal levels. Many are not taxed on state levels. This is critical if you are an investor who resides in a state that has its own taxes. The interest payments from the best known of these organizations like Freddie Mac and Fannie Mae can be taxed on a state level. The majority of others agency bonds avoid this taxation, making their rates more attractive for many investors.

The vast majority of all agency bonds outstanding, more than ninety percent, are issued by only the four largest government sponsored entities. By largest size, these are Federal Home Loan Banks, Federal Home Loan Mortgage Corporation, Federal National Mortgage Association, and Federal Farm Credit Banks. The Federal Home Loan Banks' and Federal Farm Credit Banks' agency bonds are not state income taxable.

Amortization

The word amortization is one that is commonly utilized by financial officers of corporations and accountants. They utilize it when they are working with time concepts and how they relate to financial statements of accounts. You typically hear this word employed when you are figuring up loan calculations, or when you are determining interest payments.

The concept of amortization possesses a lengthy history and it is currently employed in numerous different segments of finance. The word itself descends from Middle English. Here amortisen meant to "alienate" or "kill" something. This derivation itself comes from the Latin admortire that signified "plus death." It is loosely related to the derivation of the word mortgage, as well.

This accounting principle is much like depreciation that diminishes a liability or asset's value over a given period of time through payments. It covers the practical life span of a tangible asset. With liabilities, it includes a pre-set amount of time over which money is paid back. Like this, a certain amount of money is set aside for the loan repayment over its lifetime.

Even though depreciation is similar to amortization, they are not the same concepts. The main difference between them lies in what they cover. While depreciation is most commonly employed to describe physical assets like property, vehicles, or buildings, amortization instead covers intangibles such as product development, copyrights, or patents. Where liabilities are concerned, it relates to income in the future that will be paid out over a given amount of time. Depreciation is instead a lost income over a time period.

Several different kinds of amortization are presently in use. This varies with the accounting method that is practiced. Business amortization deals with borrowed funds and loans and the paying of particular amounts in different time frames. When used as amortization analysis, this is the means of cost execution analysis for a given group of operations. Where tax law is concerned, amortization pertains to the interest amount that is paid over a given span of time relevant to payments and tax rates.

Amortization can also be employed with regards to zoning rules and regulations, since it conveys a property owner's time for relocating as a result of zoning guidelines and pre-existing use. Another variation is used as negative amortization. This pertains specifically to increasing loan amounts that result from total interest due not being paid up at the appropriate time.

Amortization can also be employed over a widely ranging time frame. It could cover only a year or extend to as many as forty years. This depends on the kind of loan or asset utilized. Some examples include building loans that span over as many as forty years and car loans that commonly span over merely four to five years. Asset examples would be patent right expenses that commonly are spread out over seventeen years.

Angel Investor

An Angel Investor refers to an accredited investor (with over a million dollars net worth) which invests funds into entrepreneurs and smaller startups. These special investors are commonly from the friends or family of the entrepreneur. This capital which they deliver is often in the form of a lump sum one-time payment to help get the business going or to keep it funded during the challenging early stages where they are still developing and beginning to market their products.

Another characteristic of such an Angel Investor is that they offer better terms to the startup than would a comparable bank or lender in the same scenario. This is principally because they believe in the entrepreneur they are backing more than the viability of the business itself. Such investors concentrate their efforts on assisting startups with successfully making their initial business steps. They are less concerned with the potential for profit they might make off of the fledgling company. This makes most Angel Investors the diametric opposite of the venture capitalists.

There are a variety of different names which such Angel Investors go by. These include angel funders, informal investors, private investors, business angels, and seed investors. Such wealthy individuals who choose to inject desperately needed startup capital into firms do so in exchange for either convertible debt or a stake in the company's equity. There are such investors who become involved through one of the various crowd funding platforms over the Internet, and others who join with networks of other Angel Investors in order to pool their resources to be more effective (as with an Angel Investor syndicate). Angel List is a popular and well respected site that puts together angels and entrepreneurs.

Using this phrase to describe noble investors originally came from Broadway Theater. It was here that wealthy patrons would contribute money in order to advance theatrical productions. This terminology Angel Investor was first utilized by William Wetzel of the University of New Hampshire. As founder of the Center for Venture Research, he backed an extensive study on the ways that entrepreneurs are able to bring in capital.

In order to be official Angel Investors, these individuals have to meet the definition set by the SEC Securities Exchange Commission for accredited investors. This means that the interested party must possess at least a million in net worth along with an annual income amounting to at least $200,000.

Most Angel Investors will actually deploy their own funds in their investments. This puts them in direct contrast with the venture capitalists which instead gather up a pool of money from many investors and then combine this into a fund which is strategically managed. In general the Angel Investors represent actual individuals. It is also possible for the entity offering the funding to be a limited liability company, trust, business or even an investment fund.

Those Angel Investors who actually seed the entrepreneurs' startups which ultimately fail will lose their entire investment. It helps to explain why angel investors who are professionals will always be on the hunt for a clearly defined exit strategy opportunity. This might be through an IPO Initial Public Offering or an acquisition.

In truth, successful angel investors boast of portfolios with an average success rate of from 20 percent to 30 percent. This may sound costly for entrepreneurs who are involved in early stage business startups. Finding alternative cheaper sources of financing like banks are not often viable options for these fledging companies. It means that angels are often the ideal funder or backer for those entrepreneurs who find themselves still in the financially struggling days of the early startup stages in their company.

Annual Percentage Yield (APY)

APY describes the amount of compound interest which individuals or businesses will earn in a given year (or longer time period). Investments in money market accounts, savings accounts, and CD Certificates of Deposit all pay out such interest. It is the annual percentage yield that demonstrates precisely the amount in interest individuals will receive. This is helpful for people or businesses trying to ascertain which investments and banks offer superior returns by comparing and contrasting their real yields. In general, higher Annual Percentage Yields are better to have (unless one is comparing interest on credit card debts).

This APY is practical to understand and measure simply because it considers compound interest and the miracle of compounding within any account. Simple interest rates do not do this. Compounding is simply earning interest on interest that has already accrued and been paid. It signifies that individuals are gaining a greater amount in interest than the corresponding interest rate literally indicates.

It is always a good idea to consider a real world example for clarification purposes. If Fred deposits $10,000 into a particular savings account that provides a two percent yearly interest rate, then at the end of that first year Fred will have $10,200. This assumes that the interest is paid one time per year. If the bank were to figure up and pay out the interest on a daily basis, it would increase the amount to $10,202. The extra $2 may seem small, but given a longer time frame of from 10 to 30 years, this amount can add up, particularly if larger deposits are involved.

APY should never be confused with APR. They have some similarities, but APR does not consider compounding. It is once again a simpler means of computing interest. Credit card loans are an area where it is important to understand the differences between annual percentage rate and annual percentage yield. When people carry a balance, they will be paying higher APY's then the APR the firm actually quotes. This is because interest is assessed monthly, which means that interest on the interest will be computed on each following month.

The key to obtaining a better APY on investments and savings accounts lies in getting as frequent a compounding period as possible. Quarterly compounding is better than annually, yet daily is the most superior form of compounding possible. This means that as individuals are looking to increase their APY's personally, it is important to have the money compounding as frequently as they can practically achieve.

When two CD Certificates of Deposit pay out the same rate, it is best to select that one which actually pays out both more frequently and also boasts the greater APY. With CD's, the interest payments become automatically reinvested. More frequent reinvestment is always better. This will help any individual or business to earn a greater amount of interest on the interest payments already earned and paid out.

Calculating the annual percentage yield is not an easy task. Business calculators as well as computer algorithms mostly do it for people nowadays. The simplest way to find the APY for a given account is to plug in the information including the initial deposit, compounding frequency period, interest rate, and amount of overall time for the period considered. These smart calculators will then tell you both the effective annual percentage yield as well as the ending balance on the hypothetical account at the end of the given time period.

Annuity

An annuity is an investment contract that an insurance company sells to individuals. This agreement promises that it will make a regular series and dollar amount of payments to the buyer. This can be either for the rest of his or her life or for a set amount of time. The payments out are typically made after the individual retires.

Annuities have a long past that began in the Roman Empire. Roman citizens could purchase annual contracts from the Roman Emperor. The empire would then make annual payments to the citizens for the remainder of their lives. European governments revived the sale of annuities in the 1600s. They sold lump sum contracts to investors to help pay for expensive wars.

These investors also received a number of prearranged payments back from the governments that sold them. Annuities in America started as a way to support church ministries. 1912 saw the first annuity contract that was offered to the general American public by a Pennsylvania life insurance firm. These contracts continued to evolve and grow throughout the 1950s until they became commonplace in the 1980s.

Annuities offer certain tax advantages to their owners. Annuity holders only pay taxes on their contributions when they begin to take withdrawals or distributions from the funds. Every annuity contract is tax deferred. This signifies that investment earnings in such annuity accounts continue to grow tax deferred until the owners withdraw them. This also means that annuity earnings may not be taken out without paying a penalty until the owner reaches the set age of 59 1/2.

There are two general types of annuities contracts. Fixed annuities pledge to provide a guaranteed payment amount. Variable annuities do not make this guarantee. They do offer the possibility of earning higher returns in the variable annuity. Experts consider either type of annuity to be a safe but low yielding investment vehicle.

Annuities have a specific purpose. Companies developed them in order to insure the owner against the possibility of living longer than his or her retirement income. This is known as superannuation. The idea behind annuities is to help offset this risk of outliving retirement funds.

Annuities are popular with conservative investors because they continue to make payments until the holder dies. Even when the payments surpass the amount that remains in the annuity, the payments continue to be made. They are always counted as retirement savings vehicles.

The two phases of annuities are the accumulation and the distribution periods. During the accumulation phase, owners do one of two things. They can make a large lump sum payment into the annuity. They may also make regular payments into the contract. If the owner dies in this accumulation period, the heirs are given the amount of money that the owner paid into the annuity contract. Taxes owed would include estate taxes and regular income taxes.

When the owner reaches the retirement age, annuitization happens and distribution begins. At this point, the accumulated amounts convert into annuity units. The owner is changing the lump sum amount in the contract for the guaranteed series of payments. At this point he or she no longer has access to the large single amount in the account. The guaranteed income for life begins in this distribution phase.

Owners can receive their benefits as one of several options. Straight Life contracts pay calculated sums that are only based on the owner's life expectancy. These payments stop when the owner dies even if a lesser amount than the contract value is distributed. Life with Period Certain option makes payments for a minimum amount of time up to the death of the owner. Joint Life option pays benefits until both owners have died. Joint Life with Period Certain option gives payments for a guaranteed minimum amount of time until both owners have died.

Asset Allocation

Asset allocation involves diversifying an investor portfolio into a variety of different assets based on the appropriate level of risk. This procedure has investors divide up their investments between varying types of assets. Among these might be stocks, real estate, bonds, and cash.

The goal is to maximize the reward and risk balance using the investors' own goals and scenarios. This has become one of the critical ideas behind money management and financial planning today. There are several different types of asset allocation to consider. These are strategic, tactical, and dynamic.

In strategic asset allocation, the investor sets out target allocations for the desired different classes of assets. When the percentage balance deviates from the original set levels, it will involve the investor rebalancing the overall portfolio. The allocations will be reset to the original ones as they change significantly because of different returns that each class earns.

Strategic asset allocation sets these initial allocations up using a number of different considerations. Among these are the investor objectives, the intended time frame of investing, and the risk tolerance. These allocations can be changed in time as the different variables alter.

A good comparison to this form of allocating is a traditional buy and hold investment strategy. This form of strategic allocating of assets and the tactical allocation approach are both derived from modern portfolio theory. They seek diversification so that they can lower risk and boost the returns on portfolios.

Tactical asset allocating is more active than strategic forms of the discipline. Investors who follow tactical allocating will re-balance the asset percentages in different categories on a more regular basis. They will do this in an effort to benefit from market sectors that are stronger or poised for gains. They might also re-balance in an effort to capture anomalies in market pricing.

Tactical allocating is well suited to professional portfolio managers. They study the markets and look to find extra returns from scenarios that develop. This is still only considered to be a strategy that is moderately active. When the short term gains are attained, these managers go back to the original strategic asset balance of the portfolio.

Investors or managers who look for tactical asset allocators often choose ETF exchange traded funds or index funds for this purpose. The goal of these vehicles concentrates on asset classes rather than individual investments. This reduces the costs of rebalancing. The transaction costs of buying and selling index funds is far less than with many individual stocks or even several mutual funds.

For an individual investor, they allow them to pick a stock index fund, bond index fund, and money market fund. It is also possible to focus on sub-sectors within the bigger funds. There are foreign stocks, large cap stocks, individual sectors, and small cap stock funds or ETFs from which to choose.

When tactical allocating in sectors, investors can pick out those which they believe will perform strongly for either the near term or intermediate time frames. Those that believe health and technology will do well in upcoming months or even a few years might rebalance some of the portfolio into ETFs in those industry segments.

With dynamic asset allocation, investors are focused on re-balancing the portfolio to keep it near its long term goals of asset mix. This means that positions in assets classes that are outperforming have to be reduced. Those that are under-performing must then be increased with the proceeds from the outperforming assets. This restores the portfolio mix to the desired allocation. The reason investors would do this is to keep the original asset mix so that they can capture appropriate returns that meet or beat the target benchmark.

Asset Backed Security (ABS)

An Asset Backed Security is also known by its acronym ABS. This refers to a type of financial security. These are commonly backed up using either a lease, a loan, or receivables against company assets (which would not include either mortgage backed securities or real estate). With the world of investing, such ABS provide other choices for those who wish to invest in something other than common corporate debt issues.

It is interesting to note that these Asset Backed Securities are more or less identical to MBS Mortgage Backed Securities. The primary difference lies in the securities which back the two financial instruments. With the ABS, they can include credit card debt, leases, loans, royalties, and even the receivables of the company issuing the debt. Yet these mortgage based securities may never underlie the ABS.

Such an Asset Backed Security delivers to the issuer of the security a means of creating more cash for the business. It allows yield hungry investors the chance to sink their money into a great range of assets which generate income. It is worth noting that most of these underlying assets will not be liquid. This means that they can not be readily sold as stand alone assets. Yet in pooling such assets into a single conglomeration, a financial security may be created. This is done in the process referred to as securitization. This permits the asset owner to employ them in a marketable fashion.

Among the assets of such pools could be car loans, home equity loans, student loans, credit card receivables, or other anticipated cash flow items. The capacity of Asset Backed Security issuers to be creative should never be underestimated. There have even been ABS which were established utilizing the cash flow generated by movie release revenues, aircraft leases, creative works and other forms of royalty payments, and even solar energy photovoltaic revenue streams. Practically any scenario where cash is produced can be packaged up via securitization into an ABS.

It is often helpful to consider an example of this somewhat complicated Asset Backed Security topic. Consider the case of a fictitious firm Car Loans For Everybody. When individuals wish to borrow funds to purchase a car, Car Loans For Everybody will issue them the cash in a check. The individual will have to pay back the loan along with a specified interest amount at a certain time in monthly installments. It could be that Car Loans is so successful at making automobile loans that they deplete their cash reserves and can no longer issue additional loans. They have the ability to sell off their present book of loans to the fictitious investment firm Imperial Legends. Imperial Legends will then provide them with the cash they need to continue issuing new loans.

This is only where the securitization process begins. Imperial Legends investment firm would then arrange the bought out loans into a collection of parcels known in the business as tranches. A tranche effectively is a batch of loans that posses similar features. This would include interest rates, maturity dates, and anticipated rates of delinquency. After this, the Imperial Legends firm would offer new securities with features much like bonds in every tranche they created.

Finally, investors will buy such securities. They obtain the underlying cash flow out of the pool of car loans, less the administration fee, which Imperial Legends will keep to cover their costs and towards their profit.

There are three typical types of tranches in an Asset Backed Security. These are commonly referred to as Class A, Class B, and Class C. Senior most tranches belong to Class A. They are generally the biggest tranche. They will be structured in such a way as to obtain a decent investment rating so that they are easily marketable to investors.

With the Class B tranche, the credit quality will necessarily be lower. This inversely means that the yield will be higher than that of the senior tranche. Since the risk is greater, investors need to bo compensated for their appropriate risk of defaults.

Class C tranche has the lowest credit rating of all. It could be the credit quality is so poor that investors will refuse to consider it altogether. In such cases, the ABS issuer then holds the Class C tranche, collects the incoming revenues every month, and absorbs any losses themselves.

Asset Classes

Asset classes are different groups of securities which demonstrate characteristics in common, are governed by similar regulations and laws, and behave similarly in the markets. There are five principle classes which include equities (stocks), fixed income (bonds), money market instruments (cash equivalent), commodities (like gold and oil), and real estate (including land, houses, and commercial buildings), as well as some other less common alternative classes of assets.

Many times these different classes of assets are intermingled by financial advisors and analysts. They like these different types of investment vehicles to diversify portfolios more effectively and efficiently. Every asset class is anticipated to provide differing levels and types of risks versus returns among its investment characteristics. They also are supposed to perform differently in any given investment climate. Those investors who seek out the highest possible returns typically do this by lowering their overall portfolio risk by performing diversification of asset classes.

Financial professionals typically focus their clients on the different asset classes as a means of steering them into proper and effective diversification of their investment or retirement portfolios. The various classes of assets possess differing amounts and types of risk as well as varying cash flows. By purchasing into several of the competing asset classes, investors make certain they obtain a proper level of diversification in their investment choices. The importance of diversification can not be overstated. This is because all financial professionals in the know understand that it lowers risk while maximizing the opportunities to earn the highest possible return.

There are a variety of different types of investment strategies available to investors today. They might be associated with value, growth, income, or a combination of some or all of these factors. Each of them works to categorize and label the various investment options per a particular grouping of investment criteria.

There are many analysts who prefer to tie traditional valuation metrics like price to earnings ratios (PE ratios) or growth in earnings per share (EPS) to the investment selection criteria. Still different analysts feel like performance is less of a priority while asset type and allocation are more critical. They know that investments which are in the identical class of assets will possess similar cash flows, returns, and risks.

The most liquid of these various asset classes prove to be equities, fixed income securities, cash- like instruments, and commodities. This also makes them the most frequently quoted, traded, and recommended classes of assets available today. Other asset classes are considered to be more alternative such as real estate, stamps, coins, and artwork, all of which are tradable forms of collectibles. There are also investment choices such as venture capital funds, crowd sourcing, hedge funds, and bitcoin, which are considered to be even more alternative and mostly for sophisticated investors. In general, the rule is that the more alternative the investment turns out to be, the less liquidity it actually possesses.

Some of these investments, such as hedge funds, venture capital funds, and crowd sourcing can take years to exit from, if investors are able to withdraw from the investment at all. Lower liquidity does not necessarily correlate to lower return potential though. It only means that it may be a while before holders are able to find a willing buyer to sell the investments to so they can cash out of the investment.

Many of the most alternative types of investments have boasted among the highest returns over the decades, sometimes significantly better returns than the most popular two asset classes of stocks and bonds. In order to get around this lack of liquidity and often enormous investment capital requirement, many investors choose to utilize REITS. Real Estate Investment Trusts provide greater liquidity while still participating in price appreciation of the real estate asset class.

Asset Management

Asset Management refers to an organization, institution, or individual asset manager directing a client's securities, assets, and cash. It is commonly a financial services company that will do this, and especially an investment bank like Morgan Stanley, Barclays, UBS, Julius Baer, or Goldman Sachs. Such a financial institution will provide highly researched and sought after investment advice and a wide range of investment services. These would include both a variety of alternative and traditional investment product offerings. Many of these will not be available to the typical retail investor.

The financial institution will hold the account and usually offers credit cards, check writing privileges, debit cards, courtesy margin loans, and an automatic sweeping of any available cash balances into a money market fund. Brokerage services are naturally a key cornerstone of this service. Family offices and high net worth and ultra-high net worth individuals as well as institutions such as trust, pension, and insurance funds will typically be clients of asset management firms.

Because the associated investment minimums that such services demand are often in the millions of dollars, the services are typically only available to the accounts of financial intermediaries, major corporations, government entities, and wealthy families or individuals. Their products are many and vast but focus on real estate, fixed income, international investments, and commodities. Diversification is a key cornerstone to the services and investment products that good asset management offers its clients.

As these well-to-do individuals and institutions deposit their considerable sums of money into their accounts at the firm, the money is swept into a money market fund straight away. This provides a far greater return than mere checking accounts or even savings accounts offer customers. The account holders will often have the choice of either a non-FDIC backed fund (with correspondingly higher returns) or a Federal Deposit Insurance Company backed money market fund that naturally pays less since it is considered to be risk-free.

One of the principal advantages to these accounts is that these firms offer a true one-stop shop service for all of their financial needs. This includes the convenience of check writing privileges, debit and credit cards, lucrative private investments, and more all under a single roof. Both their investment and their banking needs will be serviced by the single institution instead of needing to maintain separate banking and brokerage accounts.

It was thanks to the passing of the Gramm-Leach-Bliley Act of 1997 that permitted the repealing of the Glass-Steagall Act. This Great Depression-era legislation had stopped financial institutions from providing both security and banking services to clients in an effort to protect the clients from the investment banks' rapacious greed and mis-investing of their funds.

It is always a helpful idea to look at a real-world example of the concept under discussion in order to better understand it. Consider the real-life case of investment bank Merrill Lynch, which was long the largest in the world until the Global Financial Crisis ended its near-century of successful independence and dominance in the field. Today they are a subsidiary of Bank of America.

Merrill provides its CMA Cash Management Account to meet the particular needs of its wealthy clients who want to pursue both investment and banking possibilities with only a single integrated account. This account provides customers with a personalized financial advisor as well. This financial advisor will deliver both advice and many investment options. Among these will be potentially highly lucrative IPO initial public offerings that Merrill often participates in, as well as foreign currency trades and even private investments.

The interest rates offered on such cash deposits will be tiered. This means that by linking together all deposit accounts, the eligible funds will aggregate together in order to qualify for the highest possible interest rate. The securities contained in this account will not be protected by the FDIC but instead by the umbrella of the SIPC Securities Investor Protection Corporation. SIPC will not save any owner's assets from the risk of decline or failure, but instead safeguards them from the collapse of the brokerage firm which holds them on the clients' behalves.

Back to the Merrill Lynch account example from above, the CMA account will include the ubiquitous check writing privileges and also global access to the investor's cash via any Bank of America-branded ATM automated teller machines, all without having to pay transaction fees for this convenient service. There will also be wire transfers, internal fund transfers, and bill payment services offered. The online app is called MyMerrill and it permits the account holders to have access to their accounts and engage in many of the account maintenance and management functions from their mobile device or lap top. Those accounts with over $250,000 in assets which are eligible will avoid the two fees - the annual $125 cost and the $25 assessment on every sub account the client holds.

Assets

Assets are any thing that can be owned by a company or an individual person. These are able to be sold for cash. Commonly, assets produce income or give value to the owner.

In the world of financial accounting, assets prove to be economic resources. They can be physical objects or intangible concepts that can be utilized and owned to create value. Assets are deemed to have real and positive value for their owners. Assets must also be convertible into cash, which itself is furthermore considered to be an asset.

There are several different types of assets as measured by accountants and accounting processes. These might be current assets, longer term assets, intangible assets, or deferred assets. Current assets include cash and other items that are readily and easily able to be sold to raise cash. Longer term assets are those that are held and useful for great periods of time, including such physical items as factory plants, real estate, and equipment. Intangible assets are non physical rights or concepts, like patents, trademarks, goodwill, and copyrights. Finally, deferred assets are those that involve monies spent now for the costs in the future of things like rent, insurance, or interest.

Though tangible, physical assets are not hard to conceptualize, intangible assets are often confusing for people to understand. Even though these are not physical items that may be touched, they still have value that can be controlled and sold to raise cash. Intangible assets include rights and resources which provide a company with a form of marketplace advantage. These can cover many different elements beyond those listed above, such as computer programs, stocks, bonds, and even accounts receivable.

On balance sheets, tangible assets are commonly divided into further categories. These include fixed assets and current assets. Fixed assets are objects that are immobile or not easily transported, such as buildings, office locations, and equipment. Current assets are comprised of inventory that a business holds. Balance sheets of companies keep track of a firm's assets and their value as expressed in monetary terms. These assets are both the cash and other items that the business or person owns.

Assets should never be confused with liabilities. Assets create positive cash flow that represents value or money coming into a business, organization, or individual's accounts. Liabilities are obligations that have to be paid and that create negative cash flow, or take money out of a business, individual, or organization's accounts. As an example of the difference between the two, assets would be houses that are rented out that bring in more rent every month than the expenses, interest, and upkeep of the houses. Liabilities would be homes that have payments that must be paid every month and do not provide any income stream to effectively offset this.

Bond Market

A bond market is a financial market where investors buy and sell bonds. In practice this is mostly handled electronically over computers nowadays. There are two principal types of bond markets. These are primary markets where companies are able to sell new debt and secondary markets where investors are able to purchase and resell these debt securities. Companies generally issues such debt as bonds. These markets also trade bills, notes, and commercial paper.

The goal of the bond markets is to help private companies and public entities obtain funding of a long term nature. This market has generally been the domain of the United States that dominates it. The U.S. comprises as much as 44% of this bond market on a global basis.

There are five primary bond markets according to SIFMA the Securities Industry and Financial Markets Association. These include the municipal, corporate, mortgage or asset backed, funding, and government or agency markets. The government bond market comprises a significant component of this market thanks to its massive liquidity and enormous size. Because of the stability of U.S. and some international government bonds, other bonds are often contrasted with them to help determine the amount of credit risk.

This is because government bond yields from countries with little risk like the U.S., Britain, or Germany are traditionally considered to be free of default risk. Other bonds denominated in these various currencies provide greater yields as the borrowers are more likely to default than these central governments.

Bond markets often serve a useful secondary function to reveal interest rate changes. This is because the values of bonds are inversely related to the interest rates which they pay. This helps investors to measure what the true cost of obtaining funding really is. Companies which are perceived to be riskier will have to pay higher interest rates on their bonds than companies believed to have strong and stable credit and repayment abilities. When companies or government entities are unable to make a partial or full payment on their bonds, this becomes a default.

When a company or a government needs to raise money and does not want to issue stock, it can sell bonds. These are contracts the issuers who are the borrowers make with investors who function as lenders. When investors purchase such instruments, they lend money to the issuing organization (company or government). The issuer of the bond promises to repay the original investment back along with interest in the future.

Bonds traded on these markets have many elements in common, whichever type of market they represent. All bonds have a face value. This is the amount of money which a bond would be valued at when it matures and the amount on which interest payments are based. They also have coupon rates that represent the interest rate which the issuer of the bond pays in its interest payments.

The coupon dates turn out to be the times when the issuer will pay its interest payments. Issue prices are the amounts for which the issuer sells the bond in the first place. The maturity date proves to be the exact date when the bond would be repaid. At this time, the issuer of the bond would pay the bond's face value to the bond holder.

Though a holder of a bond might keep it until maturity, this is often not the case. Many investors buy and sell them on the bond markets as their needs dictate. It is possible to sell a bond at a premium when the market value becomes greater than the original face value. Investors could also sell them at a discount to their original face value as the market price declines.

Bonds

Bonds are also known as debt instruments, fixed income securities, and credit securities. A bond is actually an IOU contract where the terms of the bond, interest rate, and date of repayment are all particularly defined in a legal document. If you buy a bond at original issue, then you are literally loaning the issuer money that will be repaid to you at a certain time, along with periodic interest payments.

Bonds are all classified under one of three categories in the United States. The first of these are the highest rated, safest category of Federal Government debt and its associated agencies. Treasury bills and treasury bonds fall under this first category. The second types of bonds are bonds deemed to be safe that are issued by companies, states, and cities. These first two categories of bonds are referred to as investment grade. The third category of bonds involves riskier types of bonds that are offered by companies, states, and cities. Such below investment grade bonds are commonly referred to as simply junk bonds.

Bonds' values rise and fall in directly opposite correlation to the movement of interest rates. As interest rates fall, bonds rise. When interest rates are rising, bonds prices fall. These swings up and down in interest rates and bond prices are not important to you if you buy a bond and hold it until the pay back, or maturity, date. If you choose to sell a bond before maturity, the price that it realizes will be mostly dependent on what the interest rates prove to be like at the time.

Bonds' investment statuses are rated by the credit rating agencies. These are Standard & Poor's, Moody's, and Fitch Ratings. All bond debt issues are awarded easy to understand grades, such as A+ or B. In the last few years of the financial crisis, these credit rating agencies were reprimanded for having awarded some companies bonds' too high grades considering the risks that the companies undertook. This was especially the case with the bonds of banks, investment companies, and some insurance outfits.

Understanding the bond markets is a function of comprehending the yield curves. Yield curves turn out to be pictorial representations of a bond's interest rate and the date that it reaches maturity, rendered on a graph.

Learning to understand and read these curves, and to figure out the spread between such curves, will allow you to make educated comparisons between various issues of bonds.

Some bonds are tax free. These are those bonds that are offered by states and cities. Such municipal bonds, also known as munis, help to raise funds that are utilized to pay for roads, schools, dams, and various other projects. Interest payments made on these municipal bonds are not subject to Federal taxes. This makes them attractive to some investors.

Capital Appreciation

Capital appreciation refers to the increase in an asset's value. This gain is based on the increase in the market price of the asset. It primarily happens as the asset which an investor backed goes for a greater market price than the investor first paid for the asset in question. The part of the asset which is considered to be capital appreciating covers the entire market value which exceeds the cost basis, or original amount invested.

There are two principle sources of returns on investment. The largest of these is typically the capital appreciating component of the return. The other return source is from dividends or interest income. The total return of an investment results from the inclusion of both the appreciation of capital and the dividend return or interest income.

There are a wide variety of reasons why capital appreciation can occur in the first place. These differ from one asset class or market to the next, but the idea is the same. With financial assets like stocks or hard assets such as real estate, this can occur similarly.

Examples of this appreciation of capital abound. If a stock investor buys shares for $20 a piece while the stock provides a yearly dividend of $2, then the dividend yield is ten percent. A year after this, if the stock is trading at $30 and the investor obtained the $2 dividend, then the investor has enjoyed a return of $10 in capital appreciating since the stock increased from $20 to $30. The percent return of the stock price increase amounts to a capital appreciating level of 50 percent. With the $2 dividend return, the dividend yield is another ten percent. That makes the combined capital appreciation between the stock price increase and the dividend payout $12, or 60 percent. This stunning total return would please most any investor in the world.

A variety of different causes can lead to this appreciation of capital for a given asset. A generally rising trend can support the prices of the investment. These can come from such macroeconomic factors as impressive GDP growth or accommodative policies of the Federal Reserve in lowering their benchmark interest rates. It might also be something more basic having to do with the company that issued the stock itself. Stock prices could rise when the firm is outperforming the prior expectations of analysts. The real estate value of a house or other property could increase because it has good proximity to upcoming new developments like major roads, shopping centers, or good schools.

Mutual funds are another investment example which seeks out capital appreciation. The funds hunt for investments which will likely increase in value because of their undervalued but solid fundamentals or because they have earnings which outperform analysts' expectations. It is true that such investments often entail larger risks than those alternatives picked for income generation or preservation of capital, as with municipal bonds, government bonds, or high dividend paying stocks.

This is why those funds which focus on capital appreciation are deemed to be more appropriate for those investors who have a higher tolerance for risk. Growth funds are usually called capital appreciation investments since they pour their funds into company stocks which are rapidly expanding and boosting their shareholder values at the same time. They do employ capital appreciation as their primary investment strategy to meet the expectations of lifestyle and retirement investors.

Capital Controls

Capital Controls refer to government intervention measures that a sovereign national government undertakes either directly, through the central bank, or another regulatory agency. They institute these in an effort to reduce the outflow of foreign capital (and sometimes the inflow as well) from the domestic national economy. There are a wide range of such controls. Among these are tariffs, taxes, volume restrictions, and literal legislation. Market forces can also be a form of capital control. Such controls can have a decisive impact on a wide range of asset classes. These include foreign exchange currency trades, stocks, and bonds.

The reason a government and its agencies would go through the trouble of implementing such Capital Controls is to normalize and standardize the rates of financial inflows and outflows from its banks and capital markets. The government comes to the decision that it must stabilize the nation's capital accounts. Such controls are not always effective on the entire economy. In fact, they can be specifically targeted towards an entire industry or even only one particular sector.

Government policies enact such controls to help ensure that the native population cannot spend their domestic currency on buying foreign assets or equities. At the same time, they impose restrictions on the abilities of foreign investors to obtain domestic securities, companies, and assets. The first example is called capital outflow controls, while the second one they refer to as capital inflow controls. The tightest of these controls often appear in nations whose economies are developing. In these states, the capital reserve base will naturally tend to be more volatile and significantly lower than in developed major economies.

There is an age-old debate still raging over capital controls. Some economists and analysts believe that they restrict and reduce economic performance and progress over time. Other economists consider them to be wise in that they provide a degree of stability to the developing economy. The majority of bigger economies pursue extremely liberal capital controls and policies. They have mostly reduced or even eliminated the stricter controls of past decades.

Despite this fact, these same liberal policy nations also maintain what they call stopgap measures. These exist to prevent a sudden and unanticipated huge capital flight in the periods of crisis or alternatively a speculative hedge fund type of attack on a national currency exchange rate. Capital controls have similarly become reduced by the twin influences of the impacts of globalization and financial market integration. Once countries choose to open their economy up to international capital this mostly permits their domestic firms and foreign firms to gain greater and simplified capital access. This can increase demand for domestic products and stocks as well.

When capital controls are deployed, this is most commonly as a direct result of economic crisis moments. A nation will make an emergency decision to stop its own citizens (as well as the guest foreign investors) from withdrawing their money from the country's economy. On June 29th of 2015, the ECB European Central Bank made the decision to freeze all support to Greek banks because of the European debt crisis.

The response from Greece was to shutter all national banks and institute capital controls on July 7th of 2015. They engaged in this series of actions out of concern that their own citizens' panic would lead to a "run on the banks" domestically. Such controls caused daily cash withdrawal limits from ATMs and banks. Overseas credit card payments and money transfers out of Greece simultaneously became restricted until further notice.

Approximately a year after the fact on the date of July 22nd of 2016, the Finance Minister of Greece announced that the country would ease its own capital controls in a measure designed to boost confidence in the domestic Greek banks. The easing increased the deposit base of the national banks of Greece as hoped for and expected by the national government.

Capital Flows

Capital Flows relate to the general movements of money and investments so that they can be invested in securities, business, or trade production. This also takes into consideration flows of such capital that occur naturally within a multinational corporation. This might result from capital spending in other divisions, investment capital allocation, acquisitions of rival companies, or R&D research and development spending.

Governments can also engage in capital flow direction by steering money they collect in tax levies into particular policies and programs as well as with their trade policies and financial policies on currency management and bilateral trade with other countries. Even individual investors can be involved in capital flow through their saving and investing personal capital into mutual funds, bonds, and stocks as well as other types of financial securities.

The United States corporate, not for profit, and government organizations direct capital flows as a result of legislation, regulation, and analysis. Economists within the U.S. and other developed nations like to study these various categories of capital inflows and outflows. This includes specific types like mutual fund flows, venture capital, asset class balancing and reallocation, federal budgets, and capital spending budgets of corporations.

In fact there are many different categories of capital flow. Within the movements in asset classes, these can be sufficiently measured as they move back and forth between stocks, cash, bonds, mutual funds, and other forms of financial securities. Venture capital can measure the shifts of investments moving around startup businesses and industries. Mutual funds will actively track the net withdrawals and additional cash deposits from and to a wide range of fund classes. With capital spending budgets, these can be studied on a companywide level. This way firms can monitor their various growth plans. Governments utilize their capital flow studies to match their budgets appropriately up with government spending plans.

Another insight that such capital flow studies provide pertains to the capital markets. They can prove the weaknesses or strengths of the various markets as economists examine the direction and pace of capital inflows and outflows. This is particularly useful for investors who can know the growth rates in specific capital flows which provide them with ideas of trends and possible opportunities. Capital spending flows will help them to know which industries and specific corporations are on the move and might be good investment opportunities. Venture capital flows reveal risks involved with venture financing of different startup industries and even specific startup operations.

Real Estate is another investment arena where capital flow direction can be most illuminating for investors. For example, during the devastating global financial crisis of 2007-2009, the capital inflows to Real Estate markets drastically slowed down. Sales did not again reach the pre-crash levels until the year 2013. By 2015, such capital flows grew as much as 45 percent compared to the levels in 2014 with regards to commercial property investment inflows.

The study of capital flows can also reveal big pictures for emerging market economies as well. As these more volatile economies often undergo rapid growth spurts and sharp contractions, the capital flow can correspondingly rise and fall steeply. Higher capital inflows often create credit booms. This leads to hot money asset price inflation. Sometimes it is offset by currency depreciation losses as exchange rates shift or equities' prices drop.

India is a classic example to consider among the developing nations of the world. The huge nation has experienced significant fluctuation periods which started back in the decade of the 1990s. Capital inflows occurred throughout the 1990s to the first years of the 2000s. This coincided with steady and positive growth. From the first years of the 2000s through 2007, capital inflows shifted into overdrive. The rapidly accompanying growth stalled out suddenly because of the peak of the global financial crisis in 2008/2009. Capital outflows became highly volatile during these several years.

Capital Gains

Capital gains refer to profits that arise when you sell a capital asset like real estate, stocks, and bonds. These proceeds must be above the purchase price to qualify as capital gains. A capital gain is also the resulting difference between a low buying price and a high selling price that leads to a financial gain for investors. The opposite of capital gains are capital losses, which result from selling such a capital asset at a price lower than for what you purchased it. Capital gains can pertain to investment income that is associated with tangible assets like financial investments of bonds and stocks and real estate. They may also result from the sale of intangible assets that include goodwill.

Capital gains are also one of the two principal types of investor income. The other is passive income. With capital gains' forms of income, large, one time amounts are realized on an asset or investment. There is no chance for the income to be continuous or periodic, as with passive income. In order to realize another capital gain, another asset must be purchased and acquired. As its value rises, it can also be sold to lock in another capital gain. Capital gain investments are generally larger amounts, though they only pay one time.

Capital gains have to be reported to the Internal Revenue Service, whether they belong to a business or an individual. These capital gains have to be designated as either short term gains or long term gains. This is decided by how long you hold the asset before choosing to sell it. When an asset with a gain is held longer than a year, the capital gain is long term. If it is held for a year or less time frame, such a capital gain proves to be short term.

When an individual or business' long term capital gains are greater than long term capital losses, net capital gains exist. This is true to the point that these gains are greater than net short term capital losses. Tax rates on these capital gains are lower than on other forms of income. Up to 2010's conclusion, the highest capital gains tax rates for the majority of investors proves to be fifteen percent. Those whose incomes are lower are taxed at a zero percent rate on their net capital gains.

When capital gains are negative, or are actually capital losses, the losses may be deducted form your tax return. This reduces other forms of income by as much as the yearly limit of $3,000. Additional capital losses can be carried over to future years when they exceed $3,000 in any given year, reducing income for tax purposes in the future. These capital gains and losses should be reported on the IRS' Schedule D for capital gains and losses.

Capital Inflow

Capital Inflow refers to money (in the form of investments) moving into a certain benefitting nation. The country which is the recipient of the inflow is best known as the host country. The source countries are the ones sending or investing the initial funds. Host nations often have a range of causes for attracting such capital inflows.

Direct foreign investment occurs when multinational corporations purchase literal tangible assets in the host country. This could come in the form of purchasing a local company outright or building a manufacturing plant locally. There could also be portfolio investment in the host nation's financial securities. This might include bonds and stocks which may be bought by international banks, foreign residents, insurance companies, pension funds, hedge funds, or other cross-border groups.

A third way that this occurs is when host governments are forced to borrow money off of international governments or foreign banks in order to pay their deficit on the balance of payments. It also occurs when domestic corporations or citizens elect to borrow from foreign banks. Finally inter-company transfers can finance investment and consumption in this category of capital inflow.

A last form of capital inflow happens when the host country has higher interest rates than the source nations' own corresponding rates. In this scenario, shorter term deposits will often flock to the banks' and money market instruments of the host nation. This could be straight up investment or speculation that the host national exchange rate will increase and so lead to a capital gain. This is the opposite of capital outflows. Outflows occur as funds move out of the host nation into other competing countries for the same reasons detailed above.

There are many beneficial effects to a country which receives capital inflows. As money comes into the host country via a business or stock purchase on the nation's stock market exchange, the recipient firm will deploy the funds either for startup purposes or to expand their existing business products and lines. This is really good for the companies which receive the funds. Such expansion of the companies in question then leads both job creation and employment growth in the host nation. Businesses will finally realize profits utilizing the original capital investment and the projects they subsequently fund with it. With these profits, the company is able to pay for additional expansion or investment in other projects and/or financial investments.

In the last few decades, foreigners have invested literally hundreds of billions worth of foreign capital into the United States economy. This has massively advantaged the American economy and workers (besides just creating countless jobs) as it boosted the international value of the dollar, lowered interest rates for American individuals and businesses, and grew the capital supply for loans which banks could make to residents and companies alike. With the onset of the catastrophic Global Financial Crisis from 2007-2009, the capital inflows to the United States dropped considerably. The subsequent Sovereign Debt Crisis in Europe dramatically decreased the capital inflow to Europe as well.

Years later by 2012, China finally surpassed the U.S. to capture the spot as the globe's greatest host of direct foreign investment . At the conclusion of 2012, the United States managed to recapture this coveted top spot. China had several reasons to steal the American thunder this way. The Chinese economy grew quicker than the United States as well as the other developed nations. Besides this, China has finally matured into a country that does not appear to be a high risk investment any longer. This has helped to draw in direct foreign investment by the hundreds of billions over the decades.

Capital Loss

Capital Loss refers to a type of loss that companies or individuals experience as one of their capital assets decreases by value. This includes a real estate or investment asset. The loss only becomes realized when the asset itself sells for less than the price for which it was originally purchased. Another way of looking at these capital losses is that they represent the difference from the asset's purchase price and the asset's selling price. In other words, for it to be a loss the selling price must be less than the original price. As an example, when investors purchase a home for $300,000 and then sell the same home six years later for only $260,000, they have taken a capital loss amounting to $40,000.

Where income taxes are concerned, capital losses often offset capital gains. Capital losses in fact reduce the personal or business income in a like dollar for dollar amount. When net losses are higher than $3,000, then the overage amount can not be applied. Instead, this amount higher than net $3,000 simply carries over against any other gains or taxable income to the following year when they will similarly offset capital gains and income. When losses are multiple thousands, they continue to carry forward as many years as it takes for them to be fully exhausted.

Both capital losses and capital gains will be reported using a Form 8949. This form helps taxpayers to determine if the sale dates allow for the transactions to be counted as long term or short term losses or gains. When such transactions are deemed to be short term gains, they become taxable by the individual's ordinary income tax rates. These ranged from only 10 percent to 39.6 percent as of 2015. This is why the shorter term losses when paired off against shorter term gains give significant tax advantages to higher income earning individuals. It benefits them when they have earned profits by selling off any asset or assets in under a year from original purchase point.

With longer term capital gains, investors become taxed by rates of zero percent, 15 percent, or 20 percent. This occurs when they take a gain which results from a position they possessed for over a year. Such capital gains also can only be offset by capital losses which they realize after holding the investments for over a year. It is also on form 8949 that these assets become reportable. Here investors list out both the gross proceeds from the sales and assets' cost basis. The two figures are compared to determine if the total sales equate to a loss, gain, or wash. Such losses become reported on Schedule D. Here the taxpayer is able to ascertain the amount that may be utilized to lower overall taxable income.

These wash sale rules can be confusing to individuals without an example. Consider an investor who dumps his IBM stock on the last day of November in order to realize a loss. The taxing authority of the Internal Revenue Service will disallow such a capital loss if the exact stock was bought again on the day of December 30th or before this. This is because investors have to wait at least 31 days before such a security can be repurchased then sold off once more in order to realize another loss.

Yet the regulation does not affect sales and re-buys of different mutual funds that possess similar positions and holdings. As an example, $10,000 worth of Vanguard Energy Fund shares may be entirely reinvested in the Fidelity Select Energy Portfolio at any point. This would not forfeit the investors' ability to recognize another loss even as they continue to own an equity portfolio (through the mutual fund) that is similar to their earlier mutual fund holdings.

Capital Markets

Capital markets refer to those marketplaces for the sales and purchase of both debt and equity financial issues. These markets move investments and savings back and forth between capital suppliers like institutional and retail investors to capital users. These are individual entrepreneurs, businesses and corporations, and governmental agencies. Economies do not function efficiently or successfully without such liquid markets of capital. This is because capital is a crucial component for producing economic output.

There are two types of such capital markets. These include the primary markets and secondary markets. In the primary markets, investors buy and sell new bond and stock instruments. Secondary markets are the ones that trade already existing securities. The two financial instruments categories are equities and debt securities. The equities are typically called stocks. The debt securities are usually called bonds. Such markets revolve around the selling of bonds and stocks for longer and medium term durations, typically of at least a year.

These capital markets in the United States function under the auspices of the Securities and Exchange Commission. In other nations, they operate under different financial regulators. In general, such markets tend to cluster in the several important financial centers of the globe. The greatest of these are London, New York City, Hong Kong, and Singapore. Despite the fact that the markets lie in these principal city centers, the majority of their trades happen via sophisticated electronic and computer trading systems. While members of the public can access some such capital centers in person, the other ones remain highly secured and regulated.

Primary markets are where these investments first appear. The companies which need to raise capital issue bonds and stocks directly to the financial institutions, businesses, and investors here. They typically buy these in a process called underwriting. Another advantage offered by companies which require capital is that they can do it there without having to hold initial public offerings (IPOs) so that the profit remains theirs. When companies do opt for IPOs, they typically sell all of their stock shares off to several underwriting investment banks through a lead investment bank and other financial firms which choose to participate.

From this stage, the new shares become a part of the secondary market. Here the investment banks, financial firms, and private investors are allowed to resell their debt and equity instruments to retail investors.

There are many entities which participate in capital markets. These include institutional investors like mutual funds and pension funds, retail investors, corporations and other organizations, governments and municipalities, and financial institutions and banks. Governments may be allowed to issue bonds on these markets, but they can never sell equity via stocks.

These markets are where supply and demand between capital suppliers and users meet and adjust. While capital users desire to raise their capital for the lowest cost they possibly can, the suppliers wish to obtain the highest return they possibly can for the least amount of risk possible.

A country's capital markets' size will be directly proportional to the economic size of the nation in question. As the biggest economy on the planet, the U.S. boasts the deepest and biggest capital markets. These markets are still interdependent on other such capital centers in the global economy of today. Small ripples in another center such as London or Hong Kong can lead to substantial waves in Singapore and/or New York City.

The downside to the interconnectedness of the financial and capital centers is illustrated by the financial and credit crisis of 2007 to 2009. It was actually the failure of the mortgage-backed securities markets in the United States that triggered the crisis and collapse. This de facto meltdown in the U.S. became transmitted around the world by the global capital markets as financial institutions, investment banks, and commercial banks throughout both Europe and Asia were holding literally trillions of U.S. dollars worth of such securities.

Capital Outflow

Capital Outflow is a phenomenon where financial assets and money move away from a given nation. All countries of the world consider this to be a negative action. It typically occurs as a result of economic and/or political instability or at least the perception of it. Such asset flight results from domestically and especially foreign-based investors choosing to sell their stakes within a certain nation. They do this as they see potential weakness in the economy or political establishment of a country. They begin to feel that greater and safer opportunities for investment lie overseas.

When such Capital Outflows become too fast and great, it is a serious indicator that economic and political turmoil is present and a primary cause of the asset and capital flight. Many governments will begin to set limitations for capital choosing to exit. The connotation of such actions tends to warn still other investors who have not left that the condition of the host nation and economy is rapidly deteriorating.

Abnormal capital outflow creates increasingly severe pressure on the macroeconomics of a country and its economy. It tends to dissuade domestic and foreign investors alike from investing in the state and its companies. There are a range of valid explanations for why such capital flight actually occurs. Among them are unnaturally low national interest rates and growing political unrest.

It often helps to look at a real world example to better understand a difficult concept. Japan chose to decrease its interest rates to actual negative levels back in 2016. This applied to all government bonds and securities. They simultaneously began unprecedented aggressive stimulatory measures to boost the growth of the GDP Gross Domestic Product at the same time. The economic problems in Japan started after massive capital outflows from the island nation throughout the decade of the 1990s kicked off two long decades of sub-par stagnated growth in the country which formerly boasted the position of second greatest economy in the world.

Often times, governments impose severe restrictions on capital flight in a valiant effort to stop the fleeing money and financial assets. This is in an endeavor to shore up the capital markets and especially domestic banking institutions and system which can fail if all the money is simultaneously withdrawn. Too few bank deposits often cause banks to crater into insolvency when a great number of assets depart all at once. Subsequently, many banks find it difficult if not outright impossible to call back in existing issued loans in order to make good on customer withdrawal demands.

Consider the sad case study of Greece. Back in 2015, the government of the world's first democracy had no other choice than to instate a week long bank holiday. Wire transfers became restricted only to those recipients with Greek bank accounts. When such events occur in developing (or sometimes third world) countries, the weakness it institutes can create a vicious downward spiral that leads to domestic public panic and foreign investment fear and resistance.

There are also dramatic effects on exchange rates. The supply of a given country's currency rises dramatically as investors cash out of the state. Investors in China have periodically sold off the Yuan in order to obtain American dollars. This drives down the value of the Chinese Yuan, which has the additional side benefit of reducing the costs of Chinese exports while simultaneously boosting the costs to import foreign goods. It unfortunately also leads to inflation since import demand will fall while exported goods demand increases. During the second half of the year 2015, Chinese assets to the tune of $550 billion departed China looking for a higher ROI return on investment. This caused not only Chinese government fears but ensuing worldwide government worries.

Similarly Argentina suffered from sudden, unexpected, and runaway capital outflows back in the decade of the 1990s following a dramatic currency realignment. Their new fixed exchange rate created a resulting recession. The nation has now become the popular example and poster country for fledgling economies and the difficulties they all too often encounter in boosting their economic development.

Capital Stock

A business' capital stock is the up front capital that the founders of the firm invest in or put into the company. This capital stock also proves useful as security for a business' creditors. This is because capital stock may not be taken out of the business to disadvantage the creditors in question. Such stock is separate from a business' assets or property that can rise and fall in value and amount.

A company's capital stock is segregated into shares. The complete number of such shares have to be detailed when the business is founded. Based on the entire sum of money that is put into the company when it is started up, each share will possess a particular face value that must be declared.

This value is referred to as par value of the individual shares. These par values are the minimum sums of money that may be issued and sold in stock shares by the business. It is similarly the capital value representation in the business' own accounting. In some countries, these shares do not contain any par value period. In this case, the capital stock shares would be termed non par value stock. Such shares literally represent a portion of an ownership in the business in question. These businesses may then declare various classes of shares. All of these could have their own privileges, rules, and share values.

The owning of such capital stock shares is proven by the possession of a certificate of stock. These stock certificates prove to be legal documents that detail the numbers of shares each shareholder owns. Other particular data of the capital stock shares, including class of shares and par value, is similarly detailed on these certificates.

These owners of the firm in question may decide that they need more capital in order to invest in additional projects that the company has in mind. Besides this, they might decide that they want to cash out some of their own holdings in order to release a portion of capital for their own private needs. They can do this by selling all or some of their capital stock to many partial owners. The ownership of one such share gives the share owner an ownership stake in the company. This includes such privileges as a tiny portion of any profits that may be paid out as dividends, as well as a small part of any decision making powers.

These shares sold from the capital stock each represent a single vote. The owners could decide to offer various classes of shares that could then have differing rights of voting. By owning a majority of the shares, the owners can out vote all of the little shareholders combined. This permits the original owners to maintain effective control of their company even after issuing shares of their capital stock to investors.

Cash Flow

Cash Flow is either an incoming revenue or outgoing expense stream that affects the value of any cash account over time. Inflows of cash, or positive cash flows, typically result from one of three possible activities, including operations, investing, or financing for businesses or individuals. Individuals are also able to realize positive cash flows from gifts or donations.

Negative cash flow is also called cash outflows. Outflows of cash happen because of either expenses or investments made. This is the case for both individuals' finances, as well as for those of businesses.

Where both individual finances and business corporate finances are concerned, positive cash flows are required to maintain solvency. Cash flows could be demonstrated because of a past transaction like selling a business product or a personal item or investment. They might also be projected into a future time for some consideration that a company or individual anticipates receiving and then possibly spending. No person or corporation can survive for long without cash flow.

Positive cash flow is essential for a variety of needs. Sufficient cash flow allows for money for you to pay your personal bills and creditors. It also allows a business to cover the costs of employee payroll, suppliers' bills, and creditors' payments in a timely fashion. When individuals and businesses lack sufficient cash on hand to maintain their budget or operations, then they are named insolvent. Lasting insolvency generally leads to personal or corporate bankruptcy.

For businesses, statements of cash flows are created by accountants. These demonstrate the quantity of cash that is created and utilized by a corporation in a certain time frame. Cash flows in this definition are calculated by totaling net income following taxes with non cash charges like depreciation. Cash flow is able to be assigned to either a business' entire operations or to one particular segment or project of the company. Cash flow is often considered to be an effective measurement of a business' ongoing financial strength.

Cash flows are also used by business and individuals to ascertain the value or return of a project or investment. The numbers of cash flows in to and out of such projects and investments are often utilized as inputs for indicators of performance like net present value and internal rate of return. A problem with a business' liquidity can also be determined by measuring the entire entity's cash flow.

Many individuals prefer investments that yield periodic positive cash flow over ones that pay only one time capital gains. High yielding dividend stocks, energy trusts, and real estate investment trusts are all examples of positive cash flow investments. Real estate properties can also be positive cash flow yielding investments when they provide greater amounts of rental income than their combined monthly mortgage payments, maintenance expenses, and property management upkeep costs and outflows total.

Cash Flow Quadrant

The cash flow quadrant is a diagram that shows four types of individuals involved in a business. These four people make up the entire business world. The four quadrants are E, S, B, and I.

The E quadrant stands for employees. Employees have the same core values in general. This is security. When any employee sits down with a manager or a president, they will always tell them the same thing. This is that they are looking for a secure and safe job that includes benefits.

The S in the cash flow quadrant represents a small business owner or a self employed person. They are generally solo actors or one person outfits. These types would rather operate on their own, as their motto is always to have something done right, you should do it yourself.

On the right side of the cash flow quadrant are the B's. B stands for Big Business people. Big businesses have five hundred or greater numbers of employees. They are completely different from the others in the quadrants, as they are constantly looking for the most intelligent and capable people, networks, and systems to aid them in running their large business. They do not want to micro manage the company themselves, rather they want good people to do it on their behalf.

The last quarter of the cash flow quadrants is the I, which stands for Investor. Investors are those individuals who make money work effectively and efficiently for themselves. The main difference between them and the B quadrants it that the investors have their money working hard while the Big Business people have other people working hard for them. Both groups of B's and I's represent the wealthy. The employees and the self employed are the people who work hard for the business people and investors on the right, or wealthy side of the quadrant.

The cash flow quadrant explains the differences between the rich and the working poor. It is useful to describe four types of income that a person can generate as well. The smartest people in the cash flow quadrant are the ones who manage to make the other people and their money work hard for their benefit. That is why they are the wealthy, while the hard working members of society on the left side are the ones who do all of the working on the wealthy people's behalf. Learning to become wealthy means effectively changing which square of the cash flow quadrant a person occupies.

Cash Flow Statement (CFS)

The Cash Flow Statement (CFS) proves to be one of three critical components in any corporation's financial reports. The other two are income statements and balance sheets. From 1987, the SEC Securities Exchange Commission has mandated that such cash flow statements be included with all corporate financial reports. This statement details the quantities of cash and cash equivalents that come into and flow out of a firm. Such a CFS permits the stake holders and potential investors alike to comprehend the way corporations' operations are functioning, how they are effectively spending the money, and from where their money originates in the first place.

There are differences that separate these Cash Flow Statements from the balance sheets and income statements. The principal one is that CFSs do not cover the future anticipated outgoing and incoming cash amounts which have already been recorded under the credit sales category. It explains why the component cash is never identical to net income. Both balance sheets and income statements cover not only cash sales, but also sales that happen on credit. In the end, a firm's cash flow is derived from three separate means of money coming in and leaving a corporation. These are cash from operations, cash from financing, and cash from investing.

Cash from Operations comprise both the cash inflow and outflow which result from the mainstay operation of the business. This means that they show the quantity of cash that the firms' services and products actually accrue to the business. Cash from operations would usually include changes to cash, depreciation, accounts receivable, accounts payable, and inventory.

The Cash from Financing component includes loans, changes in debt, and dividends. As capital becomes raised, this is a cash-in accounting item. As dividends pay out, it becomes marked as a cash-out event. As an example, when firms sell bonds on the markets, the firm obtains cash financing. As the corporation pays the associated interest out to the holders of the bonds, then the firm reduces its cash by the corresponding amount.

The final category of Cash from Investing covers all changes in assets, equipment, or company investments. These are commonly considered to be cash out events. This is because cash will be utilized to purchase new buildings, buy factory or other production equipment, and acquire other types of assets which are short term (like securities which are easily marketable). It is not always the case that these are cash negative events though. As any firms choose to sell off one or more of their assets, this creates a cash-in transaction. It would then be notated as a positive accounting item under the cash from investing category. When companies sell shares they hold in another firm, the revenue this generates becomes accounted for under the Cash from Investing.

Cash flow becomes calculated by adjustments that accountants make to net income. They simply add in (or alternatively subtract out) any differences in expenses, revenue, and credit types of transactions that appear on the income statements and balance sheets since the last accounting period. Such transactions happen every accounting period. These adjustments will be reviewed and amended as non-cash items go into the income statement under net income while liabilities and total assets go on to the balance sheet. Since not every type of financial transaction of a firm relates to real cash items, a great number of items must be reconsidered when the accountants are figuring up the cash flow from operations.

Company accountants deduce the cash flow statement calculations and compile them into official corporate report documents every reportable quarter. The SEC requires that they make this a part of every quarterly report and also each annual report which they must divulge to analysts and members of the investing public by law.

Cash On Cash Return (CCR)

Cash on cash return, also known by its acronym CCR, is an investing term. It describes a ratio of the yearly cash flow before taxes against the total sum of cash invested. This cash on cash return is expressed as a percentage.

Cash on cash return is mostly utilized to analyze any income generating asset's actual cash flow situation. This percentage is commonly applied as a simple and quick test to decide if an asset under consideration is worthy of additional study and analysis. An investor who believed that cash flow is the greatest goal would be most interested in an analysis based on cash on cash return. Others employ it to discover if a particular property or asset turns out to be under priced. This would mean that equity in a property would exist immediately upon purchase.

Cash on cash return formulas do not figure in any deprecation or appreciation of an income producing asset. This means that the cash on cash return number may be skewed to the high side if some of the cash flow produced turns out to be a return on capital. This is because return on capital is not income.

Another limitation to cash on cash returns as a measurement lies in the fact that the calculation is more or less one of simple interest. This means that it does not take into consideration the compounding of interest. As a result of this, investments that provide a lower compound interest rate might be better over time than those that provide greater cash on cash returns, which is only a simple interest calculation.

A last downside to using cash on cash returns as a means of evaluating an investment centers around the fact that they are only pre tax cash flow evaluations. This means that your tax situation as a unique investor will not be considered in the formula. Varying tax situations can determine if an investment is a good match for you or not.

Consider an example of figuring up out a cash on cash return. You could buy an apartment complex for $1,200,000 using a down payment of $300,000. Every month, the resulting rental cash flow after expenses for this property is $5,000. This means that in a year, the income before tax would amount to $60,000, as $5,000 was multiplied by twelve months. This would make the cash on cash return the cash flow for the year before taxes of $60,000 over the entire amount of money invested in the asset of $300,000. This results in an actual twenty percent cash on cash return.

Closed End Funds

Closed end funds refer to those investment companies which are publicly traded and regulated by the SEC Securities and Exchange Commission. They are similar to mutual funds in some ways. Both represent investment funds which are pooled and overseen by a portfolio manager. The closed end varieties raise fixed amounts of capital. They do this in IPO initial public offerings. Such funds will then be established and structured, listed on a stock exchange, and finally then traded, bought, and sold as a stock is on one of the exchanges.

Other names for these closed end funds are closed end mutual funds or closed end investments. These funds have things in common with the open end funds as well as characteristics which are unique to them and which set them apart from such ETF exchange traded funds and mutual funds.

Closed end funds are only able to raise their capital in a single instance by utilizing an IPO and issuing a set quantity of shares. Investors in this closed end operation will then buy the shares like stock. They do have an important difference from typical stocks. Their shares are actually a certain interest within a given portfolio of securities that an investment advisor will actively manage. Usually they focus on a chosen and particular sector, geographic area and market, or industry.

Stock prices of these closed end funds vary with the market supply and demand forces. They also fluctuate based on the changes in the values of the underlying assets or securities which the fund contains. While there are many of these particular closed end funds, among the biggest in the fund universe is the Eaton Vance Tax-Managed Global Diversified Equity Income Fund.

There are a number of important characteristics which the closed end and open end funds share in common. Management teams run their investment portfolios in the two cases. The two types similarly assess and collect their annual expense ratio. They also may both provide capital gains and income distributions to their stakeholders.

The differences between the two types of funds in this universe are important. While open ended funds have their own particulars of trading, the closed end funds will trade exactly like stocks on their respective exchanges. The open ended variants receive a value and pricing only one time per day at the end of trading. The closed end variety will be both priced and traded repeatedly all through the market trading days. The closed end funds need a broker service to sell or buy them. In marked contrast to this, investors in the open ended funds many times may buy and sell their relevant shares directly with the provider of the fund.

A closed end fund also has some unique characteristics in the ways that its shares become priced. There is a difference between the funds NAV net asset value and the trading price. The NAV will be figured up at regular intervals throughout the day by computers. The actual price for which they trade on exchanges becomes set only by demand and supply forces interacting on the exchange. The end-result of this unique set of features is that the closed end fund might actually trade at a discount or premium to the net asset value.

This might occur for several different reasons. Those funds which are closed ended might be concentrating on a sector in the markets which happens to be more popular, such as biotechnology or alternative energy sources and technology. This would allow sufficient interest from investors to bid up the price of the fund to a premium over its actual NAV. When such funds are run by a stock picker with a successful track record, they can trade for a premium. At the same time, when investor interest is insufficient or there is a negative profile of risk and return perceived on the fund, it will often trade for a discount to net asset value.

Collateralized Debt Obligations (CDO)

Collateralized Debt Obligations are one of the financial weapons of mass destruction that helped to derail the global financial system in the financial crisis of 2007-2010. They are literally securities that are supposed to be of investment grade. The backing of collateralized debt obligations proves to be pools of loans, bonds, and similar assets. These investments are rated by the main ratings agencies of Moody's, Standard and Poors, and Fitch rating companies.

The actual value of collateralized debt obligations comes from their asset backing. These asset backed securities' payments and values both derive from their portfolios of associated assets that are fixed income types of instruments. CDO's securities are divided into different classes of risk that are called tranches.

The senior most tranches are deemed to be the most secure forms of securities. Since principal and interest payments are given out according to the most senior securities first, the junior level tranches pay the higher coupon payments and interest rates to help reward investors who are willing to take on the greater levels of default risk that they assume.

The original CDO was only offered in 1987 by bankers for Imperial Savings Association that failed and became folded in to the Resolution Trust Corporation in 1990. This should have been a warning about collateralized debt obligations, but their popularity only grew apace during the following ten years. CDO's rapidly became the fastest expanding part of the synthetic asset backed securities market. There are several reasons for why this proved to be the case. The main one revolved around the returns of two to three percentage points greater than corporate bonds that possessed identical credit ratings.

CDO's also appealed to a larger number of investors and asset managers from investment trusts, unit trusts, and mutual funds, to insurance companies, investment banks, and private banks. Structured investment vehicles also made use of them to defray risk. CDO's popularity also had to do with the high profit margins that they made for their creators and sellers.

A number of different investors and economists have raised their voices against collateralized debt obligations, derivatives in general, and other asset backed securities. This includes both former IMF Head Economist Raghuram Rajan and legendary billionaire investor Warren Buffet. They have claimed that such instruments only increase and spread around the uncertainty and risk that surrounds these underlying assets' values to a larger and wider pool of owners instead of lessening the risk via diversification.

Though the majority of the investment world remained skeptical of their criticism, the credit crisis in 2007 and 2008 proved that these dissenters had merit to their views. It is now understood that the major credit rating agencies did not sufficiently take into account the massive risks that were associated with the CDO's and ABS's, such as a nationwide housing value collapse.

Because the value of collateralized debt obligations are forced to be valued according to mark to market accounting, where their values are immediately updated to the market value, they have declined dramatically in value on the banks' and others owners' balance sheets as their actual value on the market has plummeted.

Collateralized Mortgage Obligation (CMO)

Collateralized mortgage obligations are investments that contain home mortgages. These mortgages underlie the securities themselves. These CMO yields and results derive from the home mortgage loans' performance on which they are based. This is true with other mortgage backed securities as well.

Lenders sell these loans to an intermediary firm. Such an intermediary pools these loans together and issues certificates based on them. Investors are able to buy these certificates to earn the principal and interest payments from the mortgages. The payments these homeowners make go through the intermediary firm before finally reaching the investors who bought them.

The performance of collateralized mortgage obligations depends on the track record of the mortgage payers. What makes them different from other types of mortgage backed securities is that it is not only a single loan on which they are based. Rather they are categorized by groups of loans according to the payment period for the mortgages within the pool itself.

Issuers set up CMOs this way to try to reduce the effects of a mortgage being prepaid. This can often be a problem for investments based on only a single mortgage as owners refinance their loans and pay off the initial one on which the investment was based. With the CMOs, the risk of home owners defaulting is spread across a number of different mortgages and shared by many investors.

Tranches are the different categories within the mortgage pools on which the collateralized mortgage obligations are based. The tranches are often divided according to the mortgage repayment schedules of the loans. For each tranche, the issuer creates bonds with different interest rates and maturity dates. These CMO bonds can come with maturity dates of twenty, ten, five, and two years. The bondholders of each individual tranche receive the coupon or interest payments out of the mortgage pool. Principal payments accrue initially to those bonds in the first tranche which mature soonest.

The bonds on collateralized mortgage obligations turn out to be highly rated. This is especially the case when they are backed by GSE government mortgages and similar types of high grade loans. This means that the risk of default is low compared with other mortgage backed securities.

There are three types of groups who issue these CMOs. The FHLMC Federal Home Loan Mortgage Corporation issues many of them. Other GSE Government Sponsored Enterprises like Ginnie Mae provide them as well. There are also private companies which issue these CMOs. Many investors consider the ones issued by the government agencies to be less risky, but this is not necessarily the case. The government is not required to bail out the GSEs and their CMOs.

There are investors who choose to hold their CMO bonds until they mature. Others will re-sell or buy them using the secondary market. The prices for these investments on this market go up and down based on any changes in the interest rates.

The other most common type of mortgage backed securities besides these CMOs are pass through securities. Pass throughs are usually based on a single or few mortgages set up like a trust that collects and passes through the interest and principal repayments.

Collective Investment Fund (CIF)

A collective investment fund is a vehicles that manages a combined group of trust accounts. They are sometimes called collective investment trusts. Trust companies or banks operate these funds. The idea behind them is to pool together the funds and assets of organizations and individuals so that the managers can create bigger and better diversified portfolios.

Two types of these CIFs exist. A1 funds are combined together so that their operators can effectively reinvest or initially invest them. With A2 funds, trusts contribute assets that are not subject to any federal income taxes.

The main goal with a collective investment fund lies in utilizing superior economy of scale in order to reduce costs. The operators are able to combine together pensions and profit sharing funds to come up with a greater amount of assets. Banks then put these funds which are pooled together in a master trust account. The bank that controls the account then serves as executor or trustee of the CIF.

Banks that serve collective investment funds are the fiduciaries. This means that keep the legal title for the fund and all assets within it. The individuals or groups that participate in the CIF still own the results of the invested fund' assets. This makes them the beneficial owners of the relevant assets. Those who are participating within the fund do not actually own any individual assets that the CIF holds. They do maintain an interest in the aggregated assets of the fund.

Banks designed these collective investment funds so that they could improve their investment management tactics. They do this when they pull together a number of accounts' assets and merge them into a single fund with a common investment strategy. Pooling these assets into only one account allows the banks to dramatically reduce their administrative and operating costs for the fund. The investment strategy they come up with is structured to optimize the performance of the investments.

There are a number of different collective investment funds operating. Invesco Trust Company operates several of them. Examples of their funds are the Invesco Balanced Risk Commodity Trust and the Invesco Global

Opportunities Trust.

Though comptrollers use the name collective investment funds, other names sometimes refer to these vehicles. Generally applied names for them include common funds, common trust funds, comingled trusts, and collective trusts. An important characteristic of CIFs is that they are not regulated by the Investment Act of 1940 (as with mutual funds) or the SEC Securities Exchange Commission. Instead the OCC Office of the Comptroller of the Currency regulates and oversees them.

Mutual funds and collective investment funds are both pooled funds with an important distinction. These CIFs are not registered investment vehicles. Instead they exist in a class that is similar to hedge funds.

In 1927, the world's first collective fund began. Thanks to the stock market crash that occurred only two years later, CIFs became a scapegoat. They were believed to have contributed to the severe crash. This caused regulators to heavily restrict them. Banks could only provide them to trust clients or by utilizing employee benefit plans. They received a significant boost in the Pension Protection Act of 2006. This act chose them to be the standard option in defined contribution plans. Now 401(k) plans often feature them as an option for stable value.

Commercial Paper

Commercial paper proves to be a corporation-issued short term form of debt instrument which is unsecured. This paper is generally used to finance such things as inventories, accounts receivable, and other short term liabilities. The maturity dates for commercial paper vary, but they do not typically run any more than 270 days. Such paper instruments are generally issued at discounts to their face value. These discounts take into account the market interest rates that are effective when the company issues its paper.

Because commercial paper does not come with any underlying collateral, it turns out to be unsecured corporate debt. This means that only those companies that boast debt ratings which are highest quality will be able to find takers easily. Other companies must float their paper debt issues at greater discounts. This makes the funds come at a higher cost. Large organizations issue these paper instruments in significant denominations of typically $100,000 or higher. The most usual buyers of these paper instruments are banks and financial institutions, other companies, money market funds, and wealthy investors.

Commercial paper offers significant advantages for the corporations who utilize it. One of the biggest is that they do not have to register these offerings with the SEC Securities and Exchange Commission if the paper reaches maturity within 270 days or before nine months pass. This makes it a cost effective and quick way to obtain finance. While companies do have up to 270 days before the SEC is involved, typical maturity time frames for this paper only average around 30 days.

There are some restrictions to the use of commercial paper. It's funds can only be utilized for current assets and inventories. They may not be employed to purchase fixed assets like new facilities or plants unless the SEC is involved.

The financial crisis that began to erupt in 2007 involved the commercial paper market in a significant way. When investors had fears that major companies like Lehman brothers had problems with their liquidity and financial condition, markets for commercial paper seized up. Companies lost their access to funding which was affordable and simple to obtain.

This market freezing also led to money market funds "breaking the buck." As major investors in these paper instruments, the funds suffered from the suspect health of firms whose issued paper caused their own fund values to drop below the standard $1. Up to this point, money market funds had been considered risk free for investors. Government backing and guarantees were required to restore order and functionality to these markets.

A company might need additional short time frame funds in order to pay for Christmas holiday season additional inventory. The company could issue paper for $20 million in needs at $20.2 million face value. This means investors will provide it with $20 million in funding and receive $200,000 as interest when the paper matures. It would amount to a 1% interest rate. If the paper is not redeemed at its initial maturity, the interest rate would adjust the amount of principal and interest the paper would return appropriately based on the number of days it remained outstanding.

Commodities

Commodities turn out to be items that are taken from the earth, such as orange juice, cattle, wheat, oil, and gold. Companies buy commodities to turn them into usable products like bread, gasoline, and jewelry to sell to other businesses and consumers. Individual investors purchase and sell them for the purposes of speculation, in an attempt to make a profit.

Commodities are traded through commodities brokers on one of several different commodities exchanges, such as COMEX, or the Commodities Mercantile Exchange, NYMEX, or the New York Mercantile Exchange, and NYBOT, or the New York Board of Trade, among others.

Commodities are traded with contracts using a great amount of leverage. This means that with a small amount of money, a great quantity of the commodity in question can be controlled and traded. For example, with only a few thousand dollars, you as an investor are able to control a contract of one thousand barrels of heating oil or one hundred ounces of gold.

As a result of this high leverage that you obtain, the amounts of money made or lost can be significant with only relatively small moves in the price of the underlying commodity. This leverage results from the fact that commodities are nearly always traded using margin accounts that lead to significant risks for the capital invested. For example, with gold contracts, each ten cent minimum price move represents a $10 per contract gain or loss.

Commodity trading strategies center around speculation on factors that will affect the production of a commodity. These could be related to weather, natural disasters, strikes, or other events. If you believed that severe hurricanes would damage a great portion of the Latin American coffee crop, then you would call your commodity broker and instruct them to buy as many coffee contracts as they had money in the account to cover.

If the hurricanes took place and coffee did see significant damage in the region, then the prices of coffee would rise dramatically as a result of the negative weather, causing the coffee harvest to be more valuable. Your coffee contracts would similarly rise in value, probably significantly.

A variety of commodities can be traded on the commodities exchanges. These include grains, metals, energy, livestock, and softs. Grains consistently prove to be among the most popular of commodities available to trade. Grain commodities are usually most active in the spring and summer. Grains include soybeans, corn, oats, wheat, and rough rice.

Metals commodities offer you the opportunity to take positions on precious metals such as gold and silver. Changes in the underlying prices of base metals may also be traded in this category. Metals include copper, silver, and gold.

Energy commodities that you can trade are those used for heating homes and fueling vehicles for the nation. With the energy complex you can trade on supply disruptions around the world or higher gas prices that you anticipate. Energy commodities available to you are crude oil, unleaded gas, heating oil, and natural gas.

Livestock includes animals that provide pork and beef. Because these are staple foods in most American diets, they provide among the more reliable pattern trends for trading. Pork bellies, lean hogs, and live cattle are all examples of tradable livestock commodities.

Softs are comprised of both food and fiber types of commodities. Many of these are deemed to be exotic since they are grown in other countries and parts of the earth. Among the soft markets that you can trade are sugar, coffee, cocoa, cotton, orange juice, and lumber.

Commodity Broker

A commodity broker commonly is an individual who makes commodity trades for his or her customers. The term also refers to the brokerage company that manages the trades for whom this broker works. This is an oversimplification as there are several different kinds of brokers. Where the CFTC Commodities and Futures Trading Commission is concerned, there are FCM Futures Commission Merchants, IB Introducing Brokers, and AP Associated Persons who are the individuals at the various commodity broker firms.

Commodity brokers do interesting jobs. They are involved in facilitating trades done in the commodity markets on behalf of the typical investor. The main other way to place such trades is by having one's own seat on the commodities exchange or by trading in the open outcry commodity pits. For the majority of people interested in trading these markets, they will be required to utilize the broker in some fashion to place their trades.

The commodity brokers themselves have one of two ways they can route their clients' trades through to the exchanges. They may have their company's floor traders who can place the trade literally on the exchange floor. Otherwise they will possess a special direct link trading platform that will allow them to place and then execute the trades via the electronic system on the various exchanges.

The commodity exchanges depend on these commodity brokers to gather in the business and clients for them. This is because they are unable to do so directly thanks to the governing rules on the way brokers carry out their business. The exchanges find it much simpler to carry out trade with only several dozens of brokerage firms than they do with literally hundreds of thousands of different customers trying to place their particular trades at the exchange directly.

Besides this valuable introducing service which the commodity broker provides, a great number of individual investors and traders need the brokers to offer them both recommendations and general position trading advice. This is because the commodities markets are often hard to comprehend in the beginning. Without the services and assistance of a good commodity broker, many investors would simply never engage in commodities trading ultimately.

Until the 1990s, the realm of commodities trading was limited to only the commodity pits at the various exchanges. The majority of the different orders came in from what was called a full-service commodity broker. The customers would first call their introducing brokers to make them aware of a trade they wished to enter. Next this broker would write up the order and place a timestamp on it. They immediately called their FCM clearing firm which takes their orders. The broker would articulate the exact trade from the ticket which their customer had phoned in to them.

The clearing firm was receiving calls at a special phone bank directly on the floor of the relevant exchange. A clerk would be taking down the order. The clerk would then write up a ticket to hand off to one of the floor brokers. These individuals stood in the trading pits and physically filled the order. The floor broker would then hand back the ticket to a runner who would run it back to the clerk. Finally the clerk would phone the introducing broker back and provide the trade confirmation and fill price. After the broker received his confirmation information, he would contact the original client back to provide the fill price and other information.

This form of manual trading via the telephone has all but disappeared in the past two decades. Now clients simply log on to the trading platform which their broker provided. They enter the trade information and hit buy or sell using their mouse. Such orders instantly route and match up at the relevant exchange's trading platform so that the confirmation on a market order is no more than one to two seconds away. This has made the trading process far more efficient, less expensive, and faster. Other traders insist on working with the full-service broker model still so they have a professional with whom they can talk about the various trading strategies and possibilities.

Common Stock

Common stocks are shares in an underlying company that represent equity ownership in the corporation. They are also known as ordinary shares. These are securities in which individuals invest their capital. Common stock is the opposite of preferred stock.

While common stock and preferred stock both represent ownership in the company, there are many important differences between the two. Should a company go bankrupt, common stock holders are only given their money after preferred stock owners, bond owners, and creditors. Yet, common stock performs well, typically seeing greater levels of price appreciation than does preferred stock.

Common stock typically comes with voting rights, another feature that preferred stock does not have. These votes are used in electing the board of directors at the company's annual meeting, as well as in determining such things as company strategy, stock splits, policies, mergers and acquisitions, and the sale of the company. Preemptive rights in common stocks refer to owners with these rights being allowed to keep the same proportion of ownership in the company' stock, even if it issues additional stock.

Common stocks do not always pay dividends to share holders, as preferred stocks typically do. The dividends of common stocks are not pre-set or fixed. This means that the dividend returns are not completely predictable. Instead, they are based on a company's reinvestment policies, earnings results, and practices of the market in the valuing of the stock shares themselves.

Common shares have various other benefits. They are typically less expensive than are preferred stock shares. They are more heavily traded and readily available as well. The spreads between the buying and selling prices on them tend to be tighter as a result. Common stocks generally provide capital appreciation as the price of the shares rises over time, assuming that the company continues to do well and meet or exceed expectations. Dividends are often paid to common share holders when these things prove to be the case.

Common stocks can be purchased in any denominated amount. Round lots of common stocks are sold by even one hundred share amounts. This means that five hundred shares of common stock would be considered to be five lots of common stock.

Common stocks represent principally capital gains types of investments, as an investor is looking to buy them low and sell them at a higher price. This leads to a capital gain when the stock is sold at this greater level. The capital gain is the difference between the selling price and the purchasing price. Common stocks can also be cash flow types of investments when they pay a reliable stream of dividends every quarter. These income amounts are typically smaller than the one time amounts realized in capital gains, though they are obtained four times per year on a quarterly basis, or occasionally more often on a monthly basis.

Compound Annual Growth Rate (CAGR)

Compound Annual Growth Rate refers to the measurement which attempts to reduce the volatility of annual gains in growth during a set out number of years. The growth gains it considers include income, profits, customers, and more. The idea is to reduce the volatility over the years as if the growth had occurred evenly each year in the time frame under consideration. It can also be defined more technically as the average annual rate of growth for a given investment throughout a defined time period that exceeds a single year.

This means that the Compound Annual Growth Rate is not actually the real rate of return. Instead it is more like a representative figure. In other words, it is a fictitious percentage that spells out the investment return rate assuming that growth in said investment had been even and consistent over the years. In the real world, this almost never occurs. The reason to use such an artificial construct as this CAGR is to make the returns on a given investment more understandable.

Determining this Compound Annual Growth Rate is complex. It involves taking the investment value at the conclusion of the period under consideration. This must be divided by the value from the start of the period. The result has to be raised to a power of one divided by the total period length. This number that results must then be subtracted from the whole number one to get the final result for CAGR. It is a complicated formula that is difficult for most people to grasp if they are not mathematicians.

This is why looking at a tangible example makes it simpler to follow. Assume a certain corporation had three years of sales that were $300 million in the first year, $450 million in the second year, and $800 million in the third year. The growth rate was different every year. Its second year it increased by 50 percent while its third year the growth rate was almost 78 percent. Using the Compound Annual Growth Rate would smooth this out to provide a picture as if the company's rate of growth per year had been steady over the three years considered. It is the compounding part that makes the formula so complex. This also explains why investors and analysts who figure this value will use a business calculator or a program that figures out the equation for them once they plug in the appropriate numbers of starting value, end value, and number of years.

Yet the Compound Annual Growth Rate is useful to businesses, investors, and analysts in particular. It helps investors who are interested in comparing and contrasting the rates of growth (over a predetermined amount of time) for two or more funds or firms. This would not be a simple task if they instead utilized the volatile and changing year over year growth rates.

Thanks to the simplicity of this measurement, it has utility in several other cases. In its simplest form, investors or analysts can employ the CAGR to figure out the average annual growth for one investment. As an example, investments might gain in relative value each year at the varying rates of plus seven percent the first year, minus one percent the second year, then plus six percent the third year. Using this CAGR will help the investor or analyst to get a bigger picture of the three year progress made by the investment in question.

Compounding of Money

The compounding of money has everything to do with compound interest. Compounding of money through such compounding interest can become among the most potent of weapons in your investing arsenal. Compound interest allows your money to grow at a faster rate as a result of the way that the interest is added to your money's balance. Various types of compound interest are available for compounding your money.

Compounding your money with compound interest works through taking the interest that your money has earned over a time frame and adding it back to the initial amount of money. Then when the next period is figured up, this total dollar value is calculated in the next portion of interest that you will earn. Simply put, every time frame's interest is placed directly back in to the entire sum of money on which the interest will be earned. Every time the interest is figured up, your money will earn a greater amount of interest like this.

A variety of different forms of compound interest exist. These always relate to the time frame over which the interest and money compounds. Such time frames of compounding of money are comprised of yearly, monthly, and daily compounding interest. With yearly compounding interest, the interest rate is figured up each year. In monthly compounding of interest, this rate is applied to the new principal balance each month. Daily compounding of interest involves an every day accounting of the interest and new principal.

Compounding of money involves several factors. These are periodic rates of compound interest, which are the rates actually applied to your balance, and compounding periods, which are the amount of the time frame before such interest is literally applied on to your total balance. As an example, if you invested $10,000 in a .1% daily periodic rate money market form of account, then on the second day, your balance would be $10,010. The next day, this rate would then be applied to the new balance of $10,010. Figuring out the actual annual effective rate entails you taking the whole year's interest and dividing it by the amount of the investment that you started with at the beginning of the year, or $10,000 in this case.

Compounding of money through such compound interest proves to be an extremely potent weapon. This is because the interest earned is immediately added on to the account balance to be counted as principal for the next time period. Each time frame the interest rate applies to the greater balance. Accounts grow faster through the compounding of money as the interest is not held back.

This compounding of money effect multiplies when you use it with accounts that are tax deferred, such as municipal bond funds and annuities. As no penalties of taxes are paid in a given year, your money increases quicker and quicker since greater amounts are constantly in the account to receive interest.

An example of how effective compounding of money using compound interest can be is illuminating. If you put $10,000 into a simple interest account that does not compound but receives twelve percent interest, then it will increase to $46,000 over thirty years. The same money that is compounded annually will rise to about $300,000, and to as much as $347,000 if the money is compounded quarterly. Money that is compounded over a daily time frame would naturally earn the greatest amount of interest and highest principal over a period of time.

Contrarian Investing

Contrarian Investing refers to a well-known style of investing which invests against the main going and popular market trends of the day. It does so through purchasing those assets which are performing poorly to later resell them when they outperform. An individual who proves to be a contrarian investor is of the opinion that those analysts who argue the market will rise are only doing this because they have fully invested their own funds and therefore have no additional purchasing power remaining to them. This would then be the market's peak. Similarly at that point when the analysts and so-called gurus argue a downturn is overdue they have already sold out their own holdings.

Another factor of contrarian investing has to do with those securities which have fallen from favor and therefore possess lower price to earnings ratios. This strategy involves selling and buying in the opposite direction of what the mainstream investors are doing at that given moment in time. They would then choose to wade into the market as other investors feel negative on it and that the value is cheaper than its true intrinsic value.

Overwhelming pessimistic sentiment on any given stock means that the price could be unfairly punished. Contrarians feel that the risks and downsides on the issue have already been blown out of proportion. The trick lies in determining which distressed stocks they should purchase or sell as the company makes a recovery and the stock price recovers accordingly as well. It often times means that the associated stocks will regain value at a far quicker pace than is normal for mid to large cap stocks. At the same time, having an over optimistic opinion on stocks which are over hyped can cause the opposite impact.

The character trait that many different contrarians share is their eternal view of an oncoming bear market. This is called the perm bear syndrome. They may not feel the market will be negative, yet they remain cautiously skeptical on the way that the mainstream investors view the stock markets. They realize that valuations which rise too high will finally end in inevitable declines as the growing expectations of investors do not pan out in the end. Such contrarian principles may be utilized effectively not only with entire markets, but a given industry or even individual company stocks.

This also means that contrarian investing shows many of the hallmarks of classical value investing. The two types of investors are seeking out price discrepancies which would mean that a given asset class is not fairly or fully valued in the given market conditions. There are countless value investors who believe that only a fine line exists between contrarian and value investing since they are both seeking out profits on undervalued securities.

One critical difference between the two disciplines lies in the relative importance of the Price to Earnings ratio, which is centerpiece of value investing. Contrarian investors will naturally consider it but more importantly attempt to ascertain the qualitative mood on the overall market. This means that they place priority emphasis on trading volume, analyst forecasts, and the tone and substance of media commentary.

The contrarian investors also put a lot of value on the basic principles of behavioral finance. They believe that investors act as a large collective and interact with trends as such. When stocks perform badly, this means that they will remain in this trend for a while. Similarly, stronger performing stocks will stay buoyant for many market sessions until something comes along to upset this powerful market moving trend.

Convertible Bond

A convertible bond is like a hybrid between a stock and a bond. Corporations issue these bonds which the bondholders may choose to convert into shares of the underlying company stock whenever they decide. Such a bond usually pays better yields than do shares of common stocks. Their yields are also typically less than regular corporate bonds pay.

Convertible bonds provide income to their investors just as traditional corporate bonds do. These convertibles also possess the unique ability to gain in price if the stock of the issuing company does well. The reasoning behind this is straightforward. Because the bond has the ability to be directly converted into stock shares, the security's value will only gain as the stock shares themselves actually rise on the market.

When the stock performs poorly, the investors do not have the ability to convert the convertible bond into shares. They only gain the yield as a return on the investment in this case. The advantage these bonds have over the company stock in these deteriorating conditions is significant.

The value of the convertible instrument will only drop to its par value as long as the company that issues it does not go bankrupt. This is because on the specified maturity date, investors will obtain back their original principal. It is quite correct to say that these types of bonds typically have far less downside potential than do shares of common stocks.

There are disadvantages as well as advantages to these convertible bonds. Should the issuer of the bond file for bankruptcy, investors in these kinds of bonds possess a lower priority claim on the assets of the corporation than do those who invested in debt which was not convertible. Should the issuer default or not make an interest or principal payment according to schedule, the convertibles will likely suffer more than a regular corporate bond would. This is the flip side to the higher potential to appreciate which convertibles famously possess. It is a good reason that individuals who choose to invest in single convertible securities should engage in significant and extended research on the issuer's credit.

It is also important to note that the majority of these convertible bonds can be called. This gives the issuer the right to call away the bonds at a set share price. It limits the maximum gain an investor can realize even if the stock significantly outperforms. This means that a convertible security will rarely offer the identical unlimited gain possibilities which common stocks can.

If investors are determined to do the necessary research on an individual company, they can purchase a convertible bond from a broker. For better convertible diversification, there are numerous mutual funds which invest in only convertible securities. These funds are provided by a variety of major mutual fund companies.

Some of the biggest are Franklin Convertible Securities, Vanguard Convertible Securities, Fidelity Convertible Securities, and Calamos Convertible A. Several ETF exchange traded funds provide a similar convertible diversification with lower service charges. Among these are the SPDR Barclays Capital Convertible Bond ETF and the PowerShares Convertible Securities Portfolio.

It is important to know that the bigger convertible securities portfolios such as the ETFs track have a tendency to match the performance of the stock market quite closely in time. This makes them similar to a high dividend equity fund. Such investments do offer possible upside and diversification when measured against typical holdings of bonds. They do not really offer much in the way of diversification for individuals who already keep most of their investment dollars in stocks.

Corporate Bonds

Corporate bonds are debt securities that a company issues and sells to investors. Such corporate bonds are generally backed by the company's ability to repay the loan. This money is anticipated to result from successful operations in the future time periods. With some corporate bonds, the physical assets of a company can be offered as bond collateral to ease investors' minds and any concerns about repayment.

Corporate bonds are also known as debt financing. These bonds provide a significant capital source for a great number of businesses. Other sources of capital for the companies include lines of credit, bank loans, and equity issues like stock shares. For a business to be capable of achieving coupon rates that are favorable to them by issuing their debt to members of the public, a corporation will have to provide a series of consistent earnings reports and to show considerable earnings potential. As a general rule, the better a corporation's quality of credit is believed to be, the simpler it is for them to offer debt at lower rates and float greater amounts of such debt.

Such corporate bonds are always issued in $1,000 face value blocks. Practically all of them come with a standardized structure for coupon payments. Some corporate bonds include what is known as a call provision. These provisions permit the corporation that issues them to recall the bonds early if interest rates change significantly. Every call provision will be specific to the given bond.

These types of corporate bonds are deemed to be of greater risk than are government issued bonds. Because of this perceived additional risk, the interest rates almost always turn out to be higher with corporate bonds. This is true for companies whose credit is rated as among the best.

Regarding tax issues of corporate bonds, these are pretty straight forward. The majority of corporate bonds prove to be taxable, assuming that their terms are for longer than a single year. To avoid taxes until the end, some bonds come with zero coupons and redemption values that are high, meaning that taxes are deferred as capital gains until the end of the bond term. Such corporate debts that come due in under a year are generally referred to as commercial paper.

Corporate bonds are commonly listed on the major exchanges and ECN's like MarketAxess and Bonds.com. Even though these bonds are carried on the major exchanges, their trading does not mostly take place on them. Instead, the overwhelming majority of such bonds trading occurs in over the counter and dealer based markets.

Among the various types of corporate bonds are secured debt, unsecured debt, senior debt, and subordinated debt. Secured debts have assets underlying them. Senior debts provide the strongest claims on the corporation's assets if the venture defaults on its debt obligations. The higher up an investor's bond is in the firm's capital structure, the greater their claim will ultimately be in such an unfortunate scenario as default or bankruptcy.

Credit Default Swaps

A credit default swap, or CDS, is a contract exchange that transfers between two parties the exposure of credit to fixed income products. Two parties are involved in this exchange. The purchaser of a credit default swap obtains protection for credit. The seller of this credit default swap actually guarantees the product's credit worthiness. In this process, the default risk moves from the owner of the fixed income security over to the party that sells the swap.

In these CDS transfers, the purchaser of the protection gives a series of fees or payments to the seller. This is also known as the spread of the Credit Default Swap. The party selling the protection gets paid off in exchange for this, assuming that a loan or bond type of credit instrument suffers from a negative credit event.

In the most basic forms, Credit Default Swaps prove to be two party contracts arranged between sellers and buyers of credit protection. These Credit Default Swaps will address a reference obligor or reference entity. These are typically governments or companies. The party being referenced is not involved in the contract as a party or even necessarily aware of its existence. The purchaser of such protection then pays pre defined quarterly premiums, or the spread, to the party who is selling the protection.

Should the entity that is referenced then default, the seller of the protection pays the face value of the instrument to the buyer of the protection against a physical transfer of the bond. Such settlements can also be accomplished by auction or in cash. Defaults in Credit Default Swaps are called credit events. These defaults might include a bankruptcy, restructuring of the referenced entity, or a failure to make payment.

Credit Default Swaps are much like insurance on credit. The difference between them and such insurance lies in the fact that a CDS is not regulated like life insurance or casualty insurance is. Besides this, investors are capable of purchasing or selling this type of protection without having any such debt of the entity that is referenced. Resulting naked credit default swaps permit investors to engage in speculation on issues of debt and credit worthiness of entities that are referenced. These naked Credit Default

Swaps actually make up the majority of the CDS market.

The majority of Credit Default Swaps prove to be in the ten to twenty million dollar range. They typically have maturities ranging from one to ten years. The Credit Default Swap market is mostly unregulated and turns out to be the largest financial market on earth.

These CDS products were actually created in the early part of the 1990's. The market for them grew dramatically beginning in 2003. By the conclusion of 2007, the total amount of them in existence proved to be an astonishing $62.2 trillion dollars. This amount declined to $38.6 trillion in the wake of the financial crisis at the conclusion of 2008. Since then, it has been growing alarmingly again. Critics of Credit Default Swaps have consistently referred to them as financial weapons of mass destruction, capable of blowing up the financial system and world economies in the process.

Credit Derivatives

Credit derivatives refer to bilateral contracts which are privately held. These contracts permit the holders to manage their credit risk exposure. Such derivatives turn out to be financial assets. Examples of the better-known ones in the derivatives universe are swaps, forward contracts, and options. The price of these is necessarily based upon the credit risk of economic entities like governments, companies, or private investors. This means that banks which are worried about one of their customers not being capable of repaying their loan are able to purchase protection against such a potential loss in default. They do this by keeping the loan on their books at the same time as they transfer the credit risk off to a third party more commonly referred to as the "counter party."

Such credit derivatives are only one of numerous different kinds of financial instruments available to investors and financial institutions today. With these derivatives, they are merely instruments whose existence derives from underlying financial instruments. The value which underlies them comes from a stock or other asset.

Two different principal forms of derivatives exist. These are calls and puts. Calls provide the right but not obligation to purchase a stock for a pre-set price called the strike price. Puts deliver the right but not obligation to sell particular stocks for pre-arranged strike prices. With either calls or puts, investors are obtaining insurance in case a stock price rises or falls. This makes every form of derivative product an insurance vehicle and particularly these credit derivative examples.

Numerous credit derivatives exist on the markets today. Among these are CDO Collateralized Debt Obligations, CDS Credit Default Swamps, credit default swap options, total return swaps, and credit spread forwards. Banks are allowed to utilize these complicated instruments in order to completely take away their default risk from even an entire loan portfolio. The financial institutions or banks pay a premium, or upfront fee, for this accommodation.

Considering a concrete example helps to make the credit derivatives concept clearer. Plants R Us borrows $200,000 off of a bank with a ten year repayment term. Because Plants R Us shows a poor credit history, they are forced to buy the bank a credit derivative in order to be able to receive the loan. The bank accepts this product which will permit them to transfer all of the default risk to a third counter party. This means that the counter party would be forced to deliver all unpaid interest and principal on the loan in the event that Plants R Us defaults on the said loan. For this guarantee, Plants R Us pays an annual fee to the counter party for their assumed risk. Should the Plants R Us not default on the loan, then the counterparty firm keeps the entire fee. This makes it a win-win-win situation for all three parties. The bank is protected against a default by Plants R Us, which gets to have its loan. The counter party collects the yearly fee. All parties gain and benefit from the arrangement.

Credit derivatives' values vary widely depending on several factors. These include the borrower's credit quality as well as the counter party's credit quality. The biggest concern comes down to the credit quality of the third party - counter party. If the counter party defaults or is otherwise unable to honor their commitments specified in the derivatives contract, then the financial institution will not get its payment for the loan principal and interest. The counter party would naturally no longer receive its annual premium payments any longer either. This is why the quality of credit for the counter party is so much more critical than is the credit quality of the borrower (Plants R Us in the example).

Custodial Account

A Custodial Account refers to a particular type of savings account. These can be accessed via a mutual fund company, financial institution, or brokerage firm. With these accounts, an adult controls and manages the funds or assets on behalf of a minor who is less than 18 years old. State laws govern the rules that affect these special accounts. Minors may not perform transactions in such an account without first obtaining mandatory approval of the custodian. Such an account might also be one of the retirement accounts which a custodian handles for any and all employees in a firm who are eligible to have one of these.

With a Custodial Account, it is typically the guardian or parent of the minor in question who has oversight on the account. Such investments contained in these forms of accounts are limited to mutual funds or similar products that regulated investment companies offer their clients. Every company that administers such a Custodial Account will have its own particular rules on the interest rate levels and account balance minimums they maintain.

What is interesting is that any person is allowed to contribute into a Custodial Account. The minors will not have access to any choices made by the account or money in it without their guardian's consent until they attain the legal age of adult hood. At this point, the ownership of the account transfers over from the custodian(s) and on to the minor. The minor would then gain full decision-making powers over how and when to utilize this money.

Two different kinds of Custodial Accounts exist in the United States. These are the UGMA Uniform Gift to Minors Act administered accounts and the UTMA Uniform Transfers to Minors Act ones. With the UGMA, parents and other are able to provide assets to their minor children in the forms of cash, savings bonds, life insurance, annuities, or stocks. The UTMA permit parents to postpone any distributions from the account. Each state has its own age limits which can be established by the parents or guardians.

There are a number of advantages to these two types of Custodial Accounts. Withdrawal penalties, contribution limits, and income restrictions do not apply to either of them. When a single contribution in excess of

$14,000 goes into the account, this does become treated as a "gift," and the IRS will naturally then levy a gift tax on the total. Custodians also have the ability to transfer the account balance over to a 529 plan. In order to do this, the custodian first will be required to close out any investments inside the account which are not cash.

There are a few disadvantages for the minors to having one of these accounts. The government and university/college systems recognize such accounts as assets. This means that they will often decrease the ability of the minor to obtain financial aid in the college or university admissions process. This is why financial planners will often suggest that such an account should not be opened for any minor who might hope to qualify to receive financial aid packages.

Taxes will also apply to withdrawals from these accounts. Every state has its own ruling on the matter regarding whether they will be taxed at the rate of the minor or the parents' income tax bracket. Some of the unearned income becomes tax free. The rest will become fully taxable at either the child's or guardian's federal tax rate. There will also be capital gains taxes assessed on any earnings from liquidated assets in these Custodial Accounts.

Any gifts presented to such an account can not be rescinded later. The beneficiary of the account also can not be changed subsequently. The parents are required by law to file the child's tax returns when they have such an account until the minor becomes old enough to transfer over the ownership of the account. Once the minor attains the age of 18, then all dividends and earnings within the account will become subject to the minor's applicable tax rate.

Debt Fund

A Debt Fund refers to an investment pool. This might be either an exchange traded fund or a mutual fund. In it the core assets will be various types of fixed income investments. They could choose to invest in longer term bonds or shorter term ones, money market instruments, securitized products, or even floating rate debt. The debt funds feature lower fee ratios on average than do the comparable equity funds. This is in part because the total management costs prove to be significantly lower for the debt funds than for the equity funds.

The primary objectives for investing in a debt fund will commonly be the generation of income as well as preservation of the original capital. They often consider their performance against a comparable major benchmark as a means of measuring success and judging absolute returns with these debt funds. As such, they will invest in as many promising opportunities as they can find. This might include MIP's monthly income plans, liquid funds, STP's short term plans, Gilt funds, and FMP's fixed maturity plans.

In general, these debt funds will be preferred by those investors who do not want to experience scary high volatility which investing in the stock market easily often can present. It means that such a debt fund will deliver low but steady income as compared to equity funds. Yet the volatility is minor by comparison. Debt funds like these provide a number of advantages.

The tax rules have changed to favor them. Investors will have to stay invested for minimally three years in order to enjoy the advantage of lower taxed longer term capital gains. Those which are redeemed in under three years will be treated as ordinary income for taxable purposes. Debt funds thus become far more tax efficient than even fixed deposits when investors hold them for at least three years. Debt funds will only be taxed at the rate of 20 percent once they are indexed, which is often considerably lower than many investors' otherwise earned income tax rate.

There is also no tax deduction for debt funds at the source, known as TDS on any and all gains which they realize. The returns also are linked to the market performance though they do not offer corresponding returns. When interest rates rise, they can lose, though it is a remote chance of them losing. The maturity of the various holdings defines the actual volatility of the debt fund. Those funds which mostly hold shorter term bonds will not demonstrate much volatility and will still provide returns that are approximately equal to the prevailing interest rates.

Debt funds also allow individuals to invest in SIP's. These are the smartest ways to purchase equity or debt funds. With large sums, they can be sunk into a debt fund that will make systematic transfers into the plan or any fund for which an individual opts. Each month, a fixed and predetermined sum will move from the debt fund over to the other funds that the investors selected.

There will also be an exit load on debt funds. This is the tradeoff for vastly greater liquidity than with many competing investments. Individuals are able to withdraw at any point with only a day's notice. Some of the funds do assess a penalty for leaving in under a preset minimum period. Exit loads range from a reasonable .5 percent on up to a steeper two percent penalty. The minimum holding period is often anywhere from six months on out to as long as two years.

Deferred Annuity

A Deferred Annuity refers to a specific kind of annuity contract. These types of annuities delay income payments (in the form of either a lump sum or installments) to the point where the investor chooses to obtain them. There are two principal stages in these kinds of annuities. These are the savings phase and the income phase. In the savings phase, individuals put money into the contract. The income phase is the one after the annuity becomes converted so that the payments are distributed as arranged. With deferred annuities there are several sub-types. These include fixed, variable, equity-indexed, and longevity.

A Fixed Deferred Annuity operates similarly to a CD Certificate of Deposit. The main difference lies in how the interest income must be claimed. With these annuities, it becomes long-term deferred until the owners take disbursements from the contract. These fixed contracts come with a guaranteed rate of interest that all funds earn. The insurance company stands behind the guarantee. These are attractive choices for those investors who are averse to risk and who do not require any interest income until after they turn 59 and ½ or older.

A variable Deferred Annuity is something like an assortment of mutual funds. With annuities, they refer to these as sub-accounts. Each owner has personal control over the investment risk he or she engages in through selecting particular sub-accounts which may cover both stocks and bonds. The returns on these investments will influence how well the annuity performs. For most investors, it benefits them more to purchase shares in several index mutual funds. This is because deferring taxes to retirement could mean that the owners will possibly pay higher taxes when they are retired than when they are working. The fees can also be as high as greater than three percent each year with many variable annuities.

Equity indexed annuities work much like the fixed annuities but also have variable annuity-like features. They possess two features. The first proves to be a guaranteed minimum return. The second is the ability to obtain a higher return than this by gaining from a formula which is based on one of the popular indices of the stock market like the S&P 500 or the Dow Jones Industrial Average. The downside to this type is that it typically comes with expensive surrender charges that can last over a ten to fifteen consecutive year long period.

Buying one of these last categories, the longevity annuity, is akin to obtaining insurance for a long life expectancy. It is helpful to consider a real life example to better understand how this works out in practice. An investor who is 60 might decide to pay in $150,000 to one of these longevity annuities. In exchange for this consideration, the insurance company which backs it will promise to pay out a set dollar amount of income for the rest of the holder's life beginning 25 years later at age 85. The advantage to this type of arrangement is that the retirees can then spend their other retirement assets because they feel comfortable that there will be a steady income stream that will support them guaranteed the rest of their lives. All income and taxes would be deferred to the distribution age when the money begins being disbursed.

It is important to realize with these annuities that any early withdrawals realized before the owners reach their legal retirement age will come with a full 10 percent penalty tax on top of the regular income taxes which the IRS will assess. The income tax rate would be based on the tax bracket of the individual when they receive the distribution.
These deferred annuities have many interesting (but often expensive) options and features which the buyers can obtain. Some of these include future income guarantees and death benefits.

Diversifying

Diversifying refers to the means of effectively lowering your investing risk by putting your money into a wide range of various assets. A truly well diversified portfolio offers the benefits of lower amounts of risk than those that are simply invested into one or two asset classes or kinds of investments.

Everyone should engage in some amount of diversification, even if the individual proves to be one who is tolerant of risk. Those individuals who really fear the present day economic uncertainties and very real amounts of risk in the market place will perform better forms of diversification into more asset groups.

Mainstream diversification is always recommended by financial experts because of the common example of not placing all of your investment eggs into just a single basket. If you do have all eggs in the one basket and then drop the basket along the way, then they can all break. The idea is that by placing each egg into its own individual basket, the odds of breaking all of the eggs declines significantly, even if one or several of them do get broken themselves.

Portfolios that have not engaged in diversifying might have only one or two corporations' stocks in them. This proves to be a dangerous investment strategy, since no matter how good a company looks on paper, its stock could decline to as low as zero literally over night. The past few years of the financial collapse have taught many investors the extremely painful lesson that even once blue chip financial companies' stock can decline to practically nothing as they spectacularly collapse.

Any financial expert will confidently state that portfolios made up of a dozen or two dozen varying stocks will have far less chance of plummeting. This becomes even more the case when you pick out stocks from a variety of types, industries, and market capitalization sizes of corporations. Better diversifying in stocks would include some companies that are based in other countries. Diversifying does not simply stop with stocks. It steers investors into bonds, mutual funds, and money market funds as well. Though all of these different investments diversify you, they still leave you mostly exposed to the one currency of the U.S. dollar.

More thorough diversifying will put at least a portion of your investments into assets whose values are not solely expressed in terms of only the American currency. This would include commodities, such as gold, silver, oil, and platinum in particular. Foreign currencies, such as the Euro, Pound, or Swiss Franc are another fantastic means of diversifying, and they can be acquired on the world FOREX exchange in currency accounts.

Real estate, including commercial properties, residential properties, vacation homes, or even real estate investment funds, offers another way to diversify away from U.S. dollar based financial investments such as stocks, bonds, mutual funds, and money market accounts. The strongest diversifying advice is to have at least three to seven completely different investment class vehicles, preferably one or more of which is not denominated in only U.S. dollars.

Dividend

Dividends represent portions of a company's earnings that are returned to the investors in the company's stock. These are typically paid out in cash that is either deposited into the investors' brokerage accounts or can be reinvested directly into the company's stock. As an example of a dividend, every share of Phillip Morris pays around 4.5% dividends on the stock price each year.

Investing in dividend paying stocks is a particular passive income investment strategy that is also a cash flow investment. This passive, or cash flow, income means that you collect income just from holding these stock investments. This kind of strategy entails building up a group of blue chip company stocks that pay large dividend yields which add money to your account usually four times per year, on a quarterly basis. Investors in dividends tremendously enjoy watching these routine deposits in cash arrive in either their bank account, brokerage account, or the mail.

Dividend investors who understand this type of investment are looking for a number of different elements in the stocks that they buy. Such dividend stocks should include a high dividend yield. To qualify as high yields, most value investors prefer to see ones that pay more than do the interest rate yields on U.S. Treasuries. Dividend yields can be easily determined. All that you have to do is to take the amount of the dividend and divide it by the price of the stock. So a stock that offers a $2 dividend and costs $40 is paying a five percent dividend yield.

Dividend paying stocks should also feature high dividend coverage. This coverage simply refers to the safety of a dividend, or how likely it is to be reduced or even eliminated. Companies that earn their profits from a large array of businesses are more likely to be able to continue paying their dividends than are companies that make all of their money off of a single business that could be threatened.

A more tangible way of expressing the coverage lies in how many times the dividend total dollar amount is covered by the corporation's total earnings. A company with fifty million dollars in profits that pays twenty million in dividends has its dividend covered by two and a half times. Should their profits drop by ten percent or more, they will have no trouble still paying the same dividend amount to shareholders. The dividend payout ratio is another way of measuring this. On the above example it would be forty percent. Dividend investors prefer to see no more than sixty percent of profits given out as dividends, as this could signify that the company lacks future opportunities for growth and expansion.

Qualified dividends are a third element that dividend investors are looking for in their dividend paying stocks. This simply means that stocks that are kept for less than a year do not benefit from lower tax rates on dividends. Since the government is attempting to convince you to become a longer term investor, you should take advantage of these lower tax rates by only buying stocks with qualified dividends that you have held for a full year and more.

Dividend Payout Ratio

The Dividend Payout Ratio refers to a ratio of all dividends which have been paid out to the total shareholders as compared to the complete net income of the company. In the end, the percentage of earnings paid to shareholders in the form of dividends is what this amounts to. Any amount of earnings which does not become payable to shareholders remains with the company in the form of retained earnings which the company keeps in order to reinvest for expansion or in other core operations or to pay down their company debt.

This Dividend Payout Ratio may be calculated out as the annual dividend per share divided by the company's earnings per share. Another way of figuring it is by taking the number one and subtracting the retention ratio.

This Dividend Payout Ratio delivers a figure for the total sum of money which a company gives back to its shareholders as opposed to how much they decide to hold for such things as increasing cash reserves, reinvesting in growth, and paying down debt. This is commonly referred to as retained earnings.

It is always important to consider a number of factors when deciding on how to read the Dividend Payout Ratio. This starts with the maturity level of a given company under consideration. Those firms which are newer and heavily skewed towards growth will want to expand, create and launch newer products, and also attempt to grow into completely new markets. They would naturally keep to reinvest the majority of or even sometimes all of their aggregate earnings. This would excuse them maintaining an extremely low or even zero percent payout ratio.

The same does not go for a company which is older and far better established. If they return only a small percentage of their earnings to the shareholders, then investors will complain. It might not only angry the individual corporate investors, but cause the so-called activists to intervene in the company board and management in retaliation.

Consider the interesting case of Apple. In the year 2012, the technology giant finally started paying a dividend for its first time in around twenty years at that point. It was because the new Chief Executive Officer believed that the enormous cash flow of the tech giant company meant that it was no longer justifiable to offer a zero percent payout ratio. The downside to this decision is it put Apple in the somewhat awkward position of joining the ranks of those corporations which believe they have passed their strong initial growth stage and so make a large dividend ratio payout to compensate. It signals that the company share prices will not likely continue to appreciate rapidly any longer.

The Dividend Payout Ratio has another helpful use. It can be deployed in order to determine how sustainable a dividend is from a given firm. Corporations do not like to cut back their dividends once they establish them. It can cause the stock price of the company to free fall and often reflects poorly on the skills and capabilities of management. When the firm has a higher than 100 percent Dividend Payout Ratio, it means that they are giving back a larger amount of money than they are earning. This would require that they reduce the dividend or eliminate it altogether in the near future.

Companies may decide to ride out a bad year in the market place without cutting their payouts though. This is why analysts like to contemplate the future earnings expectations of a firm to calculate up a forward looking payout ratio in order to put their last payout ratios into better perspective. Longer term payout ratios are similarly significant. Those ratios which are steadily increasing might be indicative of a maturing and growing business. Spiking ones might indicate that the dividend was quickly becoming unsustainable though.

Dividend Reinvestment Plans

Dividend Reinvestment Plans are also known by their acronyms as DRIPs or even DRPs. These plans come from corporations and companies which permit their investors to take their cash dividends in the form of reinvesting options. Generally this amounts to the investors acquiring extra fractional shares or additional whole shares. It occurs on the payment date of the dividend. DRIPs are intelligent means of growing the actual value in an investment holding.

The majority of these Dividend Reinvestment Plans allow their own investors to purchase these shares directly from the company. This provides them with a commission-free buy in usually offered at a substantial price discount to the present price of the shares on the stock market exchange. The majority of them will not accept reinvestments for under $10.

These Dividend Reinvestment Plans allow their shareholders to continuously invest in differing amounts over the span of longer-term timeframe investments in publically traded companies. Stake holders are able to buy either whole shares or even fractional shares through such dividend reinvestments in the best-known, most-famous public companies for only $10 or more at a single time.

Choosing this option means that investors forego their quarterly dividend payment check. The DRIP operating entity could be a transfer agent, company itself, or brokerage company. They will utilize the money from the dividend check to buy extra shares on behalf of the investor in question in the relevant company.

When the corporations directly operate their own Dividend Reinvestment Plans, they will appoint particular times throughout the year when they will permit the DRIP program buy in of additional shares from the company stakeholders. This is generally on a quarterly basis. The corporations in question never wade into secondary markets on exchanges to buy the shares then resell them to their investors. Instead the shares proffered through the DRIP come out of the companies' treasury reserve shares.

It is also important to note that such Dividend Reinvestment Plans shares issued directly by the company in question may not ever be resold on the stock market exchanges. Investors who wish to cash out of them will be forced to resell them back to the corporation which originally issued these for the present price on the stock market. When DRIPs run by brokerage companies are involved, the firm will just buy the shares for the investors who are acquiring them out of the secondary markets then tally such share into the brokerage account. In this case, these shares may be finally resold in the secondary market where they were originally acquired.

For those companies which do not directly offer their own share holders Dividend Reinvestment Plans, these can simply be established via a brokerage company. This is because a great number of the stock brokers permit their customers to reinvest such dividend payments directly into the stock shares which they already hold within their accounts. It is important that though such dividends do not come directly to the shareholders bank accounts, the IRS still requires that they be reported on a tax return like taxable income.

Many companies actually provide some significant incentives to take dividends from their DRIPs. They might provide a substantial discount of anywhere from one to ten percent from the present market share price. This can amount to a major savings when it is added to the lack of commissions on the trade.

Longer term advantages center on the miracle of compounded reinvestments on the returns. As the dividends become higher, the stake holders will receive an ever higher amount for every share they possess. This will then allow them to buy a still greater quantity of additional shares at each dividend payment. In a longer time frame, this will significantly boost the aggregate returns of the stock investment. This can really work to the advantage of the investors if the share price goes down and they gain the ability to cost average down with their DRIP share purchases. It offers them the possibility of significant gains from their reduced cost basis.

Companies like these DRIPs because they do not have to pay out as much capital when they are able to simply issue reserve shares from their treasury in lieu of cash dividend payouts. It also increases the loyalty of the shareholders, who will more likely hold on to the shares even when there are declines in the price of the share or the overall stock market.

Dividend Stocks

Dividend Stocks refer to stocks that pay especially generous and predictable shares of the corporate earnings out to their share holders. They are especially important for those investors who require dependable continuous streams of income off of their investment portfolios, such as retirees. This is why the optimal stock portfolio for those who are officially retired includes a strong and diverse mixture of industry-leading corporations which provide consistent, generous dividend yields.

These Dividend Stocks are famous for paying out significant stock dividends as a distribution on their earnings. They may pay this in the form of additional shares or as cash, depending on the wishes of the share holder in question. Sometimes the company will declare a stock dividend instead of a cash dividend, removing the ability of the shareholder to choose the form in which the dividend actually pays. When dividends become payable strictly as more stock, they are also known as stock splits.

For the companies that declare regular cash dividends of these Dividend Stocks, with each share stake holders have, they receive a set portion of the earnings from the corporation. This is literally being paid for simply owning the stock shares.

Consider a real world example to better understand how these Dividend Stocks work out in practice. Gillette, the world famous market leader in the shaving razors industry, may pay a dividend of $4 on an annual basis. Typically these dividends will be paid practically on a quarterly basis. This means four times each year Gillette would provide a $1 payout for each share of stock which the stake holders possess. If an investor owned 100 shares, he or she would receive four checks per year of $100 each check at approximately the conclusion of each quarter.

Most dividends from these Dividend Stocks come out in cash. Investors have the option to have them reinvested into additional company stock shares. Sometimes the corporation will provide a more advantageous reinvestment price than the current market prices to encourage such reinvesting of dividends in the company stock. These plans are called DRIPS (Dividend Re Investment Plans).

There are also occasional special dividends offered on an only one-time basis. They could be provided if the company wins a large and lucrative lawsuit, liquidates its share of an investment and receives a windfall payout, or sells part of the business to another firm for cash. These dividends can be made in cash, property, or stock share dividends.

There are several important dates with which Dividend Stocks' investors need to be familiar. These are declaration date, date of record, ex-dividend date, and payment date. Declaration date is the calendar day when the company's Board of Directors announces a dividend payout. This is the point where the firm adds a liability for the dividend payout to its company books. This means that it owes money (or shares) to the stake holders. This date will be the one when they announce both the date of record as well as the dividend payment date.

The date of record is the one where the corporation will review the appropriate records to determine who is holding the shares and is thus eligible for the dividends. Only holders of record will receive the dividend payment. The ex-dividend date is the day after which any investors who wish to receive dividends must own the shares. Only stake holders who possess shares on the day before the ex-dividend date get paid. Finally dividends are literally doled out on the payment date.

While most stock companies will pay out dividends on either a quarterly or half yearly basis, real estate investment trusts are structured differently. They pay out their dividends on an every-month basis as they receive monthly income from their various commercial, industrial, and/or residential properties.

Dividend Yield

Dividend yield refers to the payout of dividend price ratio on a given company's stock. It is simply determined by taking the yearly dividend payment total and dividing it by the cost for each share. This dividend yield is commonly given out as a percentage. The reciprocal of dividend yield proves to be the price to dividend ratio.

Dividend yields vary depending on whether a stock is a preferred stock or a common stock. With preferred shares, these dividend yields are outlined specifically in the stock's prospectus. A company will generally call such a preferred class of stock by the name first given to it, which included the yield based on this initial price. This might be a five percent preferred share. Since the pricing of preferred stock shares go up and down with the dictates of the market, the current yield will vary with the changes in price.

Preferred share holders have a variety of yields that they can figure up. These depend on the eventual disposition of their preferred share security. Besides the current yield formula of amount of dividend per price of preferred share, there are present value yields and a yield to maturity. These other yields only apply to those investors who purchase preferred stock shares after they have been issued or who choose to hold them until the reach the stated maturity date.

Preferred share dividends are almost always higher than the dividend yields on common stock shares.

Common stock shares have a dividend yield that differs entirely. With such common shares, the dividend amount is not guaranteed, and could vary from one quarter to the next. These dividends that are given to you, the common stock holder, are determined by the company's management. As such, they depend on the earnings of the company for the given quarter.

With common stocks, you can not be assured that dividends will be paid in the future that match dividends paid previously, or that these dividends will be paid period. Since it proves to be so challenging to correctly predict future dividends, the figures used in determining dividend yields are the present dividend yields. This means that the present dividend yield is always determined by dividing the most current full year's dividend by the present share price.

Dividend yields can have a major impact on how much money a stock makes for its owners over time. Dr. Jeremy Siegel is a well respected professor of investments who has determined conclusively with his research that ninety-nine percent of all after inflation gains that investors realize with stocks come from only dividends that are reinvested. Reinvestment of dividends means that the dividend yield amounts are simply taken and used to purchase more shares of the stock, instead of paying them out as cash to the share holder's account. This allows for investors to compound the number of shares that they own in a company over time.

Employee Stock Option (ESO)

Employee stock options are call options that are awarded privately rather than publicly. They turn out to be the most common form of equity compensation provided to employees of a business. Companies give out these options to their employees to provide them with an incentive to build up the market value of the company. These options may not be sold on the open markets.

An ESO provides the receiving employees with the right but not obligation to buy a preset quantity of shares of the company. The contract specifies a time frame within which these must be acquired before they expire worthless. The price they employees can buy them at is the current price which becomes the strike price. These time limits for using them are generally ten years. Companies spell all of these terms out in the options agreement.

These options are only valuable to the employee if the price of the company stock increases during the exercise time-frame. This is because the employees then are able to purchase the discounted shares at the same time as they sell them for the greater price on the market. The difference between the two prices represents their profit.

If the share price of the company declines, they are unable to use them and will see them eventually expire worthless. This is why companies utilize employee stock options instead of large salaries to encourage their employees. This provides the companies with great incentive to build up the value of the company. Three principle types of ESO exist in the form of non statutory, incentive, and reload employee stock options.

Non statutory employee stock options are also called non-qualified. These prove to be the normal kinds of ESOs. In such a contract, employees are not permitted to use these options during the vesting period. This vesting timeframe ranges from one to three years. When they are sold, the employee makes the spread between current price and strike price times the number of shares he or she sells. These types of ESOs become taxable at the employee's regular income tax level.

Graduated vesting in these options allows the employees to sell a percentage of the options such as maybe 10% in the first year. Each year another 10% would become available until the full 100% level is achieved by year ten. Incentive stock options are set up to lower taxes as much as possible. Employees can not exercise the option to buy the stock until after a year. They can not actually sell the stock until another year after buying it.

This type of option creates a risk that the stock price may decline over the year long holding time frame. The advantage to the employee is that these ISOs receive far better tax treatment. The tax rate defaults to the long term capital gains rate instead of the traditional full income tax rate. Upper level management are usually the ones who receive such tax advantageous ISOs from their companies.

The third type of employee stock options are called Reload ESOs. These begin their contract lives as non-statutory ESOs. The employees engage in their first exercise of the contract where they make money on the transaction. At this point, the employees who exercise are given a special reload of the employee stock option. In this process the company issues new options to the employee. The present market price at time of issue becomes the new strike price for the reloaded options. This way the employee is constantly re-incentivized to perform for the company.

Employee Stock Ownership Plan (ESOP)

An Employee Stock Ownership Plan refers to a type of retirement plan. They are also called by their acronym ESOP. These plans permit employing companies to either provide cash or stock shares directly to the employee benefits plan. These plans hold one account for every employee who participates in them. The stock shares that the employers contribute become vested over a pre-determined period of years.

Once they are partially or fully vested, employees are able to access them. It is important to note that with these ESOPs, employees never actually hold or purchase the shares of the stock directly when they are employees of the firm. Once the employee becomes retired, fired, disabled, or deceased, the stock shares become distributed.

One should never confuse an Employee Ownership Stock Plan with an employee stock option plan. These stock option plans are not really retirement plans. Rather they only provide the right to purchase the company stock for a given, pre-determined price in a certain time period.

One benefit that makes these Employee Stock Ownership Plans popular with providers and participants alike is their tax advantaged status. The reason they are considered to be qualified is because the company participating, the shareholder who sells, and the participants are each able to enjoy varying tax benefits. This is why these ESOPs are typically utilized by companies as part of their corporate financial strategy at the same time they are employed to encourage the employees to be sympathetic to the company stakeholders and their interests.

Without a doubt, the Employee Stock Ownership Plan is part and parcel of the compensation that employees enjoy from their company. This is why they are utilized to keep the employees working for the overall good of the company as a whole. They have a stake in the stock share price rising over time since they are part owners in the company stock.

These benefits from the Employee Stock Ownership Plan accrue to the employees at no upfront cost. The shares are kept for the receiving employees in a trust to ensure they grow safely to the point where the employee resigns or retires (or is fired).

These companies are actually employee-owned to some degree. Employee-owned corporations are those that have a majority of their shares in the hands of the company employees. This makes them cooperatives but for the fact that the firm's capital is unevenly distributed. Much of the time, such employee-owned corporations do not provide voting rights to all of the shareholders. Besides this, the senior-most employees and management will always have the distinct advantage of receiving a greater number of shares than the newer employees.

There are several other competing forms of employee ownership benefits. Among these are stock options, direct purchase plans, phantom stock, restricted stock, and stock appreciation rights. Stock options give their employees the chance to purchase shares of company stock for a set price in a fixed amount of time. A direct purchase plan permits employees to buy their shares in the company using their own after tax dollars.

Phantom stock delivers special cash bonuses in reward for superior employee results. The bonus amounts equal to the sale price of a certain quantity of stock shares. Restricted stock provides employees the ability to obtain shares either in the form of gift or by buying them, once they have met certain minimum employment period benchmarks. Stock appreciation rights provide employees with the ability to increase the value of a pre-assigned quantity of shares. Such shares typically become actually payable in the form of cash.

Equities

Equities are another name for stocks and similar types of investments. Stocks turn out to be financial instruments that represent ownership, or equity position, within a given corporation. As such, they give an owner a stake in a representative share of the company's profits and assets. Such ownership in a given firm is determined by taking the total numbers of shares in the company's equities that the individual owns, and dividing it by the actual number of shares that exist.

The majority of these equities similarly give voting rights that provide representative votes in some decisions that the company makes. Not every company issues equities; only corporations engage in the practice, while limited partnerships and sole proprietorships do not. Equities can be further divided into smaller categories based on the market capitalization, or size, of the company in question.

Because they often yield greater returns over significant periods of time, they are typically characterized by higher amounts of risk than are bonds and money market funds. Because of these unique potential returns and associated risks, equities are generally considered to be their own class of assets that are utilized to a degree in putting together investment portfolios with proper diversification. Many different kinds of equities exist, including domestic equities, emerging market equities, developed market equities, and Real Estate Investment Trusts.

Domestic Equities prove to be those stocks for the publicly traded corporations that principally conduct their business in the same country in which the investor lives. When a person holds such equities, they receive their share of dividends that the corporation pays. Equities come with a higher degree of risk than do bonds, as bond holders have a greater claim on a corporation's assets should liquidation follow bankruptcy. Equity holders are commonly wiped out in such liquidation.

Emerging Market Equities are equities in corporations that are based in countries that are still developing their economies. Included in these are China, Brazil, and India. These nations feature economies that are commonly volatile and lack many protections for investors, like auditing and laws or monitoring of securities that are found in the industrialized countries.

Developed Market Equities are equities in firms that work primarily outside of an investor's home country but still in an industrialized country. For Americans, this mostly translates to European country companies, as well as those in places such as Japan, Australia, and New Zealand. Such companies and economies in these nations prove to be more stable than those in developing countries.

Real Estate Investment Trusts, also known as REIT's, are equity funds that invest in residential and commercial real estate. Because they receive lease and rent payments off of their investments, these typically pay greater percentage returns in dividends. These higher distributions mean that REIT's are much like a combination of fixed income and typical equity investments. This means that they commonly feature greater risk along with better anticipated returns than do the majority of fixed income investments.

Equity Financing

Equity Financing refers to raising capital via selling shares within the enterprise itself. This comes down to selling an ownership stake in the corporation in order to come up with much needed funds for business enterprises. This type of financing could cover a wide array of different activities in both scope and scale. It might be only several thousand dollars which an entrepreneur raises from his family and friends. It could also be enormous IPOs initial public offerings that amount to literally billions of dollars and come from such household favorite names as Facebook and Google.

The phrase is most often applied to mega financing of major public companies which are listed on a stock exchange. This could also cover financing of private companies too. Equity financing is more or less the opposite to debt financing. In debt financing, funds will be borrowed form a business to be paid back at a later date and time.

There is more to Equity Financing than only selling common shares of stock. It might also involve other forms of equity (such as preferred stock) or even semi equity instruments like convertible stock shares or equity units which come with either warrants or common shares. Startup companies that evolve into highly successful firms often go through a few rounds of such Equity Financing as they grow and mature. These startups commonly attract varying types of investors at the different points in their growth. They will often rely on differing equity instruments for the various financing needs which arise throughout the newer company's history.

Consider an example to better understand the concept. Venture capitalists and angel investors are two different investors who are commonly the initial investors in startup companies. They generally prefer convertible preferred shares of stock instead of common shares of stock for their early rounds of funding. This is because those convertible shares offer a much higher possibility for upside potential as well as a little bit of downside protection.

After the firm has expanded enough to think about going public, they might begin to sell common shares of stock equity to retail and institutional investors. It might be that later they decide they require additional capital.

At this point, they might go out for secondary equity financing. This could include rights offerings or even offering various equity units which include warrants to sweeten the deal.

Financing via equity has rules and regulations which govern it. National securities regulators such as the SEC Securities Exchange Commission have the jurisdictional authority. This is intended to safeguard the investing public from any unscrupulous practices and operators who simply trick investors out of their funds then vanish. This is why such equity financing will usually come alongside a prospectus or at least an offering memorandum.

These provide a huge amount of useful information which assists the investors in taking highly informed decisions on the merits of the company and its financing offers. This data will usually cover the activities of the firm, provide information on the directors and other officers, explain the uses for the financing proceeds, offer financial statement disclosure, and revel the various risk factors.

The appetite which investors display for the various equity financing offerings heavily depends on the equity markets status as well as the financial market demand. When there are steady equity financing deals in the works, this represents an evidence of high investor confidence. Too many financing deals might mean that optimism is exuberant and a top in the market is coming.

When the Initial Public Offerings of dot coms and technology firms touched incredibly high record levels at the end of the 1990's, the writing was already on the wall. From 2000 through 2002, NASDAQ crashed and burned in a slow motion but extremely painful train wreck from which it needed more than a decade to recover. The speed and frequency of equity financing fell off substantially after this sustained correction in the markets because investors quickly became risk averse in the wake of the massive market selloff.

Equity Securities

Equity securities prove to be those asset classes which feature shares of stock in a given corporation. Investors hold these as reported by a company's official balance sheet. Corporations issue such securities in an effort to raise business capital via the financial markets. They use this money for significant company life events, such as for product development, merger and acquisition activity, or internal expansion. The funds are seldom for daily operating needs.

When investors buy equity securities, they gain a partial stake in the underlying firm. This is a primary alternative to turning to the bond markets to borrow money in taking on debt via the publicly traded bond markets. When a company first issues such equity securities, this is called an IPO initial public offering. Companies often raise enormous amounts of cash in this means, since investors are always hunting for new stock issues that will enable them to possess a part of a new and exciting opportunity.

The total number of shares that an IPO released varies wildly. It comes down to the amounts which the companies obtain permission to issue in their financial documents which they file with the regulatory overseer for their area. Corporations are allowed to sell a specific amount of stock shares in a given price range on the actual IPO day. After these shares have been dealt out to the public via the financial markets, the price of their equity will go up and down on the stock markets every trading day. This movement all depends on the perception of investors and the accompanying demand for the shares on any given day.

It is not common for such a firm to issue its entire inventory of available stock shares in a single offering. Rather than do this, they commonly reserve a certain quantity of shares to be issued at a later date in a second offering. This is called a follow on offering or secondary offering. The management of a company would elect to do this as they know they will likely need to raise fresh additional capital in the future in order to pay for hoped for expansionary plans.

When corporations continue to issue out their equity securities via the financial exchanges there is a downside for the existing shareholders and company investors. As additional shares are available to be bought, the pre-existing stake holders have their equity stake diluted as a percentage of the total. As an example, a major share holder could possess a huge quantity of shares that equate to fully 10 percent of all outstanding company shares which can be traded. Should the company choose to boost the total number of shares which are tradable, the equity of the shareholders will immediately drop in terms of the percentage ownership of all available shares.

The main alternative to issuing equity securities lies in issuing debt securities These publicly issued bonds offered via the bond markets by a company (or even government) raise money by taking on debt which must be repaid one day, known as the maturity date. Investors who buy debt instruments like these become de facto creditors of the bond issuing entities. The main disadvantage to such issuance in debt is that the company issuing has to provide continuous interest payments to the bond holders throughout the life of the bond contract. The company is able to maintain its ownership in itself in exchange for this trade off of interest payments.

Exchange Traded Funds (ETF)

These ETF's prove to be stock market exchange traded investment funds that work very much like stocks. Exchange Traded Funds contain instruments like commodities, stocks, and bonds. They trade for around the identical net asset value as the assets that they contain throughout the course of a day. The majority of ETF's actually follow the value of an index like the Dow Jones Industrial or the S&P 500. Since their creation in 1993, ETF's have evolved into the most beloved kind of exchange traded instruments.

The first Exchange Traded Fund particular to countries proved to be a joint venture of MSCI, Funds Distributor, and BGI. This first product finally turned into the iShares name that is accepted and recognized all over earth today. In the first fifteen years, such ETF's were index funds that simply followed indexes. The United States Securities and Exchange Commission began allowing firms to establish actively managed ETF's back in 2008.

Exchange Traded Funds provide a number of terrific advantages for smaller investors. Among these are elements like simple and effective diversification, index funds tax practicality, and expense ratios that remain very low. While doing all of this, they also offer the appeal of familiarity for you who trade stocks. This includes such comfortable and helpful options as limit orders, options, and short selling the ETF's. Since it is so inexpensive to purchase, hold, and sell these ETF's, many investors in ETF shares choose to keep them over a longer time frame for purposes of diversification and asset allocation. Still other investors trade in and out of these instruments regularly in order to participate in their strategies for market timing investing.

Exchange Traded Funds boast of many advantages. On the one hand, they provide great flexibility in buying and selling. It is easy for you to sell and buy them at the actual market price any time during a trading day, in contrast to mutual funds that you can only acquire at a trading day's conclusion. Since they are companies that trade like stocks, you can buy them in margin accounts and sell them short, meaning that they can be used for hedging purposes too. ETF's also allow limit orders and stop loss orders, which are helpful for assuring entry prices and protecting profits or safeguarding from losses.

ETF's also provide lower costs for traders. This results from the majority of ETF's not being actively managed. Also, ETF's do not spend large amounts of money on distribution, marketing, and accounting costs. The majority of them do not have the fees associated with most mutual funds either.

ETF's are among the greatest vehicles for diversifying portfolios quickly and easily. As an example, with only one set of shares, you can "own" the entire S&P 500 index. ETF's will give you exposure to country specific indexes, international markets, commodities, and even bond indexes.

ETF's have two other advantages. They are both transparent and tax efficient. Transparent in this regard means that they are clear in their portfolio holdings and are priced all day long. They are tax efficient as they do not create many capital gains, since they are not in the business of buying and selling their underlying indexes. They also are not required to sell their holding in order to meet redemptions of investors.

Face Value

Face Value represents the dollar value of a given security as the issuer states it officially. It is also otherwise known as the nominal value. Where stocks are concerned, this is the certificate-displayed original value of the stock. With bonds, this amounts to the dollar amount which will be paid back to the bond holder when the bond matures. This amount for bonds is usually $1,000 par value. Where bonds are concerned, this value is also called par value or sometimes only "par." Par value is very important with bonds, while it means little to stock investors.

Par value is two completely different concepts when dealing with bonds versus stocks. With bonds, this refers to the full amount which the company will return to the bondholder at the time of maturity. This assumes that the issuer does not default on its bond principal. Despite this set face value to be returned at maturity, bonds which trade on the secondary market have market values which fluctuate every trading day based largely on the prevailing interest rates.

As an example, when interest rates prove to be greater than the coupon rate on the bond, the issue will be sold on the secondary market at a discount to par value. This means that the price will be lower than the par. At the same time, when interest rates turn out to be lower than the coupon rate of the bond, the bond sells for a premium, at higher than par. The par value still guarantees a fixed principal return in any case. Yet this value is considered to be a bad indicator of the current worth for the bond, given the fact that very few bonds actually trade for par on the secondary market.

Bond holders can make additional profits over their fixed interest rate. This opportunity lies in buying the bond at below face value, then holding it to receive the par at maturity date. This gap between sub-par purchase price on the secondary market and the par value at maturity becomes pure profit to the bond holder if they hold the bond until that eventual date is reached.

The face value where stocks are concerned is quite different from that par with bonds. The importance of stock shares' par value as stated on their shares pertains to the legal amount of capital which the business must maintain. It is a fact that only cash the company has in excess of this total amount (number of shares times the share par value) may be paid out in the form of dividends to the investors. In practice this means that the face value of the shares serves as a type of corporate cash reserve.

The law does not mandate how much the stated par value has to be when it is issued. Businesses could sidestep the reserve requirement effect by applying laughably low values to the share certificates. Examples of two prominent companies illustrate this strategy well. AT&T shares have only $1 per common share listed as their par value. Stock giant Apple shares trading at hundreds of dollars apiece list a par value of merely $0.00001 per share, a ridiculous face value amount in practice.

This is why a stock or even bond's face value rarely if ever determines the true market value of the relevant issue, especially with stocks. The market value is only based upon the market forces of supply and demand. This is decided in practice by how much investors will willingly pay for buying and selling shares on a given security at a particular snap shot moment in time. If market conditions are right, the par value and actual market value at any given moment may have little or nothing to do with each other.

With bonds and their markets, it is all about the prevailing interest rates and how they correlate to the coupon rate of the bond. This will generally decide whether the bond sells at, above, or below its par value. With zero coupon bonds, investors do not receive any interest besides buying the bond for less than its face value. These are sold for less than par as the sole means for investors to realize any profits in this case.

Fixed Annuity

A Fixed Annuity refers to a particular form of annuity contract. Insurance companies make such contracts with individuals who are mostly saving for retirement or estate planning. Two main types of these annuities exist, variable and fixed annuities. The fixed one permits investors to add money to the account which is tax deferred. The investor furnishes a lump sum of money in exchange for which the life insurance provides a fully guaranteed and fixed interest rate at the same time as they also guarantee 100 percent of the principle invested. These annuities are often popular for their ability to offer the annuity holder (annuitant) a fully guaranteed income on a regular basis. This can be arranged as a specific number of years or for the remainder of the individual's life.

The motivation for a person to turn over a large sum of money to an insurance company for such a Fixed Annuity lies in the wish to obtain guaranteed returns while not having any original principal at risk. The second factor centers on the special tax advantages that these contracts with insurance companies enjoy. They receive many of the identical tax advantages from which life insurance policies benefit. Among these are earnings growth on a tax-deferred basis. This does not mean that taxes will not be paid, only that they will not be due until the contract becomes annuitized into monthly payouts or the earnings in the account become withdrawn.

There are a number of advantages to these types of Fixed Annuity investments that continue to draw investors to them year in and out. They offer guaranteed minimum rates, competitive yields which are fixed, guaranteed income payments, withdrawal ability, tax deferred growth, and principal safety.

The guaranteed minimum rates are nice but not forever it is important to note. These exist for an initial period only. The subsequent rates becomes adjusted utilizing a certain formula or alternatively employing whatever the prevailing yield is in the investment accounts of the insurers. Some fixed annuities will also offer an extended minimum rate guarantee as a protection in case interest rates decline in the future.

Competitive yields that are fixed come from the life insurance firm's investment portfolio which generates them. These investments mostly go into both high quality corporate bonds and U.S. government bonds. This yield is usually greater than a comparable yield on another investment which comes without risk. Many times this will be guaranteed by the insurance company for anywhere from at least one to as many as ten years.

To many annuity buyers, the guaranteed income payments are the greatest benefit to them. This feature becomes activated when the holder converts the fixed annuity into what is known as an immediate annuity. They can do this whenever they wish to provide a fully guaranteed monthly income payout that can last the remainder of the annuitant's life if they so desire.

Withdrawals are possible with these forms of Fixed Annuities. Holders can take an annual withdrawal every year that is as high as 10 percent of the value of the account. Any amounts greater than 10 percent will be penalized with a surrender charge if this occurs during the surrender period (usually ranging from seven to 12 years from contract start). Every year this surrender charge amount decreases until it eventually reaches zero. At that point withdrawals exceeding 10 percent of the account become penalty-free. There would still be the IRS tax penalty which amounts to ten percent (plus regular income taxes levied as well) on any withdrawals made before the owner reaches 59 and ½ years of age.

Principal safety is a rare commodity in these financially unstable times in the world. Annuities guarantee this, but the strength of the guarantee is only as good as the life insurance company that makes it. This is why investors should only invest their money with those life insurance firms which have at least an A or higher financial strength rating.

Fixed Assets

Fixed Assets refers to tangible property which are longer term holdings by their very nature. Companies and corporations both own and utilize them in their normal everyday business operations to produce their revenues and profits. They do not typically become converted back to cash or consumed any quicker than in under minimally a year time frame. Many corporations refer to their collective fixed assets as "the plant." Classic examples of these types of assets include real estate, factories, office space and buildings, furniture, computer equipment, and other operating equipment.

There are longer term assets that do not typically qualify as fixed assets though. Among these are patents and trademarks. They are generally considered to be simply intangible assets on company balance sheets.

Such assets also go by the names of property, plant, and equipment (PP&E). Corporations purchase fixed assets to create and supply services and goods. They might also rent them out to third parties to generate a revenue stream. They could simply deploy them within the company's own internal organization as well. These often include such tangible assets as office equipment, computers, and laptops, as well as manufacturing equipment and factories. Copyrights, goodwill, patents, and trademark could fall into either the fixed or intangible assets categories, depending on the accounting method favored by the firm.

There are many different types of equipment that fall under the classification of fixed assets. Among these are office buildings and plants, software and computer equipment, land, furniture, vehicles, and machinery. It often helps to consider a real tangible example when discussing difficult concepts like this one. Think about the company Amazing Fruits and Vegetables. They sell and even deliver fresh produce. This makes their delivery vehicles a fixed asset. The firm's distribution center would also be such a fixed type of asset. Even the parking lot where customers park while they shop the fruits and vegetables stand would be considered a fixed asset.

There are several reasons why it is helpful (and often times even essential) to have reliable information on the assets of a given company. The most important is that it leads to concise and precise financial reporting, as well as a better valuation of a going concern via financial analysis. Investors rely on such reports in order to ascertain the true financial health and real value of a given company. It enables them to make well- informed choices as to whether they should trust the firm enough to loan it money or instead invest in the equity of the corporation. One thing that makes it more confusing for investors is that firms have a choice of acceptable means of recording, depreciating, and disposing of their own assets. It requires qualified analysts who are willing to read the fine print and notes on the financial statements of the company in question in order to accurately determine on what basis the numbers were compiled.

It is an inevitable fact of life that fixed assets will gradually decline in value terminally as they grow older. They do offer long term income generation, which explains why they become expensed differently than do other company items. While tangible assets become subjected to occasional depreciation, intangible assets are subjected instead to amortization. A specific portion of the costs for the asset will be expensed out yearly. The value of the asset will correspondingly diminish alongside the amount of depreciation on the balance sheet of the corporation. The firm is then allowed to match up the cost of the asset in question with the longer term value of the item.

The method that a given firm utilizes to depreciate its assets will change the book value of the firm which is based on the amount they paid for the asset. This will make the equity book value different from the current market value of the asset in question. An exception to all of this depreciation and book value discussion concerns raw real estate. Land cannot be depreciated since it does not become depleted. The exception is when it is natural resource land, as with oil land, gold or silver mining land, or timber lands. These resources are finite and become expended over time and culling.

Fund Manager

Fund managers are the individuals, investment companies, or sometimes banks that handle a mutual fund's investment decisions. These decision makers are charged with earning as much profit for their fund as they reasonably can while still following the risk parameters that the mutual fund discloses.

Fund managers are compensated differently than stock brokers who earn commissions. These managers receive their compensation based on the total dollar amounts under the management of the mutual fund. An advantage to this form of payment is that it provides motivation for fund managers to increase overall assets. A more successful manager will attract more investors and money and achieve greater returns. The management fee that the fund levies pays the fund manager. This fee appears on fund financials under the expense ratio.

A mutual fund's board of directors hires the fund manager. Fund shareholders themselves select the board of directors. These fund managers wear many hats. They oversee all of the investments that the mutual fund undertakes. They must set and manage annual meetings. They must also be responsible for the mutual fund's customer service efforts and many different elements of fund compliance. Compliance roles include offering a fund prospectus, negotiating commission rates with brokers, issuing proxies, and other important periodic and daily tasks.

Fund managers generally hire staff to help them with these many roles. Sometimes they contract out some or all of these services to another company. In practice most mutual funds are owned by families of mutual fund companies. In these cases, these companies provide their fund managers with these services at a cost.

A number of mutual funds have single managers in charge of the fund. The majority of larger funds have significant sized staffs that the fund manager leads. In such cases, these leadership positions are more like investment managers than fund managers. The biggest funds have a few fund managers who share the responsibilities and decisions. Entire investment firms act as fund managers to some mutual funds.

A fund manager is an important person to consider when investors are looking at mutual funds. One of the most important characteristics of a successful mutual fund concerns how long the fund manager has been present. Funds which boast a fund manager who has been with them a long time have a distinct advantage.

If a fund claims significant changes in its fund management, this is generally looked at as a negative factor. It might indicate that there have been problems in the fund with the performance. It could also imply that the fund manager has not properly carried out compliance and other critical issues in the daily running of the fund. Alternatively, a change in fund manager could simply mean that the fund has overhauled its investment strategy and changed its emphasis.

Hedge funds also employ fund managers. A hedge fund manager is far less restricted in the investments that he or she can pursue than is a mutual fund manager. This is because there is much less regulation for hedge funds than for mutual funds.

The hedge fund managers receive their income according to a different compensation scheme. Mutual fund managers earn their fees however the fund performs. Hedge fund managers instead are rewarded with a percentage of their earned returns. They also receive a small management fee that commonly runs between one and four percent of the fund's net asset value.

Investors who do not like paying managers for poor performance appreciate this structure for paying hedge fund managers. The disadvantage to it concerns risk. Hedge fund managers could pursue more aggressive and risky strategies to make greater returns because of their fee structure.

Future Value

Future Value refers to a current asset's anticipated value at a given specific date of the future. Such a forecast will be dependent on the rate of growth rate that the company assumes over time. As an example, a company may assume a certain guaranteed rate of growth. This would allow them to state that a $10,000 investment they make now will have a value of $100,000 twenty years from now. This would have the FV of the original $10,000 investment at $100,000. This equation takes for granted that the rate of growth will be approximately consistent and constant. It also assumes that the upfront payment is an untouched one throughout the life of the literal investment in question.

Such a Future Value calculation permits managers and analysts alike to anticipate with hopefully some accuracy the profits they can forecast earning in comparing varying investments. The weakness is that the quantity of growth which the investment generates cannot be predicted with one hundred percent certainty. Still, the returns on the investment if it were sunk into stocks versus a new product launch or other revenue accruing project will likely be vastly different from one another, which mean that the accountants will stay busy extrapolating multiple base case scenario possibilities.

It can be quite complex to accurately ascertain the future value of a given asset. This of course varies per the asset class. Such FV calculations assume that the growth rate will remain consistently stable. This is easy to determine with great accuracy when analysts are considering money put into a fixed rate of interest CD or savings account. Investments they make in securities such as stocks will provide a higher degree of volatility and fluctuating rate of return. This makes it exceedingly difficult to prognosticate with accuracy. Where the core idea is concerned though, compound and simple interest rates reflect the easiest to understand examples of utilizing a FV calculation.

These future value calculations might be compiled in two different ways, depending on the interest accruing. Look at the simple interest calculation approach. The formula for when the base case assumes simple interest is FV equals Initial principle times the result of one plus the interest rate multiplied by time in years.

It is always most illuminating to look at a tangible example on challenging concepts such as this one. Consider a $100,000 investment that the firm keeps in a simple time deposit CD account that yields five percent on a simple annual interest payment basis. In this scenario, the future value of the $100,000 would be $100,000 times (one plus .05 times five) for a final result of $125,000.

It becomes more challenging when compounded interest is taken into consideration. Under the compounding interest base case, the rate has to be reapplied on every year's cumulative account balance. Using the same example as above, if the investment in its first year realizes a five percent interest, this is $5,000 in interest. The next year, the total account value would be base of $105,000 before interest begins to accrue. Now the five percent rate would be applied to the $105,000 instead of the old $100,000 initial total. At five percent interest again, this would yield an interest dollar amount of $5,250. The calculations continue as such until the final year is reached. This means that the formula for investment earnings on a compounded interest basis is Future Value equals Initial investment times the final result of one plus the interest rate raised to the power of the time value.

Futures

Futures prove to be financial derivatives that are also called forward contracts. Such a futures contract gives a seller the obligation to deliver an asset, such as a commodity, to the buyer at a pre set date. These contracts are heavily traded on major produced commodities like wheat, gold, oil, coffee, and sugar. They also exist for underlying financial instruments that include government bonds, stock market indexes, and foreign currencies.

The history of futures goes back to Ancient Greece where the first recorded example is detailed about an olive press arrangement that philosopher Thales entered into. Futures contracts become commonplace at trade fairs throughout Europe by the 1100's. Merchants did not feel secure traveling with significant amounts of goods, so they would only bring display samples along and then sell merchandise that they would deliver in greater quantities at future dates.

Futures contracts created an enormous bubble in the 1600's with the Dutch Tulip Mania that caused tulip bulbs to skyrocket to unthinkable levels. In this speculative bubble, the majority of money that was exchanged turned out to be for tulip futures and not the tulips themselves. The first futures exchange in the United States opened in 1868 as the Chicago Board of Trade, where copper, pork bellies, and wheat were traded in futures contracts.

In the early years of the 1970's, futures trading grew explosively in volume. Pricing models created by Myron Scholes and Fischer Black permitted the quick pricing of futures and options on them. Investors could easily speculate on commodities prices through these futures. As the demand for the futures skyrocketed, additional significant futures exchanges opened and expanded around the world, especially in Chicago, London, and New York.

Futures trading could not happen effectively without the exchanges. Futures contracts are spelled out in terms of the asset that underlies them, the date of delivery, the last day of contract trading, transaction currency, and size of ticks or minimum permissible price changes. Exchanges have developed into major and predictable markets through their standardizing of all of these various factors for many different kinds of futures contracts.

Trading futures contracts involves major leverage. This means that they carry tremendous opportunities as well as risks. Futures, with their ability to control enormous quantities of commodities and financials, have been the root causes for many collapses. Enron and Barings Bank were both brought down by financial futures. Perhaps the most famous futures meltdown involved the Long Term Capital Management group.

Even though this company had the inventors of the futures pricing models Scholes and Black working for them, the company lost money in the futures markets so quickly that the Federal Reserve Bank had to become involved and bail out the company to stop the whole financial system of the Untied States from collapsing.

Futures Contracts

Futures contracts are legally binding agreements which two parties usually enter into on a futures exchange trading floor or electronic platform. They spell out the particulars for selling or buying specific financial instruments or commodities for a pre-set price at an exact moment in the future. Such contracts have become standardized to make it easy to trade them on the various futures exchanges. They provide information on the quantity and quality of the commodity, though this depends on the nature of the underlying asset.

Futures contracts can be settled in two ways. Some of them require actual physical delivery of the commodity specified. Others simply settle between the two parties in cash. These contracts specify all important characteristics for the item which the parties are trading. This makes them different from the word "futures" that more generally refers to the markets in which these commodities and instruments trade.

There are two actual types of participants in the futures markets who utilize such futures contracts. These are speculators and hedgers. Individual traders and managers of portfolios can use them to place speculative bets on the direction of price movements for the given asset that underlies the contracts. Hedgers involve buyers or producers of the contact asset itself attempting to lock in the price for which they will later buy or sell their commodity.

There are many different commodities and assets for which futures contracts exist. The most obvious of these are hard assets such as precious metals, industrial metals, natural gas, crude oil and other energy products, grains, seeds, livestock, oils, and carbon credits. Literally dozens of the more significant stock market indices around the globe have these contracts available to trade. Some major individual stocks have their own futures contract on their shares as well. The major interest rates and most important currency pairs also have such contracts and markets to trade.

Futures contracts which require physical delivery do not often result in such physical delivery. Many investors in these contracts trade them and sell them before the date of delivery. They can roll them forward by selling the imminent to expire contract and buying a further month out to replace them.

For producers of a good, these contracts provide a unique solution to the problem of fluctuating prices. Oil producers are classic examples. They might intend to produce a million barrels of oil to deliver in precisely a year. If the price is $50 for a barrel today, and the producer does not want to risk prices falling lower, it could lock it in. Oil prices have become so volatile that they could be substantially lower or higher a year from now. By selling a futures contract, the producer gives up the opportunity to possibly sell the oil for more in a year. It also eliminates the risk of receiving a lower amount.

Mathematical models actually determine the prices of futures contracts. They consider the present day spot price, time until maturity, risk free return rates, dividends, dividend yields, convenience yields, and storage costs. This might mean with oil prices at $50 that a one year futures contract sells for $53. The producer receives a guarantee for $53 million and will have to provide the 1 million barrels of oil on the exact delivery date. It will obtain this $53 per barrel price despite the spot prices at which the markets are trading on that date.

Futures Exchange

A futures exchange refers to a central clearing marketplace that allows for futures contracts as well as options on such futures contracts to be traded. Thanks to the rapid increase in electronic trading of futures, this term also finds use regarding futures trading activities directly.

There are the two most important futures exchanges in the world today. The biggest in the United States is the Chicago Mercantile Exchange, or CME. This one became established in the last years of the 1890s. In the early days, the only futures contracts available were agricultural products' futures.

This changed rapidly in the 1970s. Currency futures appeared on the major currency pairs after the breakdown of the Breton Woods Agreement. The futures exchanges of today are massive by comparison. They allow for investors to hedge all sorts of financial products and commodities. These range from stock indices and individual stocks to energies, precious and base metals, soft commodities such as orange juice and soybeans, interest rate products, and even credit default swaps.

In today's futures exchange, it is hedging financial instruments and products which create the significant majority of activity in futures markets. Today the futures exchange markets carry an important responsibility for global financial system operations, efficient functioning, and activity. The international nature of this global futures exchange has given rise to the world's first truly international futures market, the ICE Intercontinental Exchange.

ICE is massive and important in not only futures markets. They own and operate 12 different exchanges around the world, including NYSE EuroNext, which controls the famed and venerable New York Stock Exchange and EuroNext exchange (owning the Paris and Dutch stock exchanges, among others). In Europe, this is a serious rival to the historic LSE London Stock Exchange and continental powerhouse the German Deutsche Bourse. The ICE today counts 12,000 listed futures contracts as well as securities. It trades 5.2 million futures contracts every day, as well as $1.8 billion in cash equities every day.

In energies, the Intercontinental Exchange Futures commands almost half of all the traded crude and refined oil futures contracts volume for the entire planet. It is also the location of the most highly liquid market for the European interest rates short term contracts. It controls a wide variety of global benchmarks in agriculture, energies, foreign exchange, and equity indices.

ICE only launched its international futures exchange back in 2000 with the advent of their electronic trading platform. This makes it among the newer futures exchanges in the world, and yet it is a dominant international player still. Their high tech-powered rise increased the access to and transparency of the Over the Counter traded energy markets as well as the new global futures markets exchange they opened shortly thereafter. It was 2001 when they expanded to energy futures with their acquisition of the International Petroleum Exchange.

In 2002, ICE expanded heavily into Europe by opening up their ICE Clear Europe. This represented the first new clearing house in the United Kingdom in a full century. By 2007, the Intercontinental Exchange had cemented its global position in energy trade by acquiring both the NYBOT New York Board of Trade and the Canadian-based Winnipeg Commodity Exchange.

The end result today is an entire ecosystem made up of futures and equities markets, clearing houses throughout the world, listing and data centers and services, and technology-driven solutions which together work to create a full, free, and transparent accessibility to the worldwide futures, energy, derivatives, and capital markets.

Between ICE Futures U.S.'s operations and endeavors within the United States, the futures exchange is enabling and empowering markets which allow for an effective risk management throughout the world economy. Their product offerings and solutions encompass a diverse and broad variety of futures contracts. These span internationally traded equity indexes and futures; credit derivative futures; FX futures; North American oil, power, and natural gas futures; and soft commodities and agriculture futures including sugar, cotton, coffee, and cocoa.

General Obligation Bonds

General Obligation Bonds are municipal bonds which are reinforced by the full taxing powers and overall credit worthiness of the jurisdiction which issues them instead of a certain revenue stream from the associated specific project. These special general types of bonds are floated by municipalities under the belief that the jurisdiction will have the resources in the future to pay back all of its debts via general taxation or incoming revenue from other projects. With these GO bonds, there is no collateral from other underlying assets of the issuer.

What makes these general obligation bonds so appealing to investors even though they have no underlying security behind them is that the issuing government agency has promised to utilize every available resource, including tax revenues, in order to pay back the bond holders. Such pledges from local governments can include a promise to assess special property taxes so that the government entity is able to meet its obligations to the bond holders. As an example, property owners have skin in the game because of their local area property holdings and any unpaid property tax obligations.

Credit ratings agencies will analyze and rate the pledges of general obligations according to the strength of their credit qualities. They then assign them generally high investment graded ratings. When said property owners are incapable of paying in their fare share of property taxes according to the final due date, the government is permitted legally to raise the effective rates of property taxes in order to compensate for any delinquencies. On these required due dates, a general obligation bond pledge will mandate that the local government entity has to pay its owed debt using the resources which are available.

These general obligation bonds are also useful for the local area governments to be able to raise sufficient funds for needed projects which will build up revenue streams for projects including bridges and roads, equipment, and parks. Such bonds are generally utilized to pay for government infrastructure projects which will serve the general good of the public at large.

It is actually the relevant state laws which set the stage for what local governments are allowed to issue in the forms of these general obligation bonds. They can be unlimited tax obligation pledges or limited tax obligation promises to repay. Unlimited tax obligations are much like the limited tax promises. The principal difference pertains to the local government being required to raise property tax rates to levels that will service the debts, even as high as 100%, in order to cover other taxpayer delinquencies. It is up to the local residents to agree in advance to property tax increases which are needed to repay the bonds.

Alternatively the limited tax obligation pledges request that the local government issuing the bonds will increase the property taxes as needed in order to cover the debt service obligations. There is a statutory limit that provides boundaries for these. Governments are able to employ a portion of the property taxes which are already levied, increase existing property tax rates to a level that will service the debt payments, or utilize an alternative revenue stream in order to pay the debts as required by the terms of the general obligation bonds.

Such general obligation bonds are usually considered to be the safest form of municipal bonds because they are backed up by the ability of the issuer to tax. There are also other reasons that give them their aura of perceived safety. Companies may go bankrupt every day of the year, but municipalities can not.

They have therefore a far greater motivation to maintain their precious credit ratings since they can not simply go bankrupt and disappear into oblivion. They will also have to return to the bond markets periodically at other points in the future so that they can fund still more projects for their constituents. Besides this, the state laws generally detail the precise conditions under which the issuing municipalities are able to issue such general obligation bonds, as well as the kind of security they are able to utilize.

Gold Certificate

A Gold Certificate refers to the world's original paper bank notes. Beginning back in the 1600s, such certificates based on gold became first issued by various goldsmiths in both London and Amsterdam to their customers who would deposit their gold bullion with them for safe keeping. Such gold certificates became proof of the ownership of gold. After some time elapsed, such certificates became passed from one hand to the next in transactions much like cash. It avoided the inconvenience of needing to withdraw and physically transfer over the gold bullion which was bulky and expensive to ship and protect.

By the middle of the 1800s, the U.S. Treasury started offering gold certificates which people might then exchange with them for gold from within the Treasury vaults. They actually circulated as legal tender in the United States all the way through 1933. At this point, the American federal government outlawed the ownership of private gold within the U.S.

Even though they are no longer legal tender anywhere in the world nowadays, gold certificates still exist today. A few Swiss and German banks keep issuing them. Gold pool investment programs in the United States and Australia also issue such certificates. As in the earliest days of the certificates, the gold certificates today represent an ownership stake in a specific amount of gold bullion coins or bars in a vault. The gold owner receives the certificates and is then able to avoid the very considerable costs of gold trading, delivery, insurance, and storage.

Investors seem to have an ongoing love affair with gold certificates four hundred years later after they first appeared. They provide a feeling of comfort from an expensive piece of paper that stands for something of actual tangible value. Yet the critics of the concept abound. They claim that there can be many issues with such certificates. The issuer might have mistakenly issued a duplicate certificate or over issued them by accident. There are also hard to tell fakes and forgeries, poor administration, elimination of older certificates, changes of address issues, and more which can cause them to be worthless or contested.

In their defense, such certificates are now mostly also updated online in accessible databases as the gold pool publishes a daily list of gold owners which is easily accessible via the Internet and proves who owns what from the gold vault hoard. This method often utilizes nicknames to maintain the privacy and anonymity of gold ownership, which is extremely important to many holders of gold today.

The problem with gold certificates nowadays is that they represent unallocated gold claims to convert real gold into ownership through physical allocation when the investor surrenders the certificate and pays the considerable costs of transfer. Many investors and analysts do not like unallocated gold because of these limitations. Those who own unallocated gold are actually creditors to the gold pool since the gold ownership is merely a balance sheet item when all is said and done. This exposes the certificate holders to the potential insolvency of the company which owns and manages the actual gold pool over the longer term.

This is not to say that some government-guaranteed gold pools do not issue good gold certificates which investors can bank on today. The best known, most respected, and safest of these is undoubtedly the Perth Mint Certificate Program. They issue good certificates for gold coins and bullion bars which are actually there inventoried and audited independently in the vault and can be claimed upon demand and surrendering of the appropriate certificates.

Gold Roth IRA

Gold Roth IRA's are IRA's that are allowed to contain gold and other precious metals. Gold Roth IRA's make sense for many investors. This is because gold and other precious metals like silver and platinum have been considered to be the greatest form of long term storage for cash and valuables throughout history.

This means that gold in particular could be considered to be the best asset for retirement. Although there are many other types of instruments used for retirement accounts and planning, including bonds, stocks, savings, and annuities, gold is the only one whose final value does not rest on an institution or individual's performance or success. This makes physical gold an ideal means for saving for retirement.

Gold Roth IRA's are specially created either through initially funding one or by rolling over a Roth IRA or traditional IRA to a gold backed Roth IRA. Rolling over an existing employee held 401K to a Gold Roth IRA can be difficult if the employee has not left the company. This is because employees are not usually allowed to do rollovers until they separate from their company.

IRA's that already exist can be transferred to Gold Roth IRA's. They can be moved from credit unions, banks, or stock broker firms to a trust company that is allowed to hold your Gold IRA holdings. In this type of transfer, you could choose to move securities held in the account along with cash, or cash by itself.

Gold Roth IRA's must be created by sending in cash to the administrator of the IRA. They will then purchase the gold, silver, or platinum physical holdings as you instruct them. The gold must then be kept by a gold IRA custodian on your behalf. These depositories provide safe places for the gold, as well as easy access to buy or sell it. The gold kept in a Gold Roth IRA may not be sent to your house or assumed in your personal possession. Instead, it has to be liquidated before the funds from it can be accessed. Gold that is requested as a distribution will be penalized at your personal tax rate plus a ten percent penalty.

Only certain forms of gold and precious metals are allowed to be purchased and held within a Gold Roth IRA. Gold bars have to demonstrate a twenty-four karat purity to be eligible. They can be one ounce, ten ounces, a kilogram, one hundred ounces, or four hundred ounces in size. Gold coins that are permitted are twenty-four karat bullion coins from the United States, Canada, Austria, and Australia. The most heavily minted gold coins of all time, the South Africa Krugerrand's, are not permitted, as they are only twenty-two karats.

Silver bars and coins that have .999 or higher purity are permitted to be held in a Gold Roth IRA account. This allows the Canadian Silver Maple Leaf, the U.S. Silver Eagle, and the Mexican Silver Libertad one ounce bullion coins. Silver bars that are one hundred ounces and one thousand ounces are also permitted.

Government Bonds

Government bonds are debt instruments that governments issue to pay for government expenditures. Within the United States, federal government issues include savings bonds, treasury notes, treasury bonds, and TIPS Treasury inflation protected securities. Investors should carefully consider the risks that different countries' governments possess before they invest in their bonds. Among these international government risks are political risk, country risk, interest rate risk, and inflation risk. Governments generally have less credit risk, though not always.

Savings bonds are a type of United States government bonds that the Treasury department sells. They are available in an electronic form. The Treasury offers them directly from their website, or individuals can buy them from the majority of financial institutions and banks. When savings bonds reach maturity, the investors get back the bond's face value along with interest which accrued. These savings bonds may not be redeemed the first year of issue. Any investors who redeem them in their first five years of issue lose three months interest for cashing out too early.

The Treasury of the United States also issues intermediate time frame bonds known as Treasury notes or T-Notes. These notes provide interest payments semiannually at a coupon rate which is fixed. These notes typically are denominated in $1,000 face values. Those with three or two year maturity dates come in $5,000 denominations. Before 1984, T-Notes were callable and gave the Treasury the right to buy them back given specific conditions.

The U.S. government's longest term bonds are Treasury Bonds, or T-Bonds. These have maturity dates ranging from ten to 30 years time. They also provide interest payments on a semiannual basis and come in $1,000 denominated values. These T-bonds are important because they pay for federal budget shortfalls, are a form of monetary policy, and ensure the country is able to regulate its money supply. As all bond issuers, the Treasury department looks at return and risk requirements on the market when it goes to raise capital so that it can be as efficient as possible. This helps to explain the different kinds of Treasury securities and government bonds they offer.

U.S. government bonds have generally been considered to be without risk, which is why they trade so easily in extremely large and liquid markets. The downside to this is that they offer considerably lower returns than do other bonds. TIPS do provide protection against inflation so that any inflation increases will not exceed the interest rate of the bond. The prices of government bonds are based on current interest rates. This means that the fixed rate bonds will decline in value as the interest rates rise, since there is lost opportunity to obtain newer bonds at higher interest rates. Similarly, if interest rates fall, the bond's values will rise.

The federal government is able to control the money supply in part by its issue of the government bonds. If they wish to increase the money supply, they can simply buy back their own bonds. These funds then find their way to a bank and expand the money supply as banks keep small reserves and loan the rest out (in the money multiplier effect). The government is also able to lower the money supply by selling additional bonds which takes money out of circulation. If the government were to retire the funds received from the sale of these bonds, it would reduce the available money supply. More often than not, the U.S. government spends the money.

Hedge Fund

A hedge fund is an investment fund which are commonly only open to a specific group of investors. These investors pay a large performance fee each year, commonly a certain percent of their funds under management, to the manager of the hedge fund. Hedge funds are very minimally regulated and are therefore are able to participate in a wide array of investments and investment strategies.

Literally every single hedge fund pursues its own strategy of investing that will establish the kinds of investments that it seeks. Hedge funds commonly go for a wide range of investments in which they may buy or sell short shares and positions. Stocks, commodities, and bonds are some of these asset classes with which they work.

As you would anticipate from the name, hedge funds typically try to offset some of the risks in their portfolios by employing a number of risk hedging strategies. These mostly revolve around the use of derivatives, or financial instruments with values that depend on anticipated price movements in the future of an asset to which they are linked, as well as short selling investments.

Most countries only allow certain types of wealthy and professional investors to open a hedge fund account. Regulators may not heavily oversee the activities of hedge funds, but they do govern who is allowed to participate. As a result, traditional investment funds' rules and regulations mostly do not apply to hedge funds.

Actual net asset values of hedge funds often tally into the many billions of dollars. The funds' gross assets held commonly prove to be massively higher as a result of their using leverage on their money invested. In particular niche markets like distressed debt, high yield ratings, and derivatives trading, hedge funds are the dominant players.

Investors get involved in hedge funds in search of higher than normal market returns. When times are good, many hedge funds yield even twenty percent annual investment returns. The nature of their hedging strategies is supposed to protect them from terrible losses, such as were seen in the financial crisis from 2007-2010.

The hedge fund industry is opaque and difficult to measure accurately. This is partially as a result of the significant expansion of the industry, as well as an inconsistent definition of what makes a hedge fund. Prior to the peak of hedge funds in the summer of 2008, it is believed that hedge funds might have overseen as much as two and a half trillion dollars. The credit crunch hit many hedge funds particularly hard, and their assets under management have declined sharply as a result of both losses, as well as requests for withdrawals by investors. In 2010, it is believed that hedge funds once again represent in excess of two trillion dollars in assets under management.

The largest hedge funds in the world are JP Morgan Chase, with over $53 billion under management; Bridgewater Associates, having more than $43 billion in assets under management; Paulson and Company, with more than $32 billion in assets; Brevan Howard that has greater than $27 billion in assets; and Soros Fund Management, which boasts around $27 billion in assets under management.

High Yield Bonds

High Yield Bonds turn out to be bonds that possess a lower credit rating and higher yield than those corporate, municipal, and sovereign government bonds which are of investment grade. Thanks to the greater risk of them defaulting, such bonds yield a higher return than the bonds which are qualified investment grade issues. Those companies that issue high yielding debt are usually capital intensive companies and startup firms that already possess higher debt ratios. Investors often refer to such bonds as junk bonds.

The two principal corporate rating credit agencies determine the breakdown of what qualifies as a High Yield Bond and what does not. When Moody's rates a bond with lower than a "Baa" rating, or Standard and Poor's (S&P) rates then with an under "BBB" rating, then they become known as junk bonds. At the same time, all of those bonds which enjoy higher ratings than these (or the same rating at least) investors will consider to be investment grade. There are credit ratings that cover such categories as presently in default, or "D." Those kinds of bonds holding "C" ratings and below also have high probabilities for defaulting. In order to compensate the investors who take them on for the significant risks they run of not receiving either their original principal back or accrued interest payments by the maturity date, the yields must be offered at extremely high interest rates.

Despite the negative label of "junk bond," these High Yield Bonds remain popular and heavily bought by global investors. The majority of these investors choose to diversify for safety sake by utilizing either a junk bond ETF exchange traded fund or a High Yield Bonds mutual fund. The spread between the yields on the higher yielding and investment grade types of bonds constantly fluctuates on the markets. The at the time condition of the global and national economies impacts this. Industry-specific and individual corporate events also play a part in the differences between the various kinds of bonds' interest rates.

In general though, High Yield Bonds' investors can count on receiving a good 150 to 300 basis points more in yield as measured against the investment quality bonds in any particular time frame. This is why mutual funds and ETFs make imminent sense as an effective means of gaining exposure to the greater yields without taking on the unnecessary risk of a single issuer's bonds defaulting and costing the investors all or most of their original investing principal.

In the last few years, various central bankers throughout the globe have decided to inject enormous amounts of liquidity into their individual economies so that credit will remain cheaply and easily available. This includes the European Central Bank, the U.S. Federal Reserve, and the Bank of Japan. It has created the side effect of causing borrowing costs to drop and lenders to experience significantly lower returns.

By February of 2016, an incredible $9 trillion in sovereign government debt bonds provided yields of only from zero percent to one percent. Seven trillion of the sovereign bonds delivered negative real yields once adjusted for anticipated levels of inflation. It means that holding such bonds cost investors money, or provided them a real losing return.

In typical economic environments, this would drive intelligent investors to competing markets that provide better return rates. Higher yield bond markets have stayed volatile though. Distressed debts which pay minimally a yield higher than 1,000 basis points greater than a comparably maturing Treasury bond were notably affected. Energy company high yielding debt bond prices collapsed by approximately 20 percent in 2015 as a consequence of the problems in the energy sector which resulted from plummeting energy prices.

High Yield Preferred Stocks

Preferred stocks are a special type of stocks that many companies issue. These types of stocks provide investors with a different level of ownership in a given company. A preferred stock holder obtains a higher priority on the earnings and assets of a company than a common stock holder would enjoy. These preferred stocks also pay a higher dividend that has to be given out before any dividends can be paid to the common stock holders.

As such, they represent a hybrid type of security on the stock markets. They are like common stocks in that they are bought and sold as stocks and represent ownership in a company. These stocks can also trade up and down in price like a common stock. Unlike a common stock, they do not come with any rights to vote for a company board of directors or items on a company ballot at the annual meeting.

They are also like bonds in that they pay a higher dividend that must be paid out unless the company lacks the earnings to pay these holders. In this way preferred stocks have elements of bonds with their fixed rate of dividends. Every preferred stock comes with its own unique details that are set when the company issues the stock.

Preferred stocks are often higher yielding issues. They are most commonly issued by companies that are in industries such as financials, real estate investment trusts, utilities, industrials, and conglomerates. Despite this higher yield that makes them like bonds, they can be traded on the major stock exchanges. They are typically found on exchanges including the NASDAQ and the New York Stock Exchange.

As preferred stocks are a type of equity legally, they show up as equity on any company balance sheet. Both common and preferred stock holders are owners in the company. There are several advantages to preferred stocks that investors like about them.

In the past, individual retail investors were less aware of preferred stocks, but this is changing. Part of the reason they have gained in popularity surrounds market volatility. As common stocks have seen wild price swings in recent years, investors have been looking for more stable instruments in which they can invest.

Preferred stocks fit this need as they tend to be more stable in price than do common stocks. With more baby boomers looking for investments that provide higher yields, this has brought preferred stocks into the spotlight. The retirees gain the advantage of better yields and the opportunity for the price to increase in the issues as well.

Preferred stocks are not new. They have existed from the time when modern day investing began. Institutional investors have known about and invested in them for many decades. Many individual investors did not because they lacked the information they required to select and trade them.

In the past, individuals did not have any lists of preferred stocks from which to pick. The information available was difficult to come up with before the Internet made this kind of information much more readily available. Now there are tools smaller individual investors can find that provide calendar searches for ex-dividend dates.

There are also screening filters that allow individuals to narrow down their search for the best high yielding dividend preferred stocks. Preferred stocks represent another way to diversify an investor's portfolio and earn higher yields on dividends at the same time.

Index Funds

Index funds are typically exchange traded funds or mutual funds. Their goal is to reproduce the actual movements of an underlying index for a particular financial market. They do this no matter what is happening in the overall stock markets.

There are several means of tracking such an index. One way of doing this is by purchasing and holding all of the index securities to the same proportion as they are represented in the index. Another way of accomplishing this is by doing a statistical sample of the market and then acquiring securities that are representative of it. A great number of the index funds are based on a computer model that accepts little to no input from people in its decision making of the securities bought and sold. This qualifies as a type of passive management when the index fund is run this way.

These index funds do not have active management. This allows them to benefit from possessing lesser fees and taxes in their accounts that are taxable. The low fees that are charged do come off of the investment returns that are otherwise mostly matching those of the index. Besides this, exactly matching an index is not possible since the sampling and mirroring models of this index will never be one hundred percent right. Such variances between an index performance and that of the fund are referred to as the tracking error, or more conversationally as a jitter.

A wide variety of index funds exist for you to choose from these days. They are offered by a number of different investment managers as well. Among the more typically seen indices are the FTSE 100, the S&P 500, and the Nikkei 225. Other indexes have been created that are so called research indexes for creating asset pricing models. Kenneth French and Eugene Fama created one known as the Three Factor Model. This Fama-French three factor model is actually utilized by Dimensional Fund Advisers to come up with their various index funds. Other, newer indexes have been created that are known as fundamentally based indexes. These find their basis in factors like earnings, dividends, sales, and book values of companies.

The underlying concept for developing index funds comes from the EMH, or efficient market hypothesis. This hypothesis claims that because stock analysts and fund managers are always searching for stocks that will do better than the whole market, this efficient competition among them translates to current information on a company's affairs being swiftly factored into the price of the stock. Because of this, it is generally accepted that knowing which stocks will do better than the over all market in advance is exceedingly hard. Developing a market index then makes sense as the inefficiencies and risks inherent in picking out individual stocks can be simply eliminated through purchasing the index fund itself.

Individual Retirement Account (IRA)

An IRA stands for Individual Retirement Account. IRA's offer two types of savings for retirement. They can either be tax free or tax deferred retirement plans. In the universe of IRA's, numerous different types of accounts exist. These are principally either traditional and standard IRA's or Roth IRA's as the most popular types. The various IRA's are helpful to different individuals based on the particular scenarios and end goals of every person.

Standard IRA's permit contributions of as much as $4,000 every year. These are contributions that are tax deductible, giving the IRA's their primary advantage as retirement accounts. People who are older than fifty are allowed to contribute more than the $4,000 maximum for the purposes of catching up for their approaching retirement. Any money put into the IRA is used to reduce your annual income amount, which lessens your overall tax liability for the year.

The tax is really only deferred though, since monies taken from an IRA will be taxed at the typical income tax rate for the individual when they are withdrawn, even if they are held in such an account until retirement. When the money is taken out earlier than this age of 59 ½, then an extra ten percent penalty is applied as well. There are exceptions to the penalty rule though. When these early withdrawn monies are utilized to buy a home or to pay for the tuition costs associated with higher education, then they are not penalized. The typical tax rate would still apply, although the penalty is waived in these two cases. This makes IRA's a good vehicle for investments that also give you the versatility of making significant purchases with the money.

Roth IRA's are the other principal type of IRA's. The government established these types of IRA account back in 1997 in an effort to assist those Americans in the middle class with their retirement needs. Roth IRA's do not turn out to be tax deductible. The upside is that they offer greater amounts of flexibility than do the typical IRA's. These contributions are allowed to be taken out whenever you want without a penalty or extra tax. Interest that the account earns is taxed if taken out before the first five years have passed. At the end of five years, the earnings and contributions both made are capable of being taken out without having to pay either taxes or penalties. The identical housing and education allowances that permit to standard IRA's pertain to Roth IRA's. The principal attraction of Roth IRA's is that they offer tax free income at retirement time.

It is worth noting that the Roth IRA's have their particular rules that keep them from being for everybody. If your income is higher than $95,000 in a year, then you will be barred from making the full contribution, and if it exceeds $110,000, then you will not be allowed to make a partial contribution. For married, filing jointly, the limits are $150,000 for full contributions and $160,000 for partial contributions.

Initial Coin Offering (ICO)

An Initial Coin Offering refers to a non-regulated process in which the funds for new crypto-currency projects become raised. This is also popularly known by its acronym of ICO. These ICOs allow for entrepreneurs to sidestep the heavily regulated process of raising capital through more traditional means involving banks, venture capital, angel investors, or IPOs initial public offerings on stock exchanges.

With any ICO offer campaign, at least some of the crypto-currency will be sold off to those backers of the venture who become involved early. They receive this in compensation for providing traditional currency or alternative currency investment from the likes of Bitcoin. These ICOs are also known as IPCOs, or Initial Public Coin Offerings sometimes.

The process for engaging in an Initial Coin Offering is straightforward and relatively easy to do. The startup outfit begins by producing and releasing a whitepaper-based plan that reveals all of the key details on the venture. These include the needs this operation will meet when it is up and running, what percentage of the new virtual currency project pioneers will keep, what kinds of funding is allowed, the amount of cash required to make the venture a success, and what time duration the campaign will run.

In this campaign, the investors and supports of the new initiative will purchase part of the alternative coins of the new venture with real or virtual money. Such alt coins will be called tokens. They function in much the same way as do shares of stock which corporations sell their investors during an IPO initial public offering.

In cases where the funds raised are not sufficient to carry out the project requirements as set out by the firm in the white paper plan, invested sums will be given back to the investors as the ICO becomes a failure. Yet in those many cases where the funding objective are attained within the set out duration, then the money will be utilized to fund the new enterprise (or to finish it in other cases).

Naturally the upfront investors have their own motivation in purchasing such crypto-coins in the project. This is because they believe that the operation will be a success following launch. This would lead to a potentially massive gain in the value of their tokens.

One highly successful ICO proved to be the platform for the introduction of smart contracts to the world, known as Ethereum. Its coin tokens are called Ether. The Ethereum project came out in 2014. The ICO garnered $18 million worth of Bitcoins for the project's completion. This meant that the Ether tokens cost forty cents apiece. Following the live launch of Ethereum in 2015 and growing success in 2016, Ether roared higher to more than $14. In 2017, it has even topped $400 each at one point. Early investors who held to $400 realized gains of an eye-watering over 1,000 percent in less than five years.

It is true that many ICO events go off successfully. These Initial Coin Offerings are in fact highly disruptive and innovative means of fundraising. Yet they are not a serious rival to traditional stocks by a long shot. Many ICO campaigns have been deemed to be fraud. Without the imperative regulation provided by the SEC Securities Exchange Commission, their volume is likely to remain a tiny fraction of that done in IPOs on traditional exchanges for at least the foreseeable future.

ICOs have suffered from official national opposition which has hindered them as well. The People's Bank of China fully banned all ICOs in September of 2017. They declared them to be financially unstable and disruptive to an orderly economy. Banks were forbidden to provide any services having anything to do with ICOs. At the same time, these new tokens were no longer allowed to be utilized as a currency on Chinese markets. It caused the Bitcoin and Ether enthusiasts to realize that crypto-currency regulation is in the future cards. This temporarily crushed the prices of both main alternative currencies as investors realized what a serious setback it represents.

Initial Public Offering (IPO)

An IPO is the acronym for an Initial Public Offering. Such IPO's represent the first opportunity for most investors to start buying shares of stock in the firm in question. Initial Public Offerings commonly generate a great deal of excitement, not only for the company involved but also for the members of the investing community.

Private companies decide to issue stock and become publicly traded companies for a few different reasons. The main two motivating factors revolve around the need to raise more capital, as well as the desire to permit the original business owners and investors to take profits on their time and investment that they originally put into starting up the company.

It is true that private companies are limited in the amount of capital that they are able to raise, since their ownership turns out to be restricted to certain organizations and individuals. Public companies have the advantages of allowing any investor to take a stake through buying stock shares on exchanges that are publicly traded. It is far easier for them to raise money as public companies.

Initial Public Offerings that go well translate to large amounts of cash for a company. They use this for future expansion and development. Those who began the company or who were initial investors typically make enormous gains at that time in compensation for their time and effort.

Initial Public Offerings take huge amounts of preliminary work. Great amounts of paper work have to be filled in and filed with the regulatory oversight groups. A prospectus has to be created for investors to study and consider. Advertising campaigns for the first shares that will be sold must be developed. On top of these tasks, the company has to continue its normal operations. Because of this, financial firms such as Morgan Stanley or Goldman Sachs are commonly engaged to perform these tasks on the company's behalf. Such a firm is called the IPO underwriting company. With enormous sized IPO's, these tasks could even be divided up between a few different IPO underwriting companies.

Contrary to what many people think, the majority of IPO's typically do not do well initially. Besides this, a percentage of the companies will not make it, meaning that all of the investment in the IPO stock could be lost. Because of this, there is great risk and often lower rewards for sinking money into Initial Public Offerings than in traditional well established companies and stocks. Many investors buy into the enthusiasm and excitement that surrounds Initial Public Offerings. Another explanation for their euphoria may have to do with believing that there is something special in being among the first investors to acquire the next possible Apple, Coca Cola, or IBM. Whatever their reasoning proves to be, investors continue to love Initial Public Offerings and the somewhat long shot opportunities that they represent.

Institutional Investor

Institutional investors turn out to be organizations or occasionally individuals which buy and sell securities in huge enough quantities and currency totals. They benefit from lower fees and commissions as well as special treatment from the market makers.

These large and powerful deep pocketed investors experience fewer regulations from the regulatory agencies as well since they naturally assume that they have a larger knowledge base and are sophisticated enough to protect themselves in their investing strategies. There are many different kinds of investors who qualify as institutional investors. Some of them are life insurance firms and pension funds.

These entities derive their money from a variety of sources, but in all cases they pool the funds in order to buy and sell real estate, stock and bond securities, and other alternative types of investment classes such as loans, commodities, precious metals, and artwork.

There are many different kinds of institutional investors such as hedge funds, pension funds, insurance companies, sovereign wealth funds, commercial banks, investment advisors, Real Estate Investment Trusts, mutual funds, and university endowments. Other operating firms that choose to invest their extra capital in such asset classes are also covered by the term. Some institutional investors are activist. This means that they may interfere with the internal workings and governance of the firm by using their substantial voting rights in the companies in which they own larger stakes to influence corporate decisions, investments, and behavior.

Institutional investors act as intermediaries between smaller retail investors and corporations. They are also significant sources of critical capital for the financial markets. Since they pool together their member investment dollars or Euros, these larger and more powerful investors effectively lessen the cost of capital to entrepreneurs at the same time as the efficiently diversify their clients' portfolios. Since they can impact the behavior of companies as well, this helps to reduce agency costs.

Institutional investors have several significant and game changing advantages over smaller, weaker retail investors. They possess enormous resources to invest as well as specialty knowledge that pertains to a variety of different investment options. Many of these choices are not even available to traditional retail investors at all. They also have longer term investing horizons as they are not limited to accumulation and distribution requirements of individual investors who will want to transition to retirement at some point.

Such institutions turn out to be the biggest movers and shakers within both supply and demand segments in the securities markets. This means that they transact the overwhelming majority of all trades on the major stock and bond market exchanges. Their choices and actions substantially impact the prices and bid/asks of most securities on the various markets.

This has led a number of retail investors to attempt to level the proverbial playing field of investing by researching the various filings of holdings the institutions make with the SEC Securities and Exchange Commission to learn what different securities they ought to invest in for their own individual portfolios and trades.

Some of these institutional investors are critically important in specific types of countries. For example, those countries which are oil rich and exporting nations generally contain one or more massive sovereign wealth funds which possess a lion's share of the investable wealth of the nation. These are usually government controlled and administered institutional funds and investors.

They can amass even hundreds of billions of investable dollars, as have the Norwegian, Abu Dhabi, Saudi Arabian, Qatari, and Kuwaiti funds. In developed nations, it is the pension funds and insurance companies which control a substantial portion of the excess and readily deployable and investable capital.

Internal Rate of Return (IRR)

The IRR is the acronym for internal rate of return. This IRR proves to be the capital budget rate of return that is utilized in order to determine and compare and contrast various investments' profitability. It is sometimes known as the discounted cash flow rate of return alternatively, or even the ROR, or rate of return. Where banks are concerned, the IRR is also known as the effective interest rate. The word internal is used to specify that such calculation does not involve facts that are part of the external environment, such as inflation or the interest rate.

More precisely, the internal rate of return for any investment proves to be the interest rate level where the negative cash flow, or net present value of costs, from the investment is equal to the positive cash flow, or net present value of benefits, for the investment. In other words, this IRR will yield a discount rate that causes the net current values of both positive and negative cash flows of a specific investment to cancel out at zero.

These Internal Rates of Return are generally utilized to consider projects and investments and their ultimate desirability. Naturally, a project will be more appealing to engage in or purchase if it comes with a greater internal rate of return. Given a number of projects from which to choose, and assuming that all project benefits prove to be the same generally, the project that contains the greatest Internal Rate of Return will be considered the most attractive. It should be selected with the highest priority of being pursued first.

The assumed theory for companies is that they will be interested in eventually pursuing any investment or project that comes with an IRR that is greater than the expense of the money put into the project as capital. The number of projects or investments that can be run at a time are limited in the real world though. A firm may have a restricted capability of overseeing a large number of projects at once, or they may lack the necessary funds to engage in all of them at a time.

The internal rate of return is actually a number expressed as a percent. It details the yield, efficacy, and efficiency of a given investment or project. This should not be confused with the net present value that instead tells the particular investment's actual value.

In general, a given investment or project is deemed to be worthwhile assuming that its internal rate of return proves to be higher than either the expense of the capital involved, or alternatively, than a pre set minimally accepted rate of return. For companies that possess share holders, the minimum IRR is always a factor of the investment capital's cost. This is easily decided by ascertaining the cost of capital, which is risk adjusted, for alternative types of investments. In this way, share holders will approve of a project or investment, so long as its Internal Rate of Return is greater than the cost of the capital to be used and this project or investment creates economic value that is viable for the company in question.

Investment Banking

Investment Banking refers to a particular subdivision of banking. This investment type of banking pertains to developing capital for governments, organizations, and corporations. Investment banks will come up with new equity and debt securities to float and sell them on behalf of any corporation. They also facilitate mergers and acquisitions and company reorganizations. They help to sell the securities and broker major trades for private investors and institutions. Besides this, they give guidance to those issuing stocks on the placement and floating of stock issues.

A great many of the bigger investment banks prove to be associated with (or wholly or partially owned by) bigger financial and banking institutions. A number of them have evolved into house hold known names. The biggest of these famous investment banks are Goldman Sachs, JPMorgan Chase, Morgan Stanley, Bank of America Merrill Lynch, HSBC, and Deutsche Bank.

In general, such investment banking fosters huge, complex, often international in nature financial transactions. This might come with advisory services on the best ways to structure deals when the customer is interested in engaging in a sale, merger, or acquisition. Other firms may want to know how much a certain company is worth. The investment banks may need to float and sell securities in order to raise money for the groups of clients. Someone will have to develop the documents which the SEC Securities and Exchange Commission requires in order for companies to be taken public.

The investment banking groups hire investment bankers who assist their clients (the governments, organizations, and corporations) in planning for, setting up, and managing enormous projects. This saves a great deal of money and time for the clients through identifying any risks common to the project before the project starts. The idea is that investment bankers are highly trained experts in the financial services fields. They are supposed to have a wealth of knowledge, background, and advice to offer their clients for the best way to plan developments so the company can pursue the best recommendations for the current state of economics pertaining to the company's particular project.

One can also think of the investment banks as not only an advisor but a middle man. They offer the useful go-between for companies and the investing public who want to purchase such new bond and stock issues. Investment banks package together financial securities and instruments so that the companies can optimize their revenues and safely come through the often complex regulatory environments.

For example, in many cases where companies launch their first IPO initial public offering, the underwriting investment banks will purchase most or all of the new shares straight off of their client the company. They then re-sell these IPO shares on the stock markets. The company gets a big single payday upfront this way and the investment bank acts as a contractor for the actual IPO underwriting. The investment banks typically profit well, as they usually re-price the shares with a nice markup on their original purchase price. This also entails a serious amount of risk though. If they overprice the stock shares, then they may not be able to sell all the shares and instead could end up selling them at a loss to the price they initially paid for them in the first place.

It is not at all uncommon for various investment banks to compete with each other for the best new IPO underwriting opportunities, and sometimes they end up working together on enormous ones. It could lead to a higher per share price being realized for the company which is going public. When the competition for the project becomes particularly intense, it can hit the investment bank's profit margins. In these cases what often happens is that several of the major investment banks will underwrite a portion of the securities, often in different jurisdictions such as EuroNext, NYSE, and London Stock Exchange. The advantages to the investment banks are that the risk becomes spread around and reduced this way.

Investment Management

Investment Management proves to be a general term which most often relates to purchasing and selling investments inside of a portfolio. It might also be utilized to cover budgeting and banking tasks and tax management. Most of the time, the phrase pertains to managing portfolios and trading securities to reach a particular set of investment goals or objectives.

Analysts and economists also call Investment Management by the names of money management, private banking, or even portfolio management. This includes the professional money management of various assets and financial instruments. Among these are equities, bonds, real estate, and other types of securities such as gold, derivatives, and mortgage-backed securities. Successful and well-rounded management of investments works to achieve particular investment objectives for the good of the underlying investors. Such investors are not necessarily individuals, or private investors. They are often family investment offices as well as institutional investors. Among the various deep-pocketed institutional investors are governments, pension funds, sovereign wealth funds, insurance companies, and educational foundations.

The services of Investment Managers cover many functions. These include analysis of financial statements and assets, proper asset allocation and diversification, investment instruments and stocks selection, financial plan implementation, estate planning, and maintenance of existing investments in the portfolios. An entire industry has grown up around these needs for wealthy clients and investors. This is called the Investment Management industry.

For those who feel led to start an Investment Management firm, there are many important and sensitive tasks that must be successfully accomplished. This starts with hiring professional money managers. It extends to performing research on types of asset classes and particular investments. Marketing, dealing, settling, and internal auditing are all core functions on the administration side of the business. Finally, this type of firm will have to prepare regular reports and statements for the various clientele.

This means that it requires much more than simply hiring an effective asset gathering marketing team and a highly qualified and results-driven money management staff to manage the daily flow of investing. Owners of these firms must also handle the various jurisdictional regulatory and legislative environments, carefully monitor the business' cash flow, stay on top of the internal controls and all systems, and accurately record and track all fund values and any transactions performed.

This means that Investment Management firms have a certain set of stressful problems that they deal with routinely. This is the trade off for what can be substantial and highly lucrative rewards. First of all, investment management firms are highly dependent for their income on the performance of the various asset markets. In other words, the firm's profits will often come down to the progress of the markets. When asset prices suffer a substantial decline, this will undoubtedly lead to the management firm's revenues dropping off. This is particularly the case when the fall in prices is higher than the investment basis cost of the company.

There are also issues of client expectation management. When times in the markets are hard and lean, clients can become agitated, impatient, and even angry. Even fund performance which is above industry average may not be good enough to keep the clients satisfied with their portfolios' progress. This is the reason it is critical for any investment management company to attract and retain highly successful money managers. The problem with this is that top talent is costly and hard to keep loyal when the competition is always hungry for and eager to steal effective money managers.

For clients who are seriously contemplating a particular Investment Management firm, it is a common mistake to single out only the performance of one particular investment manager on staff. Instead the all-around total performance of the investment firm is what matters. This is why a successful investment company will have to retain expensive and performance-generating investment managers in order for their clientele to be willing to trust in the firm to manage their money.

Investment Trusts

An investment trust represent a type of collective investment pool generally utilized in Great Britain. These closed end funds are established as public limited companies within the United Kingdom primarily. Analysts have stated that the British investment trust was a forerunner of the American-promoted investment company.

In truth the name is somewhat of a misnomer. These investment trusts are not actually legal trust entities whatsoever. Instead they are a legal company or even individual. The reason this is important is because of the fiduciary responsibilities that trustees owe their membership.

When the fund is first established, a pool of all investors' funds becomes created. The investors then received a set amount of the fixed total number of shares that the trust floats on the launch date. Boards usually hand over the responsibility of the fund management into the care of a professional fund manager. This manager will then invest the fund's money into a vast range of individual shares of different corporations. This provides the fund investors with a massive diversification into a number of different companies that they could not possibly afford to do using their own limited resources.

These investment trusts may not have any employees, but instead count just a board of directors which is made up of exclusively non-executive directors. This has begun to change over the last few years as competition in the form of other funds emerged. Thanks to commercial property trusts and private equity groups utilizing the investment trust structure for holding vehicles, the structure of the staff and boards has changed in some cases.

Shares of investment trusts trade on various stock exchanges as do shares of typical publicly held corporations. What makes the value of these shares of the investment trusts interesting is that the offered price per share is not always the same as what the underlying share value should be based on the portfolio which the trust holds. When this happens, analysts say that the trust itself trades for a discount or a premium to its actual NAV net asset value.

This sector of the investment trust experienced significant trouble in the years from 2000 through 2003. This was because there was no set compensation plan for the industry. They then came up with guidelines for compensation packages and this cleared up many of the issues overshadowing the space.

One should not confuse investment trusts and unit (investment) trusts. There are some key differences between the two. The manager of an investment trust has the carte blanche legal ability to borrow funds in order to buy shares in company stocks. The managers of unit trusts (which are open ended funds) may not do this without first having a process for risk management established that makes rules on the ways the leverage will be considered and permitted. Such gearing can boost gains earned on investments yet also dramatically expands the risk to investors.

These investment trusts have a history going back around 150 years. The first one established was the 1868 founded Foreign & Colonial Investment Trust. Its stated goal was to "give the investor of moderate means the same advantages as the large capitalists in diminishing the risk of spreading the investment over a number of stocks."

The investment trust is classified in a breakdown by similar characteristics. This permits prospective investors to compare and contrast the various trusts within a certain category more effectively. The trusts are also further broken down according to the kinds of shares they issue. Traditional investment trusts possess only the single class of ordinary shares and enjoy an unending investment vehicle lifespan.

With the rival Splits, or Split Capital Investment Trusts, the structure proves to be more complex. They issues several varying share classes so that investors can match the shares up with their own investment objectives. The majority of such Splits begin with a preset investment life span that the fund determines when it launches. They call this the wind up date. The average wind up date of such a Split Capital Investment Trust occurs between five and ten years from the fund establishment.

Investment Value

Investment Value refers to an asset's specific value given a particular range of investment parameters. It can be defined as the property value to a given group of investors (or an individual investor) who have specific investment goals in mind. This makes it a subjective measurement of the asset or property's value.

Many times potential investors will employ the investment value metric when they have an interest in buying a certain real estate property with a particular group of investment goals and objectives. It might be they have a targeted return rate they are looking for in the investment. This is why such a value metric heavily involves motivations and beliefs in a particular investment strategy.

The reason that this investment value would have importance on a transaction concerns buyers contemplating buying a given asset when they want to compare the pricing of the real estate or asset in question to the anticipated rate of return. When they are able to use this value to consider their specific rate of return, they are able to measure up the investment final results with the projected price they will pay out for the property. This helps them to make an intelligent purchasing decision consistent with their investment objectives.

In contrast to the investment value, market value is the true value of the property (or asset) in question based on the supply and demand of the open market. It is typically determined by utilizing the appraisal process where Real Estate is concerned. This contrasts with the individual investors' value they may place on the property as it pertains to their unique goals, objectives, and needs for the property they are considering.

It is important to realize that investment value is not the same as market value in many cases. The investment values might be lower, higher, or the same to the market values. This would heavily depend on the property's specific scenario at the time. In fact the market values and investing values are typically approximately the same. Yet they can diverge.

For example, investment value might be greater than that of the market value. A certain buyer may place a higher value on the property than would a typical informed purchaser. This could happen in the real world when a firm decides to expand its premises into a larger newer building that has just gone on sale across the road from the current company offices. The company might be willing to pay a higher price than the market value so that it could ensure competitors stay out of the market and do not secure the building before they can conclude the transaction. In such a scenario, this extra value becomes derived from the strategic advantage that the firm will realize by having the property.

Where a single investor is concerned, it is also possible for investment value to exceed the market value. An example of this could be when the investors have a special tax status or situation that can not be transferred. They might also have some type of highly advantageous financing terms that do not apply to rival investors or buyers.

It is similarly possible for investment value to be under that of the market value on a property. This could happen when the given property is not a kind in which the investors normally specialize or concentrate their efforts. As an example, for multifamily developers, choosing to consider developing a hotel could cause the investment value for this particular situation to be lower than the traditional market value for the given site. This would be because of the greater costs involved in learning to develop the property. It might also be that the investors are seeking out and demand a higher than average return from a property thanks to their current portfolio diversification and allocation.

Investor

Strictly speaking, an investor is any person or entity that makes an investment. In the past, the word investors has acquired a far more specific meaning. In the world of business and finance, investors has come to characterize those individuals or companies that routinely buy debt instruments like bonds, or equity issues like stocks in an attempt to make financial profits. They hope to realize such gains in return for financing or providing capital to a company that is looking to expand.

Investors also relates to other types of individuals, businesses, or parties that put money into different types of investments. Although this is a less commonly used version of the word investors, it can relate to those engaging in currency, real estate, commodities, derivatives, or other personal property investments like art or antiques. An example of this would be a real estate investor. They purchase a piece of property or a house with the hopes of selling it for a greater amount of money than for what they purchased it. Similarly, commodities' investors are hoping to buy contracts or options on hard assets like gold, oil, or lumber cheaply to sell them later more dearly.

Investors are commonly buying such stocks, bonds, or other types of assets and holding on to them with the goal of realizing one of two types of returns, or in some unusual cases both types. These are capital gains or cash flow investments. Investors who are interested in capital gains are simply looking to sell an instrument or asset that they obtained at one price for a greater amount. When they do this, they realize a capital gain. Should they sell the investment for less than they purchased it, they would instead realize a capital loss. Capital gains can only be realized one time on an investment, as the investors will have sold the investment and have to look for another investment to begin the process anew once again.

Cash flow investors are alternatively looking for a repetitive income stream. They hope to achieve regular, smaller sums of passive income just from holding their investment. Dividends on a stock, royalties on an oil or gas investment, and rents from a residential or commercial realty property are all examples of cash flow investments and returns. So long as the investor owns the cash flow investment, he or she should be able to continuously count on a regular income stream.

The word investor commonly gives the connotation of a person who acquires these assets for the longer term. This stands in contrast to a day trader or even short term investor. Investors can be professional or self taught amateurs.

Investors also represent many entities other than individuals or even traditional businesses. They can be investment groups like clubs, venture capital investors who provide money to start up companies, investment banks, investment trusts such as REIT Real Estate Investment Trusts, hedge funds and mutual funds, and even sovereign wealth funds that invest on behalf of their respective nations.

IRA Custodian

An IRA custodian is commonly represented by some form of a financial institution. This would likely be a brokerage or a bank. These Individual Retirement Accounts' custodians have the job of protecting your assets in your IRA.

Per the rules of the Internal Revenue Service, such IRA custodians have to be financial institutions that are approved. People can not choose to perform the role of an IRA custodian. In order for institutions that are not financial in nature to perform the responsibilities of such IRA custodians, they have to receive a special approval issued to them by the Internal Revenue Service.

These IRA Custodians actually carry out the transactions that the clients request of them. They also file any and all reports, maintain all required records of anything done on the account as a custodian, and send out statements and notices for taxes, either of which may be mandated by law or the agreement for custodianship.

They sometimes will disburse the assets found in the IRA as per the wishes of the client, as well as file all necessary and relevant paper work with this action. One thing that IRA custodians do not have to do is to offer legal or investment advice to you, the IRA holder. This means that you have to provide the custodian of your IRA with clear and accurate instructions which follow the code established by the IRS.

IRA custodians can be responsible for overseeing a great range of investment securities and financial instruments. While IRS rules restrict IRA money being invested into collectibles like rare coins and artworks, or even life insurance, the custodian is able to work with various different investments like franchises, real estate, tax liens, and mortgages.

Still, a great number of financial institutions acting as IRA custodians will choose to restrict the kinds of investments that they will allow to be held in one of their IRA's under custodianship. It is important for owners of IRA's who wish to have their funds placed into investments that are not traditional for IRA's, such as real estate or franchises, to seek out and choose an IRA custodian who will allow and work with these kinds of investments. This is the particular reason that a real estate management firm might choose to attain IRS certification in order to obtain the permission for overseeing real estate investment IRA's.

Much of the time, IRA customers will just deposit their retirement money and assets into their account that the custodian holds and will supply them with overall guidelines for their investments. The IRS mandates fiduciary responsibility for IRA custodians. They have to place clients' interests first. This translates to practical requirements, such as not being allowed to put the IRA money into investments and projects that come with a great amount of risk, unless they have the customer's expressed consent.

IRA custodians are also involved with self directed IRA's. Self directed IRA's contain investments that are actively managed directly by the customer. The custodian only performs the actions that the customer requests in these cases.

Junk Bonds

Junk bonds are almost the same as regular bonds with an important difference. They are lower rated for credit worthiness. This is why in order to understand junk bonds, individuals first must comprehend the basics of traditional bonds.

Like traditional bonds, junk bonds are promises from organizations or companies to pay back the holder the amount of money which they borrow. This amount is known as the principal. Terms of such bonds involve several elements. The maturity date is the time when the borrower will repay the bond holder. There will also be an interest rate that the bond holder receives, or a coupon. Junk bonds are unlike those traditional ones because the credit quality of the issuing organization is lower.

Every kind of bond is rated according to its credit quality. Bonds can all be categorized in one of two types. Investment grade bonds possess medium to low risk. Their credit ratings are commonly in the range of from AAA to BBB. The downside to these bonds is that they do not provide much in the way of interest returns. Their advantage is that they have significantly lower chances of the borrower being unable to make interest payments.

Junk bonds on the other hand offer higher interest yields to their bond holders. Issuers do this because they do not have any other way to finance their needs. With a lower credit rating, they can not borrow capital at a more favorable price. The ratings on such junk bonds are often BB or less from Standard & Poor's or Ba or less by Moody's rating agency. Bond ratings such as these can be considered like a report card for the credit rating of the company in question. Riskier firms receive lower ratings while safe blue-chip companies earn higher ratings.

Junk bonds typically pay an average yield that is from 4% to 6% higher than U.S. Treasury yields. These types of bonds are placed into one of two categories. These are fallen angels and rising stars. Fallen angels bonds used to be considered at an investment grade. They were cut to junk bond level as the company that issued them saw its credit quality decline.

Rising stars are the opposites of fallen angels. This means the rating of the bond has risen. As the underlying issuer's credit quality improves, so does the rating of the bond. Rising stars are often still considered to be junk bonds. They are on track to rise to investment quality.

Junk bonds are risky for more reasons than the chances of not receiving one or more interest payments. There is the possibility of not receiving the original principal back. This type of investing also needs a great amount of skills in analyzing data like special credit. Because of these risk factors and specialized skills that are needed, institutional investors massively dominate the market.

A better way for individuals to become involved with junk bonds is through high yield bond funds. Professionals research and manage the holdings of these funds. The risks associated with a single bond defaulting are greatly reduced. They do this by diversifying into a variety of companies and types of bonds. High yield bond funds often require investors to stay invested for minimally a year or two.

When the yield of junk bonds declines below the typical 4% to 6% spread above Treasuries, investors should be careful. The risk does not become less in these cases. It is that the returns no longer justify the dangers in the junk bonds. Investors also should carefully consider the junk bond default rates. These can be tracked for free on Moody's website.

Keogh Plan

Keogh Plans are like 401(k) plans intended for small businesses. They are distinguished from them by having higher limits than the 401(k)s do. These tax deferred pension plans can be established by businesses that are not incorporated or individuals who are self employed.

These types of plans can be one of three types. There are money purchase plans preferred by those who are high income earners. Profit sharing plans provide yearly flexibility that is dependent on the company profits. Defined benefit plans feature higher yearly minimums.

Keogh Plans are also referred to as HR(10) plans. They are permitted to invest in the same investments as IRAs and 401(k)s. This includes stocks and bonds, annuities, and certificates of deposit. The reasons these plans are so popular for sole proprietors and small business owners has to do with their higher contribution limits. A downside to them revolves around their greater maintenance costs and more burdensome administration than SEP Simplified Employee Pension plans feature.

These Keogh Plans derive their name from the creator of the concept Eugene Keogh. He put together the 1962 Self Employed Individuals Tax Retirement Act which became named for him. The plans received a name change after the Economic Growth and Tax Relief Reconciliation Act passed in 2001. This act so altered these plans that the IRS code dropped the reference name of Keogh.

They simply call them HR(10) plans now. These retirement accounts are still utilized, but have lost many followers to the solo 401(k) and the SEP IRA. The HR(10) plans still find a good fit with professionals who are highly compensated as with lawyers or dentists who are self employed. Otherwise these plans generally do not serve retirement savers better than the competing plans.

The HR(10) plans come in two different principal breakdowns. These are defined contribution and defined benefit plans. With defined contribution plans, self employed persons can decide the amount of contribution they will make every year. This can be done either through money purchase or profit sharing plans.

Money purchase requires that the profits percentage to go in the Keogh be decided at the beginning of the year. If the employed person makes profits, these contributions must be made without changes or a penalty will be assessed by the IRS. The amounts owners contribute to their profit sharing plans may be changed every year. As much as 25% of income can be deducted and contributed every year. The limit on this amount is $53,000 for 2015 and 2016.

Defined benefit plans operate much as traditional pensions would. Business owners determine a pension goal for themselves then fund it. As much as $210,000 may be contributed in a year (up to 100% of all compensation) for the years 2015 and 2016. Business owners make all contributions in both types of Keogh plans as pre-tax. This means they these contributions come out of the taxable salary before taxes are figured.

Keoghs plans are also similar to typical 401(k)s in the way that invested monies are able to be tax deferred until retirement. This may start as early as 59 ½ years old but can not be delayed until any later than 70 years of age. Any withdrawals taken before these years are federally and potentially state taxed as regular income and also penalized at 10%. Exceptions to the penalty rules exist if certain physical or financial health issues come up for the account owner before retirement.

In order to maintain a Keogh Plan, a great amount of paperwork has to be filed each year. This includes the Form 5500 from the IRS. It requires a financial professional or tax accountant's help.

Margin Trading

Margin trading is the practice of buying investments on margin. This is accomplished through borrowing money from your broker in order to buy stocks. Another way of understanding margin trading is taking out a loan from your broker to buy greater amounts of stock shares.

Margin trading generally requires a margin account. Margin accounts differ from cash accounts that only allow you to trade with the money that your account contains. Brokers have to get a signature from you in order to open up a new margin account. This could be as an extension of your existing account and account opening forms or as a separate and new agreement. Minimum investments of $2,000 are necessary to open such a margin account. Some brokers insist on larger amounts. Whatever the final margin requirement deposit is, it is called the minimum margin.

After the margin account is up and running, you are able to purchase as much as fifty percent of a stock with margin trading money. The money that you use to buy your part of the stock is called initial margin. Margining up to the full fifty percent is entirely optional. You might borrow only fifteen or twenty percent instead.

Margin trading loans can be held for as long a period as you wish, assuming that you continue to meet the margin obligations. A stock maintenance margin has to be maintained while the loan is outstanding too. This maintenance margin is the lowest account balance that can be held by the account in advance of the broker making you deposit additional funds. If you do not meet this minimum or resulting margin call for extra funds, then the broker has the right to sell your stocks in order to reduce your outstanding loan.

Borrowing money from your broker is not done for the sake of charity. Interest has to be paid on the loan. Also, the marginable securities in the account become tied up as collateral. Unless you pay down the loan, interest charges will be applied to the loan balance. These interest amounts can significantly increase the debt level in the account with time. Higher debt levels in your account lead to still higher interest charges. Because of this, buying stocks on margin is typically utilized only for shorter time frame investments. This is true since the greater amount of time that you hold the margin loan in the investment, the higher a return you will require in order to break even on the margin trade. When you maintain such a margin based investment over a long time frame, it becomes difficult to turn a profit after the expenses are cleared.

It is also important to remember that not every stock qualifies for purchase using margin. The rules pertaining to which stocks can be purchased with margin are set by the Federal Reserve Board. In general though, Initial Public Offerings, penny stocks, or over the counter traded stocks are not allowed to be purchased utilizing margin as a result of the daily volatility and trading risks associated with such kinds of stocks. Besides this, each brokerage can restrict whichever other stocks that they wish.

Market Capitalization

Market capitalization refers to a company's total value. Analysts determine it by multiplying the number of shares in existence times the price of the stock. This concept can also be utilized to measure the full value of a stock exchange. The New York Stock Exchange market capitalization would equal the value of all publicly traded companies on the exchange added together.

Market cap is another name for market capitalization. Examples of how this is figured make it easier to understand. Companies that have 2 million shares which have been issued that sell for $20 apiece have a market cap of $40 million. If an investor had enough money and could get the stockholders to agree to sell their shares, he or she could purchase the company for $40 million total. In practice many shareholders would want more than the current share price to sell their stock.

There are three different main sizes of market capitalization among traded companies. These are large cap, mid cap, and small cap corporations. Large cap companies are generally considered the least risky ones in which to invest. They typically possess substantial financial resources to survive economic downturns. They are also generally leaders in their industries. This gives them a smaller amount of growth opportunity.

Because of this the returns for these large cap companies are often not as spectacular as with successful companies in the other two categories. They also have a significantly greater chance of paying dividends out to their share holders. Large cap corporations have $5 billion and higher capitalization.

Mid cap companies are generally less risky than the smaller companies. They still do not have the same possibilities for aggressive growth. Mid cap companies commonly possess market capitalization of from $1 billion to $5 billion. Studies have shown that mid caps have outperformed large cap and small cap corporation stocks in the past 20 years.

Small cap corporations are those which possess under $1 billion in market capitalization. These tinier companies have often completed an Initial Public

Offering in the recent past. Such companies are considered the riskiest of the three types. This is because in economic downturns, they have the greatest chance of failing or defaulting. They also enjoy plenty of opportunity and space to expand. This means that they potentially could be extremely profitable if they succeed.

Proponents of using market cap as the primary means of valuing companies have a well thought out argument. Stock prices tend to reflect the beliefs of investors and analysts in the anticipated earnings of a company. Higher earnings should cause traders and investors to bid up the price of the stock. Multiplying this price by the number of shares gives a comparable means of valuing one company against another.

A downside to valuing businesses this way is that it can give companies without profits high valuations. In the dot com bust at the turn of the century, technology companies that had never turned a profit were valued in the tens of billions of dollars. This in theory made them more valuable than reliable companies that had actual assets and earnings. Companies in slower growing industries are also typically valued less than they should be since their stock prices are often undervalued. Critics of this way of valuing companies suggest that more accurate measures would include the value of a company's assets, its annual revenues, or its earnings per share.

Companies whose market capitalization falls substantially below their asset value become takeover targets. This is because corporate raiders are able to buy a company for less money than they will realize by selling off its various parts, businesses, and assets separately.

Money Market Account (MMA)

Money Market Account refers to a type of savings account which commonly includes advantages such as a debit card and check writing privileges. Besides this, it usually has interest rates which are higher than those which normal savings accounts provide. Such money markets generally have a higher minimum account balance than the average savings accounts do. These accounts are sometimes referred to by their acronym of MMA.

For those individuals who are contemplating a safe depository vehicle for bigger sums of cash and who wish to earn some interest while keeping the funds entirely liquid, these money market accounts can be an optimal solution. Among their pros are that the balance funds are available without advance notice, that they earn a relatively higher interest rate, that they provide the capability of writing as many as six checks each month, and that the debit card attached to them can be utilized as many as six times every month.

For any person who is going to place at least a few thousand dollars into a bank account and desires the clear cut safety provided by the FDIC Federal Deposit Insurance Corporation guarantee of funds, these can be a solid choice. Both credit unions and banks offer them as a reliable place to keep customers' emergency day purpose funds. The money is kept segregated from an account holder's daily utilization checking account funds this way. It can grow quicker than money kept in a comparable savings account thanks to the higher interest rate commonly attached to these MMAs. They provide the added convenience of check writing, which allows for easily covering any unexpected or emergency expenses.

Yet these accounts should not be confused with either checking or savings accounts. In fact they have stark differences from either of the two competing types. For starters, MMAs are not at all checking accounts. They may include the debit card maximum use feature or limited check writing privileges. Yet as with a savings account, they are Federal Reserve-regulation limited to maximum of six monthly withdrawals or transfers in a given month. This includes transactions made by check, debit card, or online/in person transfer. For those individuals who will need more than these half a dozen uses, interest bearing checking accounts make more practical sense than do money market accounts.

Besides this MMAs are similarly not strictly savings accounts either because of their debit cards and check writing capabilities. For those people who do not feel the need of having checks or even the debit card convenience with the account, there are sometimes better interest rates on balances available through what are known as high yield online savings accounts.

One of these types is the CD or certificate of deposit. Cd's may require that the owners agree to tie up their funds for as little as from months to as long as for years. MMAs will certainly permit more convenient and immediate time framed withdrawals than this. Yet CDs will pay better rates for those who can afford to lock it down for some time.

Finally, such money market accounts should not be confused with money market funds. The latter are instead investments whose principal value will decline if the market plunges. All MMAs carry the full FDIC backing when they are operated by banks, and by the NCUA National Credit Union Administration when they are held at credit unions. This amount of protection is equal to $250,000 per depositor or account.

For those individuals who decide that money market accounts are well suited for them, the best policy is to pursue those that come without any associated monthly fees and that pay the highest possible interest rates. It is also critical to ensure that they do not require too high a minimum account balance. This is critical to pay attention to since some financial institutions mandate that depositors open the account with and maintain a $10,000 account balance for these MMAs.

Money Market Funds

Money market funds are investment vehicles with a unique objective of keeping a consistent NAV net asset value of $1 each share while they provide interest for their investing share holders. To accomplish this, the portfolio of a money market fund is made up of securities that are short term in nature with maturities which are under a year. These securities typically are liquid debt and money instruments that are of the highest quality. Investors can easily buy money market fund shares by going through banks, brokerage firms, or mutual funds directly.

The ultimate goal of these money market funds is to give their investors a safe haven investment for assets which are both readily accessible and equivalent to cash. In essence they are mutual funds. Among their most common characteristics are that they offer low returns and provide low risk as an investment.

Because these funds offer comparatively lower returns than many other investments, financial advisors recommend that investors not remain in these vehicles as a long term selection. Their returns will not provide sufficient appreciation on capital in order to achieve the investors' objectives over a longer time frame. Employer provided retirement plans will often sweep employees' unallocated dollars into these funds until they give orders as to where to invest them specifically.

The pros to money market funds can be significant. They offer more than simply high liquidity and lower risk. A number of investors find them appealing because there are not any fund entrance or exit fees (or loads) as with many mutual funds. A variety of them will offer investors gains which have tax advantages. These come from investments they make in state and federally tax exempt municipal securities. Other investments which these funds could hold include T-bills and other shorter time frame government debt issues, corporate commercial paper, and CDs certificates of deposit.

There are also some downsides to money market funds besides their low returns. Though they are supposed to be stable and consistent in their values, they are not insured by the FDIC Federal Deposit Insurance

Corporation. This means that in the rare cases where such funds break the buck, investors can suffer losses of principal. Competing investments like CDs, savings accounts, and money market deposits accounts provide similar returns but do offer this government backed guarantee of principal. This does not stop investors from regarding money market funds as extremely safe. The funds are carefully regulated by the Investment Company Act of 1940.

The government changed the rules on such money market funds regarding their net asset values and in what they could invest in 2014. After that year, the funds were not permitted to set their NAV permanently at $1 any longer. They did this because of the three times in the history of such funds where the $1 share price had been broken (as of 2016). It had created "bank runs" on the assets of the money market funds in 2008 when it occurred most recently in the Financial Crisis.

The American SEC Securities and Exchange Commission decided to prevent this from happening again by changing the fund management rules to provide them with more resilience and better stability. Such new restrictions more strictly limited the assets these funds were allowed to hold. The SEC also introduced triggers that would suspend redemptions and charge liquidity fees to prevent chaos in the markets. The fund managers had to start utilizing a floating NAV which created risk where it was not perceived to exist previously. Individual investors were not impacted by the floating NAV share rule since the funds are designated as retail funds and are exempt from this rule.

Money Purchase Plan

Money Purchase Plans are another type of retirement vehicle that some traditional for profit companies offer their employees. In these plans, employees and their employers both make contributions. These contributions from the employers are figured from a yearly earnings percentage.

The plans are different from Profit Sharing Plans in which the annual basis of profitability determines how large the contributions are. Money Purchase Plans' annual earnings percentages assigned for contributions stay the same ever year as set out in the originals terms of the retirement benefit plan. These plans do not enjoy a great deal of attention from the media. Despite this they are still a critical employer provided retirement vehicle that offers significant tax advantages for employees.

These plans are classified as defined contribution plans much like 401(k)s, even though the employer contributions are mandatory. Employees enjoy account control over the investments as much as the specific plan investment rules permit. Account owners also carry full responsibility for determining when any money is distributed or transferred.

The beauty of these Money Purchase Plans is that every contribution made to them is fully tax deductible while all gains in the account are tax deferred. This means the accounts are funded with pretax dollars. None of the money in the account will become taxable until it is distributed at retirement. The maximum contributions to the accounts in a year from employer and employee are $53,000 for 2016.

There are some downsides to the Money Purchase Plans. A significant one is that the retirement accounts require substantial administration costs for these types of accounts. This comes out of the account returns and earnings on investments. Besides this, account holders are unable to obtain loans from these types of plans. Most other defined contribution plans do allow for such loans to be taken. Rollovers can also be hard to accomplish with these types of plans. The level of difficulty depends on the individual guidelines of a specific plan.

It is critical for anyone considering a rollover to investigate the particular documents of the plan. The IRS does not limit rollovers from these plans. It is instead the specifics of the plans themselves that make it difficult for those who are still working for the company and under the official retirement age to transfer them. When the plan allows for them, rollovers proceed as with any other qualified retirement vehicle. They can be transferred into an individual IRA or rolled into another employer 401(k) plan.

Any individuals who attempt to take cash distributions before they reach the government set retirement age of 59 ½ will suffer substantial penalties. Besides becoming fully taxable, these funds will be subjected to the 10% early withdrawal IRS penalty. Because of the stiff penalties, direct rollovers are more sensible than indirect ones.

When individuals begin indirect rollovers, they receive a check distribution. The 60 day clock to complete the rollover then begins ticking. There are also withholding requirements when these types of indirect rollovers are attempted. Early distribution penalties can result from not completing these rollovers according to the strict IRS timetable.

Investment choices are a weak point of these Money Purchase Plans. Legally they are allowed to invest in individual government and corporate bonds and stocks, mutual funds, options, and exchange traded fund shares. The plan provider may limit these choices further as they see fit.

This means that these accounts may not invest in physical gold bullion holdings directly as with self directed or precious metals IRAs. They can participate in paper gold investments such as gold mining company stocks or mutual funds that own them. They may also purchase gold mining ETFs or gold ETFs like GLD.

Mortgage Backed Obligations (MBO)

Mortgage Backed Obligations are also called mortgage backed securities, or MBS. These are real estate-based financial instruments. They represent an ownership stake in a pool of mortgages. They can also be called a financial security or obligation for which mortgages underlie the instrument.

Such a security offers one of three different means for the investor getting paid. It might be that the loan becomes paid back utilizing principal and interest payments that come in on the pool of mortgages which back the instrument. This would make them pass through securities. A second option is that the security issuer could provide payments to the investing party independently of the incoming cash flow off of the borrowers. This would then be a non-pass through security. The third type of security is sometimes referred to as a modified-pass through security. These securities provide the security owners with a guaranteed interest payment each month. This happens whether or not the underlying incoming principal and interest payments prove to be sufficient to cover them or not.

Pass-through securities are not like non-pass through securities in key ways. The pass through ones do not stay on the issuer of the securities' or originators' balance sheets. Non-pass through securities do stay on the relevant balance sheet. With these non pass through variants, the securities are most frequently bonds. These became mortgage backed bonds. Investors in the non-pass through types often receive extra collateral as a letter of credit, guarantees, or more equity capital. This type of credit enhancement is delivered by the insurer of the mortgage backed obligation. The holder of the MBO will be able to count on the security which underlies the instruments in the event that the repayments the pools of mortgages make are not enough to cover the payments (or fail altogether) for the bond holder investors.

These offerings of Mortgage Backed Obligations, Mortgage Backed Bonds, or Mortgage Backed Securities are all ultimately backed up by mortgage pools. Analysts and investors usually call these securitized mortgage offerings. When such types of investments are instead backed up by different kinds of assets and collateral then they have another name. An example of this is the Asset Backed Securities or Asset Backed Bonds.

They are backed up with such collateral as car loans, credit card receivables, or even mobile home loans. Sometimes they are referred to as Asset Backed Commercial Paper when the loans that underlie them are short term loan pools.

With these Mortgage Backed Obligations, they are often grouped together by both risk level and maturity dates. Issuers, investors, and analysts refer to this grouping as tranches, which are the risk profile-organized groups of mortgages. These complicated financial instrument tranches come with various interest rates, mortgage principle balances, dates of maturity, and possibilities of defaulting on their repayments. They are also highly sensitive to any changes in the market interest rates. Other economic scenarios can dramatically impact them as well. This is particularly true of refinance rates, rates of foreclosure, and the home selling rates.

It helps to look at a real world example to understand the complexity of Mortgage Backed Obligations and Collateralized Mortgage Obligations like these. If John buys an MBO or CMO that is comprised of literally thousands of different mortgages, then he has real potential for profit. This comes down to whether or not the various mortgage holders pay back their mortgages. If just a couple of the mortgage-paying homeowners do not pay their mortgages while the rest cover their payments as expected, then John will recover not only his principal but also interest. On the other hand, if hundreds or even thousands of mortgage holders default on their payments and then fall into foreclosure, the MBO will sustain heavy losses and will be unable to pay out the promised returns of interest and even the original principal to John.

Mortgage Backed Securities (MBS)

Mortgage backed securities turn out to be a special kind of asset which have underlying collections of mortgages or individual mortgages that back them. To be qualified as an MBS, the security also has to be qualified as rated in one of two top tier ratings. Credit ratings agencies determine these ratings levels.

These securities generally pay out set payments from time to time which are much like coupon payments. Another requirement of MBS is that the mortgages underlying them have to come from an authorized and regulated bank or financial institution.

Sometimes mortgage backed securities are called by other names. These include mortgage pass through or mortgage related securities. Interested investors buy or sell them via brokers. The investments have fairly steep minimums. These are generally $10,000. There is some variation in minimum amounts depending on which entity issues them.

Issuers are either a GSE Government Sponsored Enterprise, an agency company of the federal government, or an independent financial company. Some people believe that government sponsored enterprise MBS come with less risk. The truth is that default and credit risks are always prevalent. The government has no obligation to bail out the GSEs when they are in danger of default.

Investors who put their money into these mortgage backed securities lend their money to a business or home buyer. Using an MBS, regional banks which are smaller may confidently lend money to their clients without being concerned whether the customers can cover the loan itself. Thanks to the mortgage backed securities, banks are only serving as middlemen between investment markets and actual home buyers.

These MBS securities are a way for shareholders to obtain principal and interest payments out of mortgage pools. The payments themselves can be distinguished as different securities classes. This all depends on how risky the various underlying mortgages are rated within the MBS.

The two most frequent kinds of mortgage backed securities turn out to be collateralized mortgage obligations (CMOs) and pass throughs. Collateralized mortgage obligations are comprised of many different pools of securities. These are referred to as tranches, or pieces. Tranches receive credit ratings. It is these credit ratings which decide what rates the investors will receive. The securities within a senior secured tranche will generally feature lesser interest rates than others which comprise the non secured tranche. This is because there is little actual risk involved with senior secured tranches.

Pass throughs on the other hand are set up like a trust. These trust structures collect and then pass on the mortgage payments to the investors. The maturities with these kinds of pass throughs commonly are 30, 15, or five years. Both fixed rate mortgages and adjustable rate ones can be pooled together to make a pass through MBS.

The pass throughs average life spans may end up being less than the maturity which they state. This all depends on the amount of principal payments which the underlying mortgage holders in the pool make. If they pay larger payments than required on their monthly mortgages, then these pass through mortgages could mature faster.

Municipal Bonds

Municipal bonds prove to be counties', cities', and states' debt obligations. They issue these in order to raise money against future tax revenues for building highways, schools, sewer systems, hospitals, and numerous other public welfare projects.

When you as an investor buy a municipal bond, you are actually loaning a state or local government or agency money. They agree to pay you back your principal, along with a certain sum of interest that is generally paid out twice a year. The principal is commonly given back on the pre arranged maturity date of the bond.

The advantage that is most commonly touted to municipal bonds is their tax free nature. The truth is that not every municipal bond actually provides income which is tax free on both state and federal levels. Many municipal bond issues are exempt from taxes from the state and local authorities but still have to pay taxes on earning to the federal government. Municipal bonds that come without any federal taxes as well are generally known as Munis. These Munis prove to be the most appealing bonds for many investors since they are generally exempt from all Federal, state, and local taxes too. Besides this, Munis are commonly investments made in the local and state infrastructure, impacting your daily quality of life and that of your community. Projects including highways, hospitals, and housing are all covered by these types of municipal bonds.

Municipal bonds can also be further subdivided into one of two general categories. These are general obligation bonds and revenue bonds. With a general obligation bond, the interest and principal that is owed to you is commonly backed up by the issuer's own credit and faith. They typically come underpinned by the taxing power of the issuer. This can be based on their limited or unlimited powers of taxing. General obligation bonds usually come approved by the voters who will pay the taxes that support their repayment.

Revenue bonds on the other hand are backed up by specific revenues for the project in question. Their interest and principal payment amounts have supporting revenues that come from tolls, rents from the facility that they build, or charges to use the facility that is built. Many different public works are built with revenue bonds. These could be airports, bridges, roads, sewage and water treatment plants, subsidized housing, and even hospitals. A great number of such bonds come issued by authorities which are specifically launched to create such bond issues in the first place.

Municipal bonds and notes commonly come with minimum investment amounts. These are typically denominated by $5,000. They can come in multiples of $5,000 increments as well. If you want to buy a municipal bond, you can buy them directly off of the bond issuer when they come out on the primary market, or alternatively off of other bond holders after they have come out, from the secondary market.

Mutual Funds

Mutual funds prove to be collective investment pools that are managed professionally. They derive their sometimes enormous capitals from the contributions of many different investors. These monies are then invested in a variety of investments and securities comprised of bonds, stocks, other mutual funds, money markets, and commodities like silver and gold.

Mutual funds all have a fund manager. His responsibility is to sell and buy the holdings of the fund according to the guidelines spelled out in the particular mutual fund's prospectus. U.S. regulations require that all mutual funds registered with the governing SEC, or Securities and Exchange Commission, make distributions of practically all income and net gains made from selling securities to the investors minimally once a year. The majority of these mutual funds are furthermore overseen by trustees or boards of directors. Their job is to make certain that the fund is properly managed by its investment adviser for the investors of the funds ultimate good.

There are really a wide variety of different securities that mutual funds are permitted by the SEC to purchase. This is somewhat limited by the objectives spelled out in the prospectus of the fund, which is comprised of a great amount of useful information on the fund and its goals. While cash instruments, stocks, and bonds are the more common types of investments that they purchase, mutual funds might also buy exotic types of investments like forwards, swaps, options, and futures.

The investment objectives of mutual funds explain clearly the types of investments that the fund will purchase. As an example, if a fund's objective claimed that it was attempting to realize capital appreciation through investing in U.S. company stocks regardless of their amount of market capitalization, then it would be a U.S. stock fund that purchased U.S company stocks.

Other mutual funds purchase specific market sectors or different industries. Utilities, technology, and financial service funds are examples of this. Such a fund is called a sector fund or specialty fund. There are also bond funds that purchase different kinds of bonds, like investment grade corporate bonds or high yield junk bonds. They can invest in the bonds issued by government agencies, municipalities, or companies.

They might also be divided up according to whether they purchase long term or short term maturities of bonds. These funds may also buy bonds or stocks of either domestic companies or global companies, or even international companies outside of the United States. Index funds are another type of mutual fund that attempts to match a certain market index's performance over time. The S&P 500 index is an example of one on which index mutual funds are based. With this type of index fund, the mutual fund would find derivatives based on the S&P 500 stock index futures so that they could match the index's performance as identically as possible.

To help investors better understand the type of fund that they are getting into, the SEC came out with a particular name rule in the 40' Act that makes funds actually invest in minimally eighty percent of securities that actually match up with their name. So a fund called the New York Tax Free Bond Fund would have to use eighty percent or more of its funds to purchase investments of tax free bonds that New York State and its various agencies issued.

Mutual Funds Dividends

Where mutual funds are concerned, dividends are quite different than they turn out to be for stocks. Mutual fund dividends are actually required distributions of both income as well as capital gains that are realized that have to be paid out to investors in mutual funds.

Mutual funds often bring in varying types of income. The challenge lies in the fact that all of these incomes come with varying tax treatments. In the majority of cases, such differences in taxes are passed through to the investors in the mutual fund. As an example, should a mutual fund own a stock for longer than a single year and then sell it to realize a capital gain, then a portion of the investors' mutual fund dividends would be classified as a long term capital gain. This would permit you to realize the advantages of such types of income's lower tax rates.

There are varying types of dividends paid out by mutual funds. One of these is ordinary dividends. These cover every type of taxable income besides the long term capital gains. This does not mean that they are always treated as ordinary tax rate income, since some of these dividends will be qualified dividends that receive preferential tax rate treatment.

Some of the distributions that come from your mutual fund could be long term capital gains. These do get the better form of tax treatment. Shorter term capital gains in these funds are generally distributed along with the regular dividends.

Some mutual funds buy into state or local government debts or municipal bonds. This results in a portion of your mutual fund distributions being treated as interest that is tax exempt. These interest payments might still impact social security benefits though, so it is wise to consult a tax professional concerning them.

Should your mutual fund be investing money into the Federal Government's debt obligations, then these distributions can often be treated as interest paid by the federal government. Such income is not given favorable Federal income tax treatment. It does become exempt from state income types of taxation.

From time to time, mutual funds will issue payments that are not income at all. This is a non dividend distribution. All that it represents is a portion of the money that was invested by you in the first place being returned to you. These distributions usually do not even have to be reported. They must be used in determining the amount of loss or gain incurred when you sell the mutual fund shares, though.

A final mutual fund dividend paid out is a capital gain allocation. These are highly unusual, since the overwhelming majority of mutual funds do capital gain distributions instead. While it is highly uncommon to see such a capital gain allocation, if you do get one, then you will have to use the special Form 2439 that your mutual fund sends to you in dealing with the particular tax rules.

MyRA Account

MyRA Account is a new form of retirement plan that the government set up under the auspices of the U.S. Department of the Treasury. They intended it for workers who do not have access to any other form of retirement plan through their workplace and who do not have a convenient vehicle of their own for saving for retirement. It is a Roth IRA and is governed by the Roth IRA rules.

It offers several advantages other forms of retirement accounts do not. There are no fees or costs to set it up or maintain it. The account is automatically invested in a government Treasury fund and pays the simple rate, so there are not any complex investment options or decisions to make. Because it is based in Treasuries of the United States government, there is no risk of losing any money. The Obama administration created and issued this MyRA account plan in 2015.

As with other types of retirement plans and accounts, participants are able to set up automatic payroll contributions to this account. When they change jobs to work for a different company, the account stays with them as it is their own personal retirement account.

The accounts also provide the distinctive advantage in allowing participants to take out the money they placed in the MyRA account whenever they wish. There is no additional tax levied or penalties assessed at any point when they do this. This means that there is no early withdrawal penalty associated with the MyRA accounts, making it more like a savings account than a government approved retirement plan.

Participants in the MyRA Account like that their money is invested in safe U.S. government Treasuries. The investment is fully backed by the United States Treasury. They state that the account will earn (with no risk) an interest rate of 1.5% APR for the month of July 2016. This is based on the Government Securities Fund. This particular fund earned a 2015 average return of 2.04% and a 2.94% average annual return in the ten year period that concluded in December of 2015.

As a starter retirement account, the MyRA account provides the unmatched benefit of no charges to set up or open it and no ongoing maintenance fees for account owners. It also allows savers to contribute any amount they like with no minimum, even $2 contributions. The investments grow with the same tax advantages as a Roth IRA with after tax dollars. This means that the interest and principle will not be taxable when it is withdrawn from the account at any point between now and through retirement.

The MyRA account does come with maximum contribution limits as do all types of retirement savings vehicles. For tax years 2015 and 2016, participants may contribute no more than $5,500 in the year. If they are older than 49 years of age, this amount increases to $6,500 for the year in catch up contribution amounts which the IRS permits. Besides the annual contribution limit amounts, there are also the same lifetime contribution limits that apply to standard Roth IRA accounts.

Critics of this account have warned that this plan represents an all too easy mark and tempting target for the U.S. government if it runs into financing troubles. In the event that Treasury needs ready to access funds, it would not be able to find any that were easier to seize than the ones it is holding itself on behalf of American account holders. They also accuse the government of setting up a plan that props up and creates demand for Treasuries using Americans' retirement funds as the vehicle to do this.

Offshore Bonds

Offshore Bonds are sometimes called offshore investment bonds. These investment vehicles allow individuals to gain control over what point they pay tax, to whom they will pay such tax, and how much they will ultimately pay in the end. These types of bonds are offered internationally from some of the mega global multinational life insurance firms like Britain's Old Mutual International and Friends Provident International, Genarali Worldwide, RL360, and Zurich International.

Such Offshore Bonds would not ever be domiciled in the United Kingdom or the United States. Rather they would be based in such offshore tax havens as Luxembourg, Guernsey in the Channel Islands, or the Isle of Man. More and more these days, international expatriates choose Dublin, Ireland for a domicile for these investments. This is because of the perception that Ireland offers tax efficiency and effective regulatory protection.

When money like this is not brought back into most countries (beside the United States) where the citizen is from in the form of either capital appreciation or income, then it will not be subject to those jurisdictions' taxes. This is why investors have to consider the tax jurisdiction where they are residents when they cash out their Offshore Bond. It means that selecting the best location and provider of the bond is extremely critical, since this will determine which access and taxation rules apply in the event of a cash out scenario.

A great number of the Offshore Bonds prove to be inexpensive, completely transparent, and tax efficient planning investment vehicles. Investors still have to be careful that they are not abusing this type of tax and investment vehicle. Reality is that whether a bond is offshore or onshore, it truly is an investment masquerading as an insurance contract. This delivers to the investors an array of some helpful tax benefits.

There are a number of good reasons for why investors (and especially those who are not U.S. citizens who can not escape from their own taxing regime the IRS no matter where they live unless they give up their citizenship) utilize such investment vehicles as Offshore Bonds. For starters, an offshore bond will not be considered an income generating asset. Because of this truth, trustees and individuals do not have to fill in any tax returns which require self assessment.

Income which is reinvested in the Offshore Bonds will not produce income tax events. These bonds have advantages over pensions and retirement accounts as well, since investors can assign them to another individual or legal entity at will. Money kept inside of the bond may be switched around and still will not require any Capital Gains Tax payment or even tax reporting situations.

There are similarly income tax-free events with these Offshore Bonds. It is possible to draw out as much as five percent of the premium originally deposited or paid without creating any taxing liability. This can be done over a span of 20 consecutive years. When owners make their five percent withdrawals, this is not an income-generating event, but instead simply a return of original capital to the bond holder. These bonds may also be put inside of a trust and then removed from it without creating an income taxing event.

Without a doubt, these Offshore Bonds have proven to be enormously popular with expatriates living abroad. They provide tremendous possible tax advantages for anyone who will reside outside of their native country (besides for citizens of the U.S.). The reason for this is that investors are able to claim tax relief for those gains which they make when residing offshore. This significant benefit is known as time apportionment relief.

For British residents as an example, they are able to lower the tax which must be paid commiserate with the amount of time they resided outside of the United Kingdom. So if they were bondholding residents of Spain for half the life of holding the bond, then this would lower the amount of taxes they had to pay for any income or gains in Britain by half.

The danger of course is that some commission-based financial advisors will try to take advantage of the investors in this type of program. When they are not correctly established with extreme transparency, the unscrupulous financial advisor may draw out a significant amount of the savings percentage wise. This transfer of wealth is not illegal, as it is merely a case of high fees and commissions. These Offshore Bonds can be dangerously opaque if investors are not careful.

Options

Options are contracts on stocks, indexes, currencies, commodities, or debt instruments. There are two principle types. These are call options and put options. Call options give holders the ability to purchase a set amount of the underlying instrument for a specific price in a certain amount of time. This specific price is known as the strike price. Put options grant holders the ability to sell the exact amount of the underlying instrument at a fixed price in a given period of time.

With options on stocks, the set amount of the underlying shares that calls and puts cover are typically 100 shares. Option contracts have two parties to them. The first are the sellers who are also known as writers of the option. The buyers are the holders of the option.

Option values are made up of two components. These are intrinsic value and time value. Intrinsic value is the amount that the option is in the money. For an option to be in the money, the stock price must be higher than the strike price for calls. For puts, the stock price has to be lower than the strike price. The value that is left after subtracting intrinsic value is the option's time value. When an option has no intrinsic value, one hundred percent of its value is time value.

Investors can buy and sell options until they run out of time. At this point, they expire either with some intrinsic value or worthless. They can also be exercised. When an option is exercised, the seller must transfer the underlying shares to the holder of the option. When the instrument is not able to be transferred over, then the parties settle in cash instead.

Investors like this financial tool because they give buyers peace of mind. The most an option holder is able to lose is the total price that they paid when they bought the contract. If options are not exercised or sold within the given time frame, then they expire. An option that expires worthless does not involve any exchange of shares or cash.

Buyers and sellers have different potential profits with options. Profit potential is limitless for the buyers. For the sellers, the profit is limited to the price which they receive for the contract. Sellers have unlimited loss potential unless they own the underlying shares or instrument. When a seller of an option holds the underlying instrument, the option is covered.

There are two main reasons that investors buy options. These can be to gain leverage or to obtain protection. The leverage benefit means that the option holder can control a larger amount of equity for a much smaller price than it costs to actually buy the shares. This exposes the buyer to a far smaller potential loss.

Options provide protection to investors who own the shares that underlie the contract. While the owners of the option hold the contract, they gain protection against adverse price movements in their shares. This is because the contract provides the ability to obtain the stock at a certain price during the option's contract time-frame. In this case, the cost of the option is the premium that the owner pays.

There are several downsides to options. The trading costs for options are higher than with buying the underlying shares of the stock or other instrument. This is because the spread between the bid and ask is higher for options. Option commissions also cost more than do stock commissions.

Option trading is more complicated than stock trading too. Options also have to be watched more closely than do stocks generally. The time involved to trade and maintain option strategies can be significant.

Paper Assets

Paper assets have three different meanings depending on whether you are discussing business, investments, or fiat currencies. Where business is concerned, paper assets are assets that you can not easily use or change in to cash. These paper assets possess extremely low liquidity, meaning that they are difficult to sell too. The term in this case literally arises from assets that are valuable on paper, or that have a paper only value.

In investments, paper assets mean something entirely different. They refer to assets that are representations of something. Paper assets in investments literally are pieces of paper that define ownership of an asset. Classic examples of investing paper assets prove to be stocks, currencies, bonds, money market accounts, and similar types of investments. For paper assets to have a tangible value, there must be a working financial system in order to back them up and exchange them. In the cases where a financial system collapses, paper assets commonly sharply decline along with it. The majority of Americans have placed an overwhelming percentage of their money in paper assets, and as the Financial Crisis of 2007-2010 showed, this makes them extremely vulnerable to economic calamities.

Paper assets stand apart in contrast to hard assets. Hard assets contain actual value in the nature of the item itself. There are many forms of hard assets, but among the most popular are gold, silver, diamonds, oil, platinum, land, and other such physical holdings. While financial collapses can cause a set back for the value of hard assets, these types of assets almost always hold up far better than do paper assets.

Many people are shocked by the fact that the U.S. dollar is also a paper asset, as are all Fiat currencies in the world except for the Swiss Franc. These paper currencies are no longer backed up by the long running gold standard. Instead, they only have value because their respective issuing governments, as well as the underlying currency users, say that they do. The Swiss Franc is a lonely exception. The Swiss constitution requires that for every four paper or electronic currency Swiss Francs in existence, there must be one Swiss Franc worth of gold in the Swiss National Bank vaults. Since the Swiss only value their gold holdings at around $250 per ounce, and gold has been trading between $1,300 and $1,400 per ounce for some time now, the Swiss actually have a greater gold backing to their currency than one hundred percent.

Paper Investments

Paper investments can be several things. Where businesses are concerned, paper investments turn out to be investments in commercial paper. Commercial paper investments prove to actually be money market instruments that companies and banks sell to raise money. There are many large issuers with good credit who offer these types of paper investments to interested investors. They represent inexpensive other sources of short term funding as opposed to standard bank loans.

Commercial paper investments come with a fixed maturity of from one day to two hundred and seventy days. These types of paper investments are generally regarded as extremely secure, although they are unsecured loans. The companies that take advantage of them are commonly utilizing these short term operating funds for working capital or inventory purchases.

Corporations like to utilize commercial paper because they are able to quickly and effectively raise significant sums of money without having to get involved with costly SEC registration through selling paper investments. This can be done through working with independent dealers, or on their own efforts directly to investors. Institutional buyers commonly prove to be significant buyers of these types of paper investments.

Such notes come with amounts and maturity dates that can be specifically crafted to meet particular needs. The key features of these types of paper investments are that they are of short term maturity, commonly ranging from only three to six months of time. They liquidate on their own, with no action being required by the investing party in question. There is little to no speculation involved in their intended use as well. This gives them an appeal of clarity.

Offering this type of paper investments offers several advantages for the issuer as well. The issuer is able to access cash at rates that are lower than those offered at the bank. Companies taking advantage of commercial paper are able to leave open reserves of borrowing power at their area banks. Finally, they are capable of getting cash on hand which will allow them to benefit from trade creditors who offer special discounts for those who pay for supplies and other needs with cash.

Where traditional investments are concerned, paper investments also prove to be investments whose value is stated on and represented by paper. A number of different kinds of popular investments in the United States qualify as paper investments. These include stocks, bonds, mutual funds, certificates of deposits, and money market accounts. Shares of stock are pieces of paper that relate a certain percentage of ownership in a publicly traded company.

Most any type of investment that does not have a physical component of the investment associated with it is considered a paper investment. Commodities, as well as futures and options on futures that permit you to take delivery of the underlying commodities if you wish, represent examples of investments that are not only paper investments. These types of investments, along with real estate holdings, are considered to be physical, or hard, investments.

Penny Stocks

Penny stocks are those securities that usually trade for comparatively lower prices, off of the big stock exchanges, and with smaller market capitalizations. Many analysts and investors look at these securities as higher in risk and extremely speculative. This is because they feature significant bid and ask spreads, less liquidity, smaller followings, and lesser capitalization and disclosure requirements. Many of these smaller stocks trade on the pink sheets or OTC Bulletin Board in what is known as the "over the counter market."

Penny stocks used to be those which traded for under a dollar, but thanks to the SEC this is no longer the case. The SEC altered the definition so that all stock shares which trade for less than $5 are now considered to be a penny stock. These companies have fewer listing requirements, regulations, and filings which govern them.

It is important to remember that penny stocks best suit investors who can stand more risk. They come with greater amounts of volatility which can lead to steep losses or possibly greater returns. The lower volumes and greater amounts of risk are why the moves in these stocks can be staggering. These companies struggle with fewer resources and less cash, but sometimes achieve breakthroughs that can catapult their share prices higher. It is safer to trade or invest in penny stocks which are listed on the NASDAQ or the AMEX American Stock Exchange because these exchanges more vigorously regulate their constituent companies.

Four factors make these micro cap stocks so much riskier than traditional blue chip stocks. The information which the public has access to is usually lacking. It is harder to make well informed decisions on companies that do not provide sufficient information. Other information that is offered on such micro cap stocks can come from less than reputable sources.

Another feature that makes penny stocks so risky is that they do not have a common set of minimum standards. Neither the pink sheets nor the OTCBB require these companies to live up to minimum requirements to stay listed. They will have to file certain documents in a timely manner with the OTCBB, but not with the pink sheets. These standards traditionally offer a safety cushion that helps to protect investors. They are a benchmark for other smaller companies to achieve.

A third difficulty with these micro cap stocks is they lack history. A great number of such companies could be nearing bankruptcy or recently founded. This means that their track records are either non existent or poor at best. A lack of historical data compounds the difficulty of assessing a company's future and their stock's near and long term possibilities.

A final danger with penny stocks is their lack of liquidity. This creates two problems. An investor may not be able to sell out of the stock at an acceptable price. With low liquidity, there may be no buyer available at any price. Lower liquidity also leads to the possibility for traders to manipulate the prices of the stocks themselves. They can purchase enormous quantities of the issue, promote it themselves, and then sell it at higher prices to other investors who become stuck with it. This is called a pump and dump strategy.

Pension Funds

Pension funds are retirement plans which mandate that an employer must do contributions for the benefit of their employee's future. They contribute such money into a pool of funds. This pool then becomes invested for the employee's benefit. All earnings which the investments make accrue to the workers once they reach retirement.

Besides these mandatory contributions, there are pension plans which have components of voluntary contributions. Pension plans can permit workers to contribute a portion of their wages and income into the investment plan to help prepare for their retirement. It is also customary and encouraged for an employer to match some part of the yearly contributions of the employees. The limitations on this amount which they can contribute by matching funds are set by the Internal Revenue Service or IRS.

Two primary kinds of pension funds exist today. With defined benefit plans, the companies promise their staff will obtain a minimum benefit amount when they retire. These kinds of plans deliver the minimum regardless of how poorly the investment pool that underlies the fund actually performs. This means that the employer will be required to make a particular pension payment guarantee for their retired employees in these cases.

There is a formula that determines the precise amount. It is typically built on the combination of years in service and aggregate earnings. In the cases where the pension plan assets are insufficient to pay out the defined and guaranteed minimum benefits, then it is the firm which will have to make up the balance of the minimum payment.

Such employer sponsored pension plans and pension funds in the United States hail from the decade of the 1870s. At their peak in the roaring 1980s, they amounted to a participation rate of almost 50 percent of the total workers in the private sector. Around 90 percent of all public employees as well as approximately 10 percent of the private ones receive the coverage of this kind of defined benefits plan nowadays.

The second type of pension funds are defined contribution plans. With these, the employing company engages in particular set contributions to the retirement plans of their employees. They typically will match to some degree their employees' contributions to the plan. The ultimate payouts which the staff receive while retired come down to the investment results of the plan. In these cases, the firms which sponsor them do not have additional minimum payout liability after they make their pre-set contributions.

The reason these are so much more popular now is that they prove to be far less costly for employers than do traditional forms of pensions. This is because companies are not backing whatever benefits the funds are unable to produce. More and more private corporations and firms have moved over to this form of plan and have closed out their defined benefit plans. While there are a number of defined contribution plans, the 401(k) plan is the most well-known one. For the benefit of not for profit workers, the equivalent plan turns out to be the 403(b) plan.

When the phrase is utilized, "pension plan" typically refers to these more traditional forms of defined benefit plans. These payouts remain established, controlled, and ultimately funded 100 percent by the sponsoring employer. There are corporations which provide a choice from both plan types. Some will even permit their workers to roll over their 401(k) plan balances to their defined benefit or "pension" plans.

A final version of these is the pay as you go pension plan. Employers set these up themselves. Such plans are entirely funded during the accumulation phase by the workers. They may choose to make either a lump sum contribution (as with an annuity) or regular salary-deducted contributions. Besides these capabilities, such plans prove remarkably similar to other 401(k) plans. One disadvantage to them is that they lack a company matching participation program.

Portfolio Income

Portfolio income proves to be money that is actually brought in from a group of investments. The portfolio commonly includes all of the various types of investments that an investor owns. These include bonds, stocks, mutual funds, and certificates of deposit. These various financial instruments earn a variety of different types of passive income, such as dividends, interest income, and capital gain distributions. Such portfolio income returns are generated by the holdings of the various investment products in the portfolio.

Portfolio income varies with the types of investments that an investor picks. You as an investor will commonly look at two different factors when assembling a portfolio for portfolio income. These turn out to be the money that the investment itself will produce, which is also known as an investment's return, and the investment's risk level that it contains.

As an example, stocks are frequently deemed to be investments with considerable risk, yet the other side of the risk return equation is that they provide income from a company's dividends, or distribution earnings returned to the shareholders, as well as an increase in the stock price as the stock value gains with time. Certificates of deposit and bonds create interest income that is paid out on the investment that you hold. Still different kinds of investments produce other types of income, although this depends on the characteristics of the investment in question.

To maximize the portfolio income while reducing the amount of risk involved, individuals commonly choose to invest in numerous different kinds of investments. This is known as diversifying your portfolio and portfolio income. This way, you can combine both safer investments that provide lower real returns with riskier investments that offer greater investment returns. Your total collection of investments is the portfolio that makes your portfolio income for you.

This portfolio income is also classified as passive income, or income that does not require you to perform any work in order to make the money. The upfront investment actually creates the income without you having to be actively involved in the money making process. This stands in contrast to incomes that are earned through active involvement, or active income that you must expend both energy and time to create.

The ultimate goal for you with your portfolio income will probably be to build up enough of it that you are capable of living off of only the income that the portfolio generates. Once this point is reached, you would be able to not receive a payroll check any longer. Instead, you would support yourself in retirement from the dividends, interest, and capital gains created by the investments in the form of portfolio income. The best and safest way to do this is to only draw on the portfolio income itself, without drawing down the original principal.

By not touching the investment principal, you allow your portfolio and resulting portfolio income to build up over time. If you do not take out the portfolio income, then the total value of the portfolio will grow faster with time, allowing you to compound your investments for retirement. It is critical to have enough money saved for retirement that you do not need to take out this principal to support yourself. Sufficient portfolio income should be generated to cover the monthly retirement expenses. In this way, you will not be reducing your principal and risking the very real danger of your portfolio running out of money while you are still alive to need it.

Portfolio Manager

Portfolio managers are individuals who invest the assets of a fund. They generally handle either an ETF exchange traded fund, a mutual fund, or a closed end fund. Their responsibility is to carry out the daily trading of the portfolio and to put into practice the fund's investment strategy.

When investors are considering different funds in which to invest, among the most critical elements to think about is the name, reputation, and track record of the portfolio manger. This is especially true if they are involved in active portfolio management as opposed to passive management. Though there are numerous active fund managers in the markets, the track records of historical performances are not encouraging. Only a small minority of them are successful in beating the main market indices.

These managers engage in portfolio management as part of their daily routines. This is the science of making difficult decisions regarding the funds objectives. They must weigh investment mix against objectives, carefully balance the fund risk versus performance, and allocate the assets for the funds customers.

The management of a given portfolio revolves around opportunities, risks, weaknesses and strengths of various categories. These include deciding between equity investments as opposed to debt instruments, international versus domestic securities, and safety as compared to growth. There are numerous trade offs involved in this type of management as a manager makes tough choices in an effort to increase returns to the optimal point for the risk the investors are willing to take.

Passive management is the form of managing a portfolio where the holdings of a fund track an index in the markets. This is most often known as index investing or indexing. Active management is the opposite form. It requires that either one manager, a few managers working together, or even a management team strive to try to outperform the market's return. They try to do this by managing the portfolio actively. They make choices and investment decisions utilizing research on individual securities and positions. Among the different actively managed funds are closed end funds and many mutual funds.

In passive management, the style is to have the holdings of the fund identically reflect the benchmark index. This is the direct opposite of an active style of management where the managers are buying and selling securities in the portfolio according to different investment strategies.

Passive managers and the followers of this particular management type hold with the efficient market hypothesis. This idea says that the markets always reflect and factor in all relevant information all of the time. It believes that picking stocks out individually is a waste of time. Followers of this premise believe that the best method for investing is to put investment funds into index funds. History shows that these funds have performed better than most of the funds which are actively managed.

Active management still has a significant following. It utilizes the human efforts of the management team, co managers, or single portfolio manager to manage the funds portfolio on a daily, weekly, and monthly basis. These active managers work with forecasts, analytical research, and their own personal experiences and judgments to engage in the buying, selling, and holding decisions of the various securities.

The sponsors of these actively managed funds and their investment companies hold that a really good manager can beat the market. This is why they employ professional fund managers to actively handle the portfolio funds. Their goal is to beat those returns of their benchmark. For a large cap stock fund this would mean outperforming the S&P 500 index. Despite the best efforts of a considerable majority of active fund managers, they have not been able to do this successfully.

Preferred Stock

Preferred stock is referred to as preference shares or preferred shares as well. Preferred stock is the name used for a particular equity security which exhibits both characteristics of a stock equity as well as an instrument of debt. Because of this, preferred stocks are commonly deemed to be hybrid types of instruments. In the claims on a company's assets in the event of default or bankruptcy, preferred stocks prove to be higher ranking than mere common stocks, yet subordinated to bonds.

Preferred stocks have a number of interesting properties. They typically come with a dividend that is often fixed. They also enjoy preference versus common stocks where dividend payments are concerned and at any liquidation of the company's assets. A downside to preferred stocks is that they do not include voting rights as do common stock shares. Some preferred stocks offer convertible features that turn them into common shares of stock at a certain time. There are preferred stocks that may be called in early at the wishes of the issuing company. All terms for a preferred stock are listed out specifically in the Certificate of Designation.

Since preferred stocks are somewhat like bonds, the big credit rating companies all rate them for quality of credit. Preferred stocks generally garner lower ratings than do bonds, as the dividends of preferred stocks are not guaranteed as are bonds' interest payments. Preferred stocks are also subordinated to all of the creditors, making them less secure.

Dividends are a key feature of preferred stocks and the main motivating factor in acquiring them. Preferred stocks come with dividend payment preference over other shares. While this does not guarantee that the stated dividends will be paid, the company has to pay such dividends to the preferred share holders before they are allowed to issue any common stock shares' dividends.

These dividends for preferred stocks might be either noncumulative or cumulative. Cumulative preferred stocks mandate that companies who neglect to cover stated dividends up to the full rate must cover them fully at a later date. In each passing dividend time frame, the dividends continue to accumulate. This might be on an annual, semi annual, or quarterly basis.

Dividends that are not paid on time are labeled dividends that have passed. These passed dividends for cumulative stocks are called dividends that are in arrears. If a stock does not possess these cumulative features, then it is called a straight preferred stock, or a noncumulative dividend stock. With these types of non cumulative preferred stocks, the dividends that become passed simply vanish for good if they are not paid on time.

Besides these preferred stock features, they have various other rights. Some types of preferred shares do include a particular group of voting rights for the approval of unusual events like the ability to issue and sell extra shares, to approve the company to be sold, or even to choose the board of directors' members. In general, preferred stocks do not have voting rights. Many preferred shares also come with a liquidation value that states what sum of money was put into the issuing corporation as the shares became issued.

Private Equity

Private Equity refers to an investment capital source that comes from those institutional investors and accredited individual investors who boast high net worth. The goals of these investors are to gain a significant equity ownership in corporations. The partners at these firms raise funds and then manage them to gain higher than average returns for their client shareholders. They commonly pursue this goal via an investment time frame of from four to seven years. Private equity is therefore not for those who require that their investment positions be readily liquid.

Such mega funds are often utilized to buy private companies or to privatize publically listed corporations in order to de-list them from the stock market exchanges in a go private arrangement. Each firm sets its own minimum investment threshold for the fund investors. This ranges depending on the needs of the funds being raised. There are many funds with a minimum $250,000 in smallest investment permitted, while still others look for at least millions of dollars per contributing investor.

The private equity industry has a long and storied history of gaining the best possible talent from the corporate world throughout America. This includes top-delivering CEOs and directors even from Fortune 500 firms as well as the best management consulting and top strategy firms. This is why private equity hiring managers often scout out major corporations, law firms, and accounting companies when they go recruiting for new talent. They require legal experience and accounting skills to provide the many support services that such large enterprises require in order to put together major corporate mergers and acquisitions and to properly advise the management companies on the effective management of their newly acquired portfolios holdings.

There are quite high fees involved with such firms. Typically they receive first a management fee and then a performance fee. This generally amounts to annual management fees at around two percent of all assets under management. The performance fees add up to 20 percent of all gross profits when they sell a company. There can be a great deal of variety in the ways that such firms receive their compensation and incentives to outperform.

It is not hard to understand why private equity has been so successful at recruiting and keeping the very best talent based upon the money they have to offer by way of compensation for performance. Consider that these firms which have a billion dollars' assets under management would likely have around only two dozen professional investment personnel. They receive $20 million in annual fees just for the assets under management. Add on to this the 20 percent performance fees based on all gross profits, and it is not hard to understand how they generate additional tens of millions of dollars in performance fees for the company.

Middle market level managers and associates generally expect to earn six-figure salaries and bonuses. The vice presidents pull down half a million dollars easily. Principals rake in a cool over million dollars per year in both realized and unrealized compensation.

Given the incredible rewards at stake, it should not come as any surprise that there are a range of types of private equity firms operating today. Many choose the route of passive investing to be strictly financiers. They depend on their appointed management to increase the size and profitability of the firm in which they invest so that the owners will realize generous, outsized returns. Other kinds of these firms choose to be more active investors. They deliver operational support to the management to ensure that they can build up a stronger and more profitable firm which they can then resell or spin off.

These private equity firms pride themselves on their expansive list of contacts and relationships with corporate boards. They leverage these CFO and CEO relationships to help them grow the company revenue as well as to recognize synergies and operational combination opportunities. One of the kingpins of private equity remains Goldman Sachs, the legendary investment bank. They facilitate the biggest deals and concentrate their time on forging acquisitions and mergers that have billions of dollars in notional values. For other smaller investment banking companies, the majority of deals run in the range of from $50 million to $500 million, while lower middle-market transactions vary from $10 million to $50 million in total.

Private Equity Fund

A Private Equity Fund refers to a fund that is not carried by a public stock exchange and which does not have to be regulated by the SEC Securities Exchange Commission. Private equity itself is made up of the range of investors and funds who choose to invest directly in privately held companies. They might also pursue mergers and acquisitions to cause public companies to be delisted by taking private the companies which were public.

The capital for such private equity comes from retail and institutional investors. Such funding is useful for many types of purposes. It might bolster working capital, make possible research into a new technology, provide for acquisitions of public or other privately held companies, or simply improve a given company's balance sheet.

Such private equity funds derived most of their resources from accredited investors and institutional investors. These deep pocketed entities are able to allocate enormous amounts of money into an investment (that might possibly fail) for longer term time frames. Generally these longer investment holding time frames become necessary for such private equity investments. This is because working with distressed companies or waiting on liquidity events like IPO initial public offerings or selling the private company to a public one needs time.

This private equity fund market has grown rapidly from the 1970s to date. Nowadays, funding pools can be started by private equity firms so that they can take enormous public companies private. A substantial quantity of these private equity operations engage in what analysts call LBO leveraged buyouts. With an LBO, large purchases can be affected in the markets thanks to the pooling of enormous resources. Once the transaction is completed, the private equity firms will do their very best to better the profits, prospects, and all around financial condition of the newly privatized company. Their greatest hope and plan is to resell the company back via an initial public offering or alternatively through selling the company to another larger firm.

It is worth noting that the fee arrangements of these private equity funds are different from one fund to the next. They generally start with a management fee and add a performance-based fee to the costs as well. Some firms will assess an approximately two percent management fee each year based on the value of the assets under management. They usually also get 20 percent of all profits realized when selling any companies.

When investors hand over their money to one of these private equity funds, they are throwing their lot in with an adviser that is actually a private equity firm. These funds are something like a hedge fund or mutual fund in many respects. All three of them are comprised of pooled resources that an advisor combines to utilize for investment purchases for the common good of the fund. There are differences between these types of pooled funds though.

Private equity firms will usually concentrate their efforts on longer term time framed investment possibilities. They will often look for those assets that require significant amounts of time in order to sell investments. This given investment horizon will require many times at least 10 years and sometimes significantly longer than this.

A common strategy of investing with these private equity funds proves to be engaging in minority stake investments in startups or companies which are rapidly expanding in a promising industry. Others focus solely on the previously mentioned leveraged buyouts. In either case, transparency of these funds is an issue that has been growing since 2015. The high incomes for these funds have raised questions about what they are doing with the enormous sums of money they receive.

From 2016, some states began to pursue regulations and bills that provided more clarity on what the inner workings of such private equity firms is really like. The congress has so far resisted these investigations and tried to limit the ability of the SEC Securities and Exchange Commission to access the funds' privately held proprietary information.

Proprietary Trading

Proprietary Trading refers to a type of trading in which the bank or other financial institution invests its own funds for its own benefit. They do this instead of investing the money of and for their clients and gaining a commission fee for trading for their customers. Such trading happens as a firm makes the choice to engage in market profiteering instead of existing on the tiny commissions which they realize for taking and processing others' trades.

Those banks and companies which pursue such proprietary trading feel certain they enjoy some from of competitive advantage. It is this which provides them with the confidence in their own abilities to make outsized returns versus other traditional investors.

Proprietary trading is actually a dangerous and risky type of trading. Rather than safely carrying out the orders of their clients and collecting their fair commissions, the bank traders take on real positions using the capital of the company. In other words, they will enjoy the entire profit or suffer from the brunt of the full loss of such a position. These firms will do this entirely electronically to boost their speed of execution. They will employ the firms' own leverage in order to multiply the size of their positions as well as the hoped for returns or actually realized losses which they incur.

This actually occurs because the company's own trading desk at these huge financial institutions decides they can do it for themselves. These companies are typically investment banks or brokerage firms. They will then utilize their own corporate balance sheet and capital of the company in order to make transactions in the financial or stock markets. Such trades are commonly speculative. The products in which they trade are commonly complicated and dangerous investment vehicles such as derivatives and credit default swaps.

Naturally these financial companies receive benefits from proprietary trading on their own behalf. The biggest one is that they often do enjoy higher profits, at least until a financial crisis hits like with the one in 2007-2009 that nearly overthrew most of the American, British, and continental European banking system financial institutions. With these proprietary trades, the brokerage firm or investment bank gets to keep all of the investment gains which they realize from their investments.

A second benefit which these large financial firms enjoy is that they will be capable of inventorying an impressive array of securities. It allows them to offer their speculative inventory directly to their clients who could not have obtained it any other way. It also helps the institutions to be well-supplied with securities in the event of illiquid or declining markets when it is more difficult to buy such securities on the free markets.

The last benefit pertains to the second one. With such proprietary trading, financial firms can evolve into an important market maker. They gain the ability to offer liquidity for a particular security or even range of securities through dealing in such investments. They can realize profitable spreads and fees when acting in this capacity.

The ugly truth is that this proprietary trading has led to enormous losses for the investment banks in particular. Thanks to the likes of such one time investment banking firms as Merrill Lynch, Bear Stearns, Lehman Brothers, and others engaging in such dangerously over-leveraged proprietary trading schemes before the outbreak of the financial crisis, they nearly brought down the entire financial system.

The Lehman Brothers moment refers to the point where the company failed completely. All other investment banks began to crater at this point. Bear Stearns ceased to be a going concern. Merrill Lynch the one-time largest investment bank and brokerage had to be bought out by Bank of America in order to survive. Both Morgan Stanley and Goldman Sachs, the only remaining two of the big five, were forced to change into traditional banks, backstopped by the FDIC, This helped them to stave off total collapse at the height of the Global Financial Crisis of 2008/2009.

Because of these unmitigated disasters, the Dodd-Frank Legislation and Volcker Rules were passed. These made it increasingly more difficult to engage in such trading for a financial firms' own benefits and with their leveraged balance sheets and company capital.

Rate of Return

In the worlds of finance and business, the rate of return, also known by its acronym ROR, proves to be the ratio of money lost or gained pertaining to an investment and the sum of money that is originally invested in it. This rate of return is also called the rate of profit or more commonly the return on investment, or ROI.

The sum of money that is lost or gained could be called the loss or profit, interest, or even net loss or net income. Regarding the money that is actually invested, it is sometimes called the capital, asset, or principle. It is also referred to as the cost basis of an investment. Rate of return or Return on Investment is commonly stated as a percentage and not a fraction.

This rate of return is one measurement of how much cash is made or lost as a direct result of the investment in question. It quantifies the amount of income stream or cash flow that moves from the investment itself to the investor as a percentage of the original amount that the investor put into the investment. Such cash flow that accrues to the investor comes in a number of forms. It might be interest, profit, capital gains and losses, or dividends received. These capital gains and losses happen as the investment's sale price is greater or less than its initial purchase price. The use of the term cash flow includes everything except for the return of the original invested money.

Rates of return can be figured up as averages covering a number of different time periods. They may also be determined for only one time frame. When these calculations are being made, it is important not to mix up annualized and annual rates of return. Annualized rates of return prove to be geometric average returns figured up over several or even numerous periods. Annualized returns might be the investment return on a period less than or greater than a year, for example for six months or three years. The rates of return are then multiplied out or divided in order to come up with a one year rate of return that can be compared against other annual rates of return. As an example, if an investment possessed a one percent rate of return per month, then this might be more appropriately expressed as an annualized rate of return of twelve percent. Or, if you had a three year rate of return amounting to fifteen percent, then you could say that this is a five percent annualized rate of return.

Annual rates of return are instead returns figured up for single time frame periods. These time frames are commonly one year periods running from the first of January to the last day of December. Alternatively, they could cover any year long period, regardless of what month and day they started and ended.

Real Estate Investment Trusts (REIT)

Real Estate Investment Trusts are also known as REITs. These turn out to be investment companies which finance or outright own real estate that produces income. REITs were created along the model of mutual funds. They give all levels of investors the access to the benefits that real estate typically provides.

This includes diversification, income streams, and capital appreciation longer term. Usually these REITs pay their investors 100% of their taxable income in the form of dividends. The shareholders are responsible for paying taxes on the dividends as income tax.

The beauty of Real Estate Investment Trusts lies in the ability for any investor to participate in major properties. They are able to do this by buying shares of stock to become involved as they would with any other industry Just as a shareholder obtains benefits through stock ownership in companies, the stock holders in a REIT gain a percentage of the income that the underlying real estate produces. They do not have to locate, purchase, or finance any of the properties in the process.

The majority of Real Estate Investment Trusts trade on the bigger stock exchanges. Despite this, some of them are privately held or public companies that are not exchange listed. With these REITs there are two principle types, Mortgage and Equity REITs.

The mortgage REITs buy mortgage instruments or outright mortgages that are connected to residential or commercial properties. The Equity REITs produce their income by collecting rent from and selling properties they hold over longer time frames.

Real Estate Investment Trusts have expanded into practically every part of the economy today. There are REITs connected to timberlands, student housing, storage centers, shopping malls, company offices, nursing homes, infrastructure projects, industrial facilities, hotels and resorts, hospitals, and apartments. Every state in the United States has properties which are owned by REITs. Ernest and Young has funded a study that shows REITs provide for around 1.8 million jobs in the United States every year.

These American REITs have become so successful that they are now a model for other countries. Over 30 nations throughout the globe have approved legislation that allows the Real Estate Investment Trust.

Real Estate Investment Trusts offer diversification that does not correspond to the overall stock market and its performance measured longer term. Their dividends give investors a reliable stream of income. They are so liquid because these stock exchange based ones may be simply and quickly purchased and sold.

Their performance is standout. REITs which are publically listed and traded have outperformed the Dow Jones Industrial Average, the S&P 500, and the NASDAQ Composite when measured over the longer term. Like publically traded companies, they offer the transparency and oversight of quarterly financial reporting and commonplace regulatory standards.

There are many qualifications a company must meet to be considered a Real Estate Investment Trust. They have to place minimally 75% of all assets they possess into real estate. They also must obtain 75% or more of their gross income from sales of real estate, rents on property, or interest on mortgage holdings that finance property. These companies have to pay out a minimum of 90 % of their taxable income as dividends to shareholders every year.

The prospective REIT must have the status of corporation that is taxable. It must also have either trustees or a board of directors that manage it. They can not have over 50% of their entity shares owned by less than six individuals. The REITs also must possess at least 100 different shareholders.

Return on Assets (ROA)

Return on Assets is also known by its acronym ROA. It is also sometimes called return on investment. This proves to be an indicator of a company's profitability compared to its aggregate asset base. With ROA, investors and analysts can learn about the big picture of the efficiency of an organization's management compared to the deployment of their company assets which produces earnings.

This is figured up relatively easily. To calculate the ROA, simply take the corporation's annual earnings (or income) and divide these by the firm's total assets. The final answer is the percentage amount of ROA. Other investors will do a slight variation on the formula by adding back in the corporate interest costs to the net income. This allows them to employ operating returns before the net cost of debt.

Thanks to Return on Assets, analysts and investors can learn the amount of earnings that the invested capital or assets produced. Such a figure ranges dramatically from one publically traded company to the next. Every industry's ROA varies substantially. For this reason, analysts prefer to compare and contrast the ROA primarily against the company's own prior figures or alternatively versus another company which is both similar and in the same industry.

Company assets are made up of equity and debt together. The two kinds of financing will jointly fund most corporations' various operations and projects. Because of this Return on Assets number, investors are able to discern the efficiency with which the firm converts its investable money into actual net income. Higher ROA numbers are always considered to be superior. They mean that the corporations can bring in larger revenues and earnings on a smaller amount of investment.

Consider a real world example for clarification. If Imperial Legends Strategy Games produces a net income of $2 million on aggregate underlying assets of $6 million, then it has a Return on Assets of 33.3 percent. Another company Joy Beverages may enjoy the same earnings but against a full asset base of $12 million. Joy Beverages would have an ROA of only 16.7 percent in this scenario. This means that ILSG does twice the job of converting its all around investments into profits as does Joy Beverages. This matters because it speaks volumes of the quality of management. There are not too many managers who are able to turn over significant profits utilizing small investments.

The Return on Assets provides observers with a snapshot and analysis of a business that is distinctive from the usual return on equity formula. Consider that certain industries need to pay more careful attention to the ROA figure than other ones do. In banking, some firms managed to avoid the various banking crises of the last few decades. The ones that sidestepped the problems better than others had something in common. It was that they were more conservative based on the ROA they deployed. The more successful banks did not allow their return on assets numbers to become too unnaturally high. They did this by contemplating the underlying fine details in the loan book. Too many loans that yielded too high a return indicated that management was taking excessive risks. Yet in the business of software development firms, these enterprises are not leveraged, so this ROA comparison is less important.

An important difference separates asset turnover from Return on Assets. Asset turnover specifies that companies have sales which amount to a certain amount per asset dollar on the corporate balance sheet. Conversely, the ROA explains to investors the amount of post tax profit that a firm creates for every $1 of assets it has. This is to say that the ROA compares all of the company earnings relating to the entire resource base the company claims, including both long-term debt and the capital from shareholders. This makes the relevant ROA a strict test of shareholder returns. When companies possess no debt, then their two figures of ROA and ROE Return On Equity will be identical.

Return on Equity (ROE)

Return on equity proves to be a useful measurement for investors considering a given company. This is because it takes into account three important elements of a company's management. This includes profitability, financial leverage, and asset management. Looking at the effectiveness of the management team in handling the three factors gives you as an investor a good picture of the kind of return on equity that you can expect from an investment in such a company.

Return on equity is very easy to calculate. You can figure it up by collecting two pieces of information. You will need the company earnings for a year and the value of the average share holder equity for the same year. Getting the earnings' figure is as simple as looking up the firm's Consolidated Statement of Earnings that they filed with the Securities and Exchange Commission. Alternatively, you might look up the earnings of each of the last four quarters and add them up.

Determining share holder equity is easiest by looking at the company's balance sheet. Share holder equity, which proves to be the difference of total liabilities and total assets, will be listed for you there. Share holder equity is a useful accounting construct that reveals the business assets that they have created. This share holder equity is most commonly listed under book value, or the quantity of the share holders' equities for each share. This is also an accounting book value of a corporation that is more than simply its market value.

To come up with the return on equity, you simply divide the full year's earnings by the average equity for that year. This gives you the return on equity. Companies that produce significant amounts of share holder equity turn out to be solid investments, since initial investors are paid off using the money that the business operations generate. Companies that create substantial returns as compared to the share holder equity reward their stake holders generously by building up significant amounts of assets for each dollar that is invested into the firm. Such enterprises commonly prove to be able to fund their own operations internally, which means that they do not have to issue more diluting shares of stock or take on extra debt to continue operating.

The return on equity can also be utilized to determine if a corporation is a cash generating machine or a cash consuming entity. The return on equity will simply show you this when you compare their actual earnings to the share holder equity. You can learn at almost a glance how much money the company's present assets are producing. As an example, with a twenty percent return on equity, every original dollar put into the company is creating twenty cents of real assets. This is also useful in comparing subsequent cash investments in the company, since the return on equity percentage will demonstrate to you if these extra invested dollars match up to the earlier investments for effectiveness and efficiency.

Return on Investment (ROI)

ROI is the acronym for return on investment. This return on investment is among the most often utilized methods of determining the financial results that will arise from business decisions, investments, and actions. ROI analysis is used to compare and contrast both the timing and amount of investment gains directly with the timing and amount of investment costs. Higher returns on investment signify that the results from investments are positive when you compare them against the costs of such investments.

Over the past couple of decades, this return on investment number has evolved into one of the main measurements in the decision making process of what types of assets and equipment to buy. This includes everything from factory equipment, to service vehicles, to computers. ROI is similarly utilized to determine which budget items, programs, and projects should be both approved and allocated funds. These cover every type of activity from recruiting, to training, to marketing. Finally, return on investment is often employed in choosing which financial investments are performing up to expectations, as with venture capital investments and stock investment portfolios.

Return on investment analysis is actually used for ranking investment returns against their costs. This is done by setting up a percentage or ratio number. With the vast majority of return on investment calculation methods, ROI's that are higher than zero signify that the returns on the investment are higher than the associated expenses with it. As a greater number of investments and business decisions compete for funding anymore, hard choices are increasingly made using the comparison of higher returns on investment. Many companies believe that this yields the better business decision in the end.

There is a downside to relying too heavily on the return on investment as the only consideration for making such business and investment decisions. Return on investment does not tell you anything regarding the anticipated costs and returns and if they will actually work out as forecast. Used alone, return on investment also does not explain the potential elements of risk for a given investment. All that it does is demonstrate how the investment or project returns will compare against the costs, assuming that the investment or project delivers the results that are anticipated or expected. This limitation is not unique to return on investment, but similarly plagues other financial measurements. Because this is the case, intelligent investment and business analysis also relies on the likely results of other return on investment eventualities. Other measurements should also be used along side the return on investment to help measure the risks that accompany the project or investment.

Wise decision makers will demand more from return on investment figures than simply a number. They will require effective suggestions from the person making the return on investment analysis. Among these inputs that they will desire are the means of increasing an ROI's gains, or alternatively the means for improving the ROI through decreasing costs.

Revenue Bonds

Revenue Bonds are municipal bonds. Their payments on principal and interest come from a special project's revenue. This could be from a highway toll, toll bridge, or area stadium receipts. Whatever the specific project may be, its revenues are what support the underlying bond issues.

These revenue bonds are utilized to finance projects which will eventually produce income for the issuing authority. Generally any government agency or even government fund which they run like a business will be able to issue these types of bonds. Such bonds stand in contrast to those competing types called general obligation bonds, or GO bonds.

General obligation bonds may be paid back by drawing on a number of different tax sources. Those investors who purchase such GO bonds are relying on the "full faith and credit' by which the municipality promises to repay them with any means necessary. This makes the revenue bond issues riskier. They only can promise the revenues from a particular project. Because of this fact, the revenue bonds pay a higher interest rate than do the GO bonds.

Municipalities structure revenue bonds in a particular way. They possess maturity dates of from 20 to 30 years most of the time. The issuers offer them in standard $5,000 even increments or amounts. There are a number of these bonds which include maturity dates that stagger. This means their maturities will not be on the same day and year. Bond aficionados call these serial bonds.

A toll road is a classic example of such revenue bonds. A municipality might issue this in order to pay to construct a new toll road. The revenue which would secure this issue would be the tolls they collect in the future from those drivers who utilize the road. The construction expenses will have to be covered before the bond holders are completely paid off at maturity.

These revenue bonds became popular because the issuing authorities' debt limits are set by legislation. They may only borrow so much money according to the laws. These types of bonds allow them to side step the legal debt limit restrictions so that they can build new improvements within their jurisdiction.

This also means that government groups which rely only on only tax dollars can not issue such bonds. Public schools are one example of this. They would not be able to pay off a revenue bond since they would not have any income off of a specific project.

These revenue bonds should not be confused with combination bonds. The combination ones are usually municipal bonds with two sources of financial backing. On the one hand, they enjoy revenue off of an existing or a future project. At the same time, they are covered by the full faith and credit of the issuing municipality or agency. This makes them a true combination of both revenue and general obligation bonds. Naturally, these types of bonds are deemed to be considerably safer. Such lower perceived risk results in the agency paying a lesser interest rate than they would have to give investors on comparable revenue or even general obligation bonds.

It is helpful to consider a real world example of a revenue bond. The MTA Metropolitan Transportation Authority of New York chose to float Green Bonds back in February of 2016. MTA announced it will put this $500 million in total proceeds towards covering the costs of renewal projects on infrastructure. This includes upgrades to their various railroads. The bonds were issued by the Transportation Revenue Bond of the MTA. They received backing from the income of the MTA transportation service. This income comes from two sources, subsidies which the State of New York provides and operating revenues of the agency.

Risk-Weighted Assets

Risk-Weighted Assets refer to those which are utilized to decide on much capital financial institutions like banks must hold in order to decrease the chances of becoming insolvent. Regulators determine the capital amount required using a complicated risk assessment of every individual kind of asset the bank holds. As a simple example, the loans which have been secured by only letters of credit will be deemed to be far riskier than those loans which are instead backed up by tangible collateral. These would similarly require a greater amount of additional capital than the ones with real collateral.

The concept of Risk-Weighted Assets is relatively new and only dates back to the aftermath of the Global Financial Crisis. At this time following the worldwide financial meltdown from 2007-2009, the banking industry faced stark and rigorous new regulation as a drastic change following the crisis.

The government regulators, spurred on by Congress with their Dodd-Frank banking reform act, came out with massive new and complex capital requirements for the financial institutions in the United States, Great Britain, and Europe especially. As a direct result of this historical phenomenon, today's banks must hold far greater capital cushion levels than ever before. The dilemma for them is that the accounting rules surrounding these new regulations are extremely complex. Few investors nowadays are able to understand them really, yet they are critically important for investors in banks to grasp.

The central pillar of the revised and still fairly-new calculations is the Risk-Weighted Assets. It would be next to impossible to work out the numbers here, but it is instructive and helpful to concentrate on the general meaning of the idea and to show some examples of how it works generally in practice. Investors can not understand a bank's balance sheet any longer without having some command of the topic.

Because the 2007-2009 financial crisis occurred mainly as a result of the banks and other financial institutions choosing to heavily back the subprime mortgage home loans, they suffered from massively higher defaults than regulators, investors, and government officials conceived was possible.

These massive consumer defaults led to enormous capital sums being lost by the banks, which were too highly leveraged at the time. This caused some of the largest of them to become insolvent. Among these were Washington Mutual Bank (the largest savings and loans institution in history), Wachovia Bank, Bear Stearns, Lehman Brothers, Merrill Lynch, and many more.

So that this problem can be avoided in the future, regulators force every bank now to combine their assets into categories which are similar by asset risk level. The idea is to stop the greedy banks from suffering devastating capital losses again as a single asset class plunges severely in value. Regulators use a few different kinds of tools in order to determine the level of risk for a given category of assets. As a huge percentage of assets the banks hold are loans, the regulators look at the loan repayment sources and the collateral value which underlies them.

For example, commercial building loans generate both principal and interest payments. They do this using income from tenants in the form of lease payments. When buildings are not completely leased out, it is possible that the property manager will be unable to service the loan payments due to a lack of enough regular income. The building itself represents collateral against the loan. The regulators will contemplate the building's value as part of the determination for Risk-Weighted Assets.

Another example surrounds United States Treasury bonds. These are backed up by the federal governments' ability to generate taxes. Since these government securities come with a higher credit rating than do the commercial building loans, the regulators will expect less capital to be carried for the bonds than they would for the commercial loans.

Regulators understood these differences in risk levels and so decided that the only sufficient way to guarantee sufficient capital for a bank is to make them vary their capital requirements according to the risk they were taking with different types of assets. This is how the risk-weighted assets came into being in the first place.

Rollover IRA

An IRA is the acronym for Individual Retirement Account. These accounts represent a form of government-approved and -created savings account for retirement. They have several advantages, the main one of which is the significant tax breaks they receive in tax deferment. This makes them the optimal way to put cash aside towards eventual retirement. It is important to know that IRAs are not investments. Instead they are more like the basket in which individuals maintain their mutual funds, stocks, bonds, and other assets. When one retirement account is transferred to another one, this is known as a Rollover IRA.

Generally people open such a Rollover IRA themselves. There are also a few types which small business owners and the self employed can open. Among the various types of Individual Retirement Accounts in existence are the Roth IRAs, traditional IRAs, SEP IRAs, and SIMPLE IRAs. Not all of these can be accessed by every individual in the U.S. This is to say that every one of them has specific eligibility requirements which revolve around the type of employment and income level. What they do all have in common is the caps on the amount individuals are allowed to contribute every year. They also mostly share steep penalties for withdrawing funds ahead of the government set age of retirement.

The greatest benefit to these accounts lies in their ability for all of the assets within the plan to gain in value while not being taxed by the U.S. Federal government. This means that all income generated by capital gains, dividends, and interest will compound every year with no tax bite. Taxes on the majority of these forms of IRAs only become due as the owners take qualified (or unqualified with a penalty) distributions. There are two different forms of this. With the majority of the IRAs, individuals are able to commit pre-taxed dollars to the account. With Roth IRAs, the dollars are after-taxed, but then no additional taxes on them will be required upon withdrawals at retirement. Using the Rollover IRA concept, individuals can switch from one type of IRA to another.

The Internal Revenue Service strictly limits how much money people can put into such accounts. The majority of individuals who are less than 50 are not permitted to contribute over $5,500 each year as of 2016. These limits become higher once the holders attain an age greater than 50. They call this "catch up contributions," and the limits are typically raised by $1,000 to $1,500 more in this decade immediately before holders reach retirement age.

Practically all individuals are allowed to make contributions each year to a traditional form of IRA. So long as either the holder or spouse earns taxable income and is less than 70 and a half years old, they can participate.

The various kinds of IRAs are important to understand. A ROTH IRA does not provide tax deductions on contributions. There are also income restrictions which in 2016 amounted to under $184,000 for married filing jointly families or $117,000 for single heads of households or those who are married filing separately and not living with their spouses.

Both SEP and SIMPLE IRAs apply to only small business owners and the self employed. Only employers who claim fewer than 100 employees can set up these SIMPLE IRA accounts. Any individual who possesses freelancing income or who owns a business can open an SEP IRA.

While individuals can always withdraw their contributions (and even earnings) at any point once they have deposited them to their IRAs, there are penalties if they are less than 59 and ½ years old. The penalty is an extra 10 percent above the that-year tax bracket of the individuals who take distributions early. The government's point is to discourage people from utilizing their retirement accounts like ATM machines or credit cards.

Roth IRA

A Roth IRA is a particular type of Individual Retirement Account. These Roth IRA's prove to be special retirement plans that are given favorable tax treatment. The tax laws of the United States permit tax reductions on restricted amount savings for retirement accounts.

Roth IRA's are different from other IRA's in several ways. Among the chief of these is that tax breaks are not given on monies that are put into the plan and account with a Roth IRA. Instead, these tax breaks are given out on the money and its investment gains when they are taken out of the account at retirement. This chief appeal of Roth IRA's is that they provide completely tax free income at retirement.

Other Roth IRA benefits over traditional forms of IRA's exist as well. The restrictions placed on the kinds of investments that they are allowed to contain are fewer. You can turn them into gold IRA's and annuity account IRA's. Roth IRA's can also contain all of the usual forms of investments that IRA's contain, such as mutual funds, stocks, bonds, and certificates of deposit. More unusual investments such as real estate, mortgage notes, derivatives, and even franchises are allowed to be purchased with Roth IRA's. These investment choices do depend on the capability and allowance of the Roth IRA trustee, or firm with which the plan is set up. Roth IRA's also permit you to make un-penalized withdrawals of all direct contributions that you make, after the first five years of the account have and plan have passed, which is certainly not the case with traditional IRA's.

These distributions, or withdrawals, are not taxed because they are taxed before the contributions are made. The penalties are waived for principal, as well as interest and earnings in the account, if the distributions are for purchasing a house or for disability or retirement withdrawal uses. If there is not a justified reason for the distribution, then the account earnings and income made above contributions will be taxed.

All IRA's contain specific limits on the dollar amount of contributions that the government permits. This amount changes per year, and is set through the year 2011 now. Presently, you can put $5,000 per year into Roth IRA's. There are income restrictions that govern whether you are allowed to make this full contribution as well. Individuals who make less than $106,000 are permitted to make full Roth IRA contributions, and those who make under $121,000 may make a partial contribution. Married couples who file together are allowed to earn less than $167,000 to make their full contribution to the Roth IRA, while those who make under $177,000 can do a partial contribution.

Roth IRA conversions from traditional IRA's have been allowed by the IRA in the past, although with certain income restrictions. Beginning in 2010, this policy changed. Now the IRS permits any persons, regardless of how much money that they make, to convert their traditional IRA's into Roth IRA's.

SDR Denominated Bonds

SDR denominated bonds are a fairly recent phenomenon. These are bonds issued in special drawing rights currency units. SDR units are a basket of the world's most important currencies including the U.S. dollar, Euro zone euro, Japanese Yen, British pound sterling, and the Chinese Yuan. The International Monetary Fund's executive board approved a framework to issue such bonds to member nations and central banks back on July 1, 2009.

The principle of these SDR denominated bonds was intended to be allocated in SDRs. The market for such bonds was established initially as the official sector of IMF members. This meant it was to include primarily the member nations, relevant central banks, and another 15 holders of SDRs.

Included in these 15 prescribed holders are four central banks which were regional, eight developmental organizations, and three monetary agencies which were intergovernmental. Others allowed to trade in them were the fiscal agencies of the members. This means that a number of sovereign wealth funds were allowed to participate as there are not always distinguishing lines between national monetary authorities and their sovereign wealth funds. This is the case with Hong Kong and Saudi Arabia.

The IMF issued SDR denominated bonds were to start with three month maturities that could be extended to as long as five years. Interest payments on these instruments were quarterly. China signed an agreement to buy upwards of $50 billion of them, while Russia, India, and Brazil intended to buy as much as $10 billion each.

SDR denominated bonds again gained the international spotlight in August of 2016 when the World Bank's IBRD International Bank for Reconstruction and Development priced the first such bond in the Interbank Bond Market of China. This bond raised 500 million SDR units, which were equal to about $700 million US dollars. These bonds came with a three year maturity date. Their coupon interest payment rate was .49% per year. What made them most notable was that the payments are issued in Chinese Yuan.

This group of bonds is only the first batch. The full size of the issue approved by the World Bank SDR Denominated Issuance Program in August 12, 2016 is for 2 billion SDR's, making them equal to roughly $2.8 billion US dollars.

Even in China, placing so many SDR denominated bonds is a challenge. This is why the joint lead managers for the Interbank Market were several important banks with great depth in China. These included HSBC Bank of China Company Limited, the Commercial Bank of China Limited, China Development Bank Corporation, and China Construction Bank Corporation.

The issue was a great success. The significant interest in them led to a 2.5 times oversubscribing. Orders amounted to roughly 50. Fifty-three percent of them came from bank treasuries, 29 percent from central banks and official institutions, 12 percent from asset managers and securities firms, and six percent from insurance companies. These bonds will mature on September 2, 2019 with all payments coming from the World Bank's IBDR to be made to bond holders in Chinese Yuan.

Securities Markets

Securities Markets refer to either literal physical or virtual online places for traders and investors to buy and sell securities. These markets have been dramatically changing in the last several decades in order to best meet the requirements and wishes of investors and traders alike. Traders must have such markets which are easy to access, highly liquid, and that levy the most competitive transaction costs possible. These three core needs of traders have combined to create several different kinds of market structures around the globe. Among these are markets which are order driven, quote driven, hybrid, and brokered.

Many Securities Markets are order driven. With these markets, the sellers and buyers on the exchanges match directly up, typically using a computer system. The middle man is eliminated in such a market structure. This makes them the opposite of markets which are quote driven. Price discovery is accomplished thanks to the traders' limit orders on every security. The majority of such order-based markets utilize an auction system. Naturally sellers will be seeking the highest possible price while buyers are on the hunt for the best possible bargain. When they match, execution of trades happens.

The two kinds of such markets are the continuous auction and the call auction markets. The greatest advantage to this style of market is the massive quantities of investors and traders who will offer to sell and buy a security. This means that prices are competitive and provides superior prices for all traders. It does have a downside. When a security has only a few members trading, then liquidity is often weak. The TSX Toronto Stock Exchange of Canada represents a market that is order driven.

Securities Markets which are quote driven are also referred to as dealer markets. In such market structures, the sellers and buyers have a transacting middle man in between them in the form of a dealer or market maker. It is up to the market makers to provide the ask and bid quotes on stocks for which they are willing to sell and purchase shares. These market makers have exclusivity in their market functions (many times) and receive special privileges. Among these are low to no exchange fees, specific order book and order flow information, and the unique ability to post the stock quotes. Such markets are most common with OTC over the counter markets like the NASDAQ and London's SEAQ, the FOREX market, and the bond markets. Nowadays NASDAQ has become more of a hybrid type with elements of order-driven structures in place.

The greatest advantage to such quote-driven securities markets appears when stocks or markets are illiquid. Dealers are able to boost the traders' liquidity with their intervention, as they often keep a security inventory on hand. They get to enjoy the spread between the bids and ask as a compensation for this accommodation.

Hybrid markets are also popular structures with many Securities Markets. They are sometimes called mixed markets. The NYSE New York Stock Exchange is a well-known example of this category. Naturally this system will utilize characteristics from the two order-driven and quote-driven arrangements. When they have low liquidity periods, these markets are able to fall back on the dealer-provided liquidity to improve transactions.

A final type of Securities Markets is the brokered markets. Brokers represent middle men who engage in discovering counterparties for any trade. As customers request of a broker to help them complete an order, the brokers will go through their extensive networks in an effort to locate an appropriately matching client. These types of markets are mainly for those securities which do not have a traditional public market. Illiquid and unique securities fall into this category. Where huge block trades of highly illiquid stocks or bonds are concerned, brokered markets are employed. Direct real estate is another classic example of such a brokered type of market. Real estate brokers are the ones who fill the service of matching up a unique seller and interested buyer in this case.

Self Directed IRA

Self directed IRAs prove to be special kinds of individual retirement accounts. They are different from traditional IRAs because they provide the account holder with a significantly greater variety of investment choices and control over decisions on the account. With these types of IRAs, the owner or an investment advisor makes a variety of investment decisions. They then deliver these instructions to an IRA custodian who executes them.

Federal law allows these types of IRAs to invest in a tremendous range of investment vehicles. It is IRS section 408 that restricts the few categories that are not allowed. The IRS forbids investments of IRA funds in life insurance and collectibles such as rugs, art, gems, etc. It does allow a wide range of investment choices that cover most anything else.

Self directed IRAs may purchase real estate, mortgages and trust deeds, energy investments, gold and other precious metals in bullion form, privately held stock, privately owned LLCs and Limited Partnerships, and corporate debt or promissory notes. When accounts such as these are opened primarily to purchase precious metals bullion, they are typically known by the name of their primary metal in which they invest.

These Precious Metals IRAs can be called Gold IRAs, Silver IRAs, Platinum IRAs, and Palladium IRAs. Such self directed IRAs can even purchase franchises such as Subway or Timothy Horton. All of these different investment choices allow for superior and broad based asset diversification of investors' retirement funds.

These types of IRAs also provide all of the usual benefits which are commonly associated with Traditional IRAs. Money saved in these plans is contributed on a tax free or tax deferred basis. No taxes will be paid on either the money deposited, or the gains made on these investments within the account, until they are withdrawn at retirement or under early withdrawal rules and limitations. Self directed IRAs are still subject to the same yearly maximum contribution limits of $5,500 in 2016. They allow for larger contributions of $6,500 to be made as catch up once the account holders reach age 50.

Early withdrawals from these IRAs as with traditional ones are penalized. It is often more advantageous to take a loan against the value of the IRA rather than suffer the financial consequences of early withdrawal. When loans are taken, there is no penalty. A repayment plan is established to put the borrowed funds back in the account in installments. Loans can be approved for a variety of expenses, such as home purchase, educational needs, or health care related expenses.

When an actual early withdrawal is taken, two penalties are assessed. First the money in the account is taxed as ordinarily earned income. Next a 10% penalty is levied by the IRS on all monies which the owner early withdraws.

These types of IRAs do have some limitations. The custodian must physically hold all assets in the account. This means that the account owners are not allowed to keep their real estate or mortgage deeds, stock certificates, or precious metals bullion at home in a safe. There have been offers made by some companies to help investors become their own IRA custodian by forming a special LLC company. This is a gray area which the IRS has not yet come down on with a hard ruling. In the future, they are likely to rule that investors absolutely can not be a custodian for their own gold, silver, platinum, or palladium bullion using either a safe deposit box or a home based safe.

The IRS requires that owners of these accounts begin taking distributions no later than at age 70. They can start withdrawing them as retirement funds at 59 ½ if they wish to begin using the money earlier.

SEP IRA

SEP IRAs are special simplified employee pensions that permit employers to contribute money to the retirement plans of their employees. If individuals are self employed, they may also set up and fund one of these accounts for their own benefit. These plans compare favorably to the more popular and utilized 401(k) plan. SEPs offer greater contribution amount limits. They are also much less complicated to establish and maintain than are the 401(k)s.

Any type of employer is allowed to create an SEP IRA. This means that businesses which are not incorporated, partnerships, and sole proprietorships can all work with and utilize them. Even self employed individuals who are employed elsewhere as well (with retirement plans at their other workplace) can make their own SEP.

SEP IRAs offer several advantages to owners and contributors. They provide significant tax benefits for employees and employers. Employer contributions give tax deductions to the employer during the tax year in which they make the contribution. Self employed individuals also can take this tax deduction for themselves. SEPs are also popular because they do not require any annual paperwork to be filed with the IRS. The paperwork that creates these accounts also offers the plus of being simple and minimal.

Individuals can make contributions for SEP IRAs in the year after the contribution applies. Deadlines for these contributions may also be stretched to the tax return due date. As far as establishing these accounts goes, deadlines are for the tax return due date and any extension that the IRS grants on the taxes.

In general, these accounts have to be opened and all contributions should be made by the April 15th that comes after the year in which the income was attained. Any taxpayers who take an extension on their tax returns to October 15th would receive a similar grace period for opening and funding the SEP IRA.

The contribution amounts for SEPs are quite flexible. No set percentage has to be contributed as with some of the rival retirement accounts like

Keoghs. One could contribute nothing or as much as 25% of his or her income for the year (on as high as a $265,000 income amount). The full contribution for a single individual is not allowed to be greater than $53,000 in the year 2016. This amount contrasts with the typical standard IRA contribution limits of $5,500 for the year 2016.

The SEP limits are also substantially higher than the contribution limits on 401(k)s that come in at $18,000 for 2016 or at $24,000 for those who are at least 50 years old. SEPs do not have any provisions for catch up, as with other forms of IRAs or 401(k)s. Thanks to the higher contribution limits for every given year, this does not usually present a problem for those who are behind on their retirement accounts and want to put in more.

Employers are required to treat all employee contributions equally. This means that they must give the same contribution percentage for each employee who has made at least $600 in the year, who is 21 years or older, and who has worked for the company minimally three out of five prior years.

The only point where contributions to SEP IRAs get complicated centers on maximum contribution amounts. The 25% of income limit mentioned earlier is not figured out of gross revenue, but from net profits. Besides this, deductions on the half of self employment tax have to be first taken off of the net profit number before the limit for maximum contributions can be accurately determined off of the net profits.

Simple IRA

Among the stable of various types of IRAs American savers for retirement can take advantage of is a less common plan called the SIMPLE IRA. These kinds are a combination of traditional IRAs and employer offered plans like 401(k)s. The word SIMPLE in this case is actually an acronym that stands for Savings Incentive Match Plan for Employees. This is the most common name for the employer offered tax deferred retirement savings account.

SIMPLE IRAs were created to help smaller employers who have 100 or less employees. The idea was for them to offer their workers retirement plans. The IRS knew that the bigger packages of benefits all too often involved long and difficult opening procedures with mountains of complicated paperwork. Smaller employers simply did not have the time or resource capacity to complete and maintain these types of plans.

Among the advantages of SIMPLE IRAs is that they are not governed by ERISA, the Employee Retirement Income Security Act. This means that they are able to sidestep substantial expenses and significant amounts of paperwork in establishing them. The contributions to these kinds of IRA accounts are also fairly straightforward. Employers must make specific minimum amount contributions to the accounts of the employees.

They can accomplish this by establishing a match program at a minimum of 3% of their employee contributions. Alternatively they might set a 2% of his or her salary flat rate and offer it to every employee who participates.

When employees become part of a company SIMPLE plan, they are basically establishing a traditional IRA via their employing company. A significant disadvantage to these types of IRAs centers on their lower contribution limits. These are less than comparable 401(k) plans or other plans which employers sponsor. The limits amount to $12,500 for a single year in tax years 2015 and 2016.

Rolling over from these types of IRAs is also more complicated. They can not be started without a waiting period first being observed. Once employees start their participation with the plans, they can not do a rollover for generally two years on from their participation dates. The only exception to this rule pertains to transfers between SIMPLE IRAs.

These can be done at any time since they are considered to be a tax free transfer from one trustee to another. In the even of any other type of transfer within the two years waiting period, these are deemed as distributions by the IRS. While most penalties for tax deferred plans are set at 10% withdrawal penalties, these particular IRAs carry a more punishing 25% withdrawal tax penalty.

After the conclusion of the two year time frame, individuals may then move their funds from the SIMPLE plan to a different kind of IRA. The only restriction is that they can not move them to a Roth IRA which is funded with pre-taxed dollars. The current SIMPLE plan as well as the new plan must also allow for the transfer to occur.

As with any kind of retirement plan, early withdrawal penalties apply. If any withdrawals occur before the official retirement age of 59 ½ is attained, the early withdrawal penalties of up to 25% will be assessed against the account withdrawals.

When rollovers are done, direct rollovers are much preferred to indirect rollovers. If account holders pursue indirect rollovers there are tax withholding requirements. It is also possible that the account owner will inadvertently fail to complete the transfer in time or at all and then suffer from the substantial early withdrawal tax penalties of up to 25%.

Solo 401(k) Plan

Solo 401(k) plans function much as their standard 401(k) plan cousins do, but display some important differences. These retirement savings plan vehicles for the self employed are also called One Participant 401(k)s, Self Employed 401(k)s, Individual 401(k)s, and Uni-Ks.

These particular 401(k)s provide business owners and spouses who do not have any employees beyond themselves with the ability to be a part of a 401(k) type of tax deferred plan. The plans are fairly new. Congress unveiled them as part of their 2001 Economic Growth and Tax Relief Reconciliation Act. At the time, these became the first specially tailored employer sponsored retirement plans intended for the self employed. Before their introduction, these self employed persons could only rely on such plans as IRAs, Keogh Plans, or Profit Sharing Plans.

These Solo 401(k)s possess practically identical requirements and rules as do the normal 401(k) plans. There are two important exceptions to this. The owner and the business do not find themselves governed by the expensive and complicated requirements of the ERISA Employee Retirement Income Security Act. Besides this, the company is not permitted to employ additional employees who are full time workers contributing 1,000 hours or more each year to the business.

Contributions also have their own particular rules with these Solo plans. The account owner is also both the employee and employer. For the 2016 tax year, employee contributions are limited to $18,000 (or $24,000 per year in the case of those who are fifty years of age or older). Other contributions can be put in as employer contributions. Whichever type a business owning participant wants to call these contributions, the limit for both employee and employer contributions may not be more than $53,000 for a given year.

One benefit that holders of these Solo 401(k) plans enjoy is that they do not have to employ a custodian as with IRAs. Instead they can work with practically any financial institution or bank as their account trustee. Assuming that the trustee will handle it, these plans are able to invest in a wide range of alternative asset types. This includes mutual funds, individual bonds and stocks, ETFs, CDs, real estate, life insurance, S corporations, and precious metals bullion such as gold or silver. Solo Plans are almost unique in their ability to invest in life insurance, which even the self directed IRA plans are not enabled to do.

This all makes the Solo 401(k)s practically unrivalled in their capability to provide retirement plans with low costs, that are easy to make transactions in, with great flexibility, and with generous contribution limits all at once. The downsides to the Solo 401(k) are two. Most workers are not allowed to participate with them. They also need a great deal of paperwork and account maintenance when measured up against numerous other types of retirement plans.

Rollovers are easy to do with these Solo plans. They are able to receive such transfers from other kinds of accounts and IRAs. Account holders may also transfer or roll them over to another kind of retirement account. It is important to check with the rules of an individual's particular plan, as some plans do not accept rollovers from the Solo 401(k)s. Besides this, there are Solo 401(k)s that specifically do not permit rollovers.

Business owners should take care when setting up these types of accounts. Rolling over these types of retirement vehicles will not incur any IRS tax penalties, so long as they are done according to the IRS rules and regulations. An individual has 60 days to finish the procedure and may only engage in it one time per year. Failing to abide by these rules will incur regular income taxes plus the 10% penalty for early withdrawals, unless the individual is older than the 59 ½ years retirement age.

Stock Buybacks

Stock buybacks occur when companies repurchase their own company shares from the markets. They are sometimes called share repurchases. A buyback is like a company choosing to invest in itself, since it is actually employing its own cash reserve to purchase its own stock.

Companies may not be shareholders in themselves, which means that their shares are absorbed back into the company. This has a net effect of decreasing the quantities of stock share which are outstanding. This also increases the size of each owner's stake in the company as there are not as many shares and claims on the company's earnings.

There are two means in which stock buybacks occur. They can be done via tender offers or open market purchases. In a tender offer, all shareholders receive such a tender offer from the company to submit some or all of their shares by a specific deadline. Such an offer divulges the quantities of shares which the company wishes to buy back as well as the price range they are agreeable to offer.

These tenders are nearly always at premium prices versus the current market level. Investors who are interested in participating will let the company know how many shares they wish to sell them at the price they will take. The company involved in the share repurchase would then put together the right combinations so that it could purchase the shares it wants for the lowest price.

Companies can also enter the open markets to engage in stock buybacks. They do this precisely as individual investors by buying shares at the going market price. The difference between the company and an individual investor doing this is that the market sees a company repurchasing its own shares as a significantly positive action. This generally leads to the stock prices rising quickly.

A company management will state that the share repurchase is their best option for deploying the firm's excess capital at that given point in time. The management of a firm is supposed to be interested in maximizing the returns for their stake holders. These stock buybacks do usually boost the value of shareholders. There are other motives for company managements buying back shares. They may believe that the stock market has overly discounted the prices of its stock shares.

Stock prices can decline from many different causes. These might be that earnings were less than anticipated, the economy is poor, or there are negative rumors surrounding the company. Firms that pay out millions of dollars to invest in their own shares show that the company management feels the market has punished their share prices unfairly with the discount. This is always seen positively.

Stock buybacks can also create better fundamentals for a company's balance sheet. Since the repurchased shares become either cancelled or treasury stock, this lowers the number of outstanding shares as a result. This decreases the balance sheet assets as the cash is spent. With fewer assets on the balance sheet, the return on assets ROA goes up in the process. Return on equity ROE also grows as the outstanding equity is reduced. The markets generally prefer higher ROAs and ROEs. Managements that do share buybacks just to boost their balance sheet fundamentals are looked at negatively and as problematic.

Stock Market Index

A stock market index refers to a collection of stocks which are combined together to create a bellwether for a group of similar companies in the market. The idea is to present an index which tracks a certain sector, market, currency, commodity, bond, or other type of financial asset.

Stocks which are collected in such an index are put into a so-called basket. An example of this is easy to understand. A person who wished to invest in the DJIA Dow Jones Industrial Average index would buy into the shares of the index basket that represented the 30 component companies. This means that the investor would then own 30 different companies' stock shares.

The idea behind indices is that they track the underlying assets or market. The XAU Gold and Precious Metals Index is comprised of those companies which mine precious metals including gold. Purchasing shares in this index means that an investor has the benefit of exposure to the entire gold mining sector. They achieve this without having to acquire shares in all of the gold mining firms of the globe. It is accomplished because shares in XAU represent all of the gold mining shares in the form of the entire industry.

These indices were fashioned to imitate particular markets. This does not mean they will ever be accurate all of the time nor even 100 percent at any given point. This is because there are a wide range of factors that can change the market course which indices will not always capture with perfection immediately.

Not every stock market index is liquid. This means that it could be hard to get in and out of some index-based positions. It is also the case for some stock company securities too. Because of these problems, there are alternatives to a stock market index. These are called ETF Exchange Traded Funds. Such ETFs have the advantage of being constructed in order to imitate an index. This is done in the same way that indices imitate stock markets and various other assets. The ETF has the advantages of being immediately ready for trade and a pre-arranged package. This makes an ETF a true mini portfolio available for an affordable price with reasonable fees (especially as compared to mutual funds).

There are many stock market indices that are well-known throughout the world. The most famous of these is surely the DJIA Dow Jones Industrial Average. This 30 stock company index trades every day on the NASDAQ and NYSE New York Stock Exchange. The component companies of this most famous of indices on the planet include such internationally respected giants as the Walt Disney Company, General Electric Company, Microsoft Corporation, McDonald's, and Exxon Mobile Corporation.

Another internationally followed index is the S&P 500. It measures the values of 500 of the large cap stocks of the United States. The NASDAQ Composite index follows the fortunes of fully 4,000 different company stocks as they trade daily. Yet another stock market index often called the total market index is the Wilshire 5000. While somewhat less famous than the other three, this index of indices follows the performance of every publicly traded corporation which is headquartered within the U.S. The four indices mentioned here address the daily progress of the large American companies. A competing index the Russell 2000 follows the performance of an impressive 2,000 smaller corporations of the U.S. markets.

The market index values are called points. This means that if the London FTSE 100 rose 150 points in a single day that the value increased versus the prior day's close to that point. It means that the total net gains of all the composite companies collectively increased by a net of 150 points.

Indices such as these assist investors by helping them to keep tabs on the health of various industries in which they may have interests or capital invested. If the DJIA continues to drop repeatedly for a period of many weeks or a month, investors could reasonably conclude at least some of the companies within the underlying index have run into serious trouble. This would be a prescient warning to evaluate the portfolio and perhaps liquidate some of the holdings in favor of other ones which were performing better.

Tax Sheltered Annuities 403(b)

Tax sheltered annuities are retirement savings programs and vehicles that the Internal Revenue Service allows for under the 403(b) section of their tax code. They were created for the benefit of employees who work for churches, educational institutions, and specific not for profit agencies.

They offer the advantage of permitting employees who are eligible to participate to contribute nearly all of their annual income towards retirement savings and investments in the plan. As an example of the generous limits with these particular plans, employers who choose to contribute can put in as much as $53,000 as of 2016 for any single tax year.

This supplemental program for retirement savings gives participating individuals a variety of ways in which they can choose to contribute funds. They may invest on an after tax basis, as with a Roth plan. They may also choose to contribute using funds that are pre-taxed. They can also opt to use a combination of the two methods. These plans and their participating contributions are entirely voluntary. Employees generally make the majority of these contributions as there is not always an employer match involved with them.

A variety of employees of eligible organizations may participate in these tax sheltered annuity plans. Employees of public schools, universities, and state colleges are allowed to participate. Many employees of churches are also allowed to become involved. Those who work for the school systems run by Indian tribes and their governments may participate. Not for profit 501(c)(3) churches' and organizations' ministers are included in them, as are ministers who are self employed who serve as part of a tax exempt organization. Chaplains are also usually qualified to participate.

There are several good reasons to become involved with these tax sheltered annuity plans. With automatic payroll deductions, it is a simple and relatively painless means of building up extra savings which individuals will require to increase their after retirement income.

They can get involved in a low cost program that is flexible enough to offer a good selection of investment choices. People can make contributions on a Roth after tax basis, a pre tax basis, or a combination of the two. Finally these plans are portable, meaning the owners can take their retirement vehicles with them when they move to a different job or another not for profit organization.

Thanks to these plans and vehicles, account holders are able to invest tax money that would otherwise go to the IRS. They can move money between the various funds in the plans without suffering from capital gains taxes or additional fees. This gives these TSA pre tax accounts a greater return than a taxable account would enjoy if it earned similar returns. For any individuals who use these account vehicles as Roth after tax accounts, all qualified distributions at retirement will be enjoyed completely tax free.

Money from these accounts can not be taken out without penalties until the individual reaches the government mandated minimum retirement age of 59 ½. They must begin taking distributions by the time they turn 70. An exception to the minimum retirement age is for individuals who stop working for their not for profit company before they reach retirement age. In this case, they are allowed to go ahead and begin receiving distributions without having to pay the extra 10% early withdrawal penalty tax. Only any taxes that were due for monies which had been contributed as pre tax dollars would apply in this particular case.

Tenure Annuity

A Tenure Annuity is a type of reverse mortgage monthly payment plan. This program delivers cash payments that are consistent to the home owning seniors for an unlimited amount of time until they pass away or move out of the house. The agreement remains in force up to the point that both spouses leave the house that backs the loan. Tenure payment amounts are usually fixed based on the primary borrower's age.

Such a tenure annuity can be crucial for those seniors who do not have much monthly income or savings. They likely still want to take advantage of activities which provide an active and enjoyable retirement. The monthly payments from these tenure annuities can be used at the discretion of the borrower. They might use them to supplement benefits from social security. Medical costs can be paid with them. Seniors can work to pay down debts using the funds or to improve, renovate, or repair their home. They can even put them to use for leisure activities and travel opportunities.

Financial planners often advise seniors to increase their retirement income streams using a tenure annuity. This is because the income from private pensions and/or social security is often insufficient to meet their expenses and desires. There are many benefits to these plans. One of the most important is that they deliver a guaranteed and predictable monthly payment that boosts other income sources.

A tenure annuity has numerous other advantages. The money will be provided for as long as the borrowers live in the house, whether this is for from a few months to several decades. The arrangement is fully covered and backed by the FHA Federal Housing Administration. The borrowers continue to enjoy complete and unrestricted use of their house that is tied to the reverse mortgage. There is no burden of monthly mortgage payments as with a traditional mortgage loan. Finally, there are no additional collateral requirements besides the house itself.

One of the valuable characteristics of a tenure annuity is that the debt builds up against the home slowly. The equity for the future payments remains in the house until it is needed. This means that the estate of the borrowers will be significantly greater if they die early than for a senior who simply took out the maximum cash value in the reverse mortgage.

A tenure annuity also provides flexibility for the senior borrower. These participants are able to modify the transaction by simply paying a minor $20 fee to the loan servicer.

As an example, a borrower who determines he or she will not require the monthly tenure payment amount for some time can change the house's unused equity over to a credit line. The credit line increases in size every month as the payment amounts of the annuity build up in the line. In a case where the opposite is true, seniors who require bigger payment amounts are able to switch over into the term annuity from the line of credit.

Another useful feature of the tenure annuities is that they protect the value of the property from declining. Whether the borrower chooses the monthly payments, the credit line, or switches back and forth, the protection remains the same. Thanks to the FHA coverage of the reverse mortgage, the borrower is not liable for any declines in the value of the home.

Term Deposit

Term Deposit refers to a special type of deposit which individuals or businesses maintain at a bank or other financial institution. These are unique from standard deposits in that they include a fixed term. Such terms are usually shorter-term in nature. Their maturities could vary from a single month to several years or even five years. Term deposits are purchased. The lender is the customer, who makes a loan to the bank. The money is only allowed to be pulled back out once the term has concluded. Some contracts will allow an individual to provide a pre-set amount of days in notice if they need to withdraw the money early. Such kinds of financial instrument products are available at credit unions, thrift institutions, and commercial banks.

There are several other designations by which these term deposits go. They can be called bonds, time deposits, and certificates of deposit as well. Britain calls them bonds. Such deposits (by whatever name they go) represent an incredibly safe form of investment. This is why risk-averse and conservative investors find them appealing. Besides the bank backing up these terms and investments, The National Credit Union Administration and the Federal Deposit Insurance Corporation jointly insure them and backstop them against any losses to principal. Banks like them because the guaranteed amount of time they have to utilize the funds means that they can invest the money in financial products which feature larger gains.

The tradeoff for this is that the financial institutions themselves will have to offer a larger interest rate to the customer lender. The majority of banks will provide only fixed rates, yet this does not mean that variable rate CDs do not exist. In the early years of the 2000's, banks sold CDs whose interest rates could be single-time bumped up but not lowered. The interest rates usually correspond to the amount of time existing in the time deposit.

For example, with a term deposit that has three years on it, the rate will be considerably higher than one that is only a three month term product. Similarly, larger CD amounts will receive higher interest rates. Jumbo CDs are those that come in increments starting at $100,000. They obtain much greater interest rates than do $1,000 amount certificates of deposit. Smaller institutions also tend to pay higher interest rates as well. Uninsured banks will provide the very largest interest rates on the products available.

The irony to these financial products lies in their name. Certificates of deposit imply that an investor will actually obtain a certificate on the terms of the deal. Usually this is not the case though. Originally, banks would deliver a type of certificate to the holder, but nowadays they are mere book entries on a bank statement. It is still possible to demand a paper statement that details the interest rate, principal, and amount of time remaining on the CD. These terms were mutually agreed upon by the financial institution and the customer lender after all.

There are penalties for those who decide to close out their term deposit before the time has fully elapsed. Breaking the maturity includes a loss of interest on principal. The penalties for early withdrawal are clearly marked on the documentation at the opening of a term deposit. This is required by congressional act according to the Truth in Savings Regulation. There are times however when interest rates have increased dramatically enough that the financial institution's penalties may not deter the individual investor from withdrawing their CD to open a new one at the significantly higher rate elsewhere.

As the maturity date of the CD approaches, the bank will commonly dispatch a letter requesting direction from the customer lender. The investor may pull out the original principal plus interest completely penalty free at this point. They could also allow the instrument to roll over. When the owners do not provide any response and instructions, the financial institution has the right to simply roll it over automatically and reinvest the principal as they see fit.

Term Life Insurance

Term life insurance is a form of life insurance. It offers coverage for a preset and limited amount of time that is called the relevant term. The coverage provided is a fixed rate of payment coverage. Once the term expires, the individual's coverage at the rate of the premiums that were charged before are not assured any more.

The client will be forced to drop their term life insurance coverage or to get a different coverage with varying payments and terms. Should the person who is insured die within the term, the death benefit amounts are paid out to the insured person's beneficiary. This term life insurance proves to be the most affordable means of buying a major dollar value of death benefit coverage based on the premium cost charged.

Term life insurance turns out to be the first type of life insurance created, and it stands in contrast to permanent forms of life insurance like universal life, whole life, and variable universal life. These coverage types promise an individual pre set premiums that can not go up for the person's entire life. People do not usually employ term insurance for strategies involving charitable giving or their needs for estate planning. Instead, they are thinking about a need to replace an income if a person passes away on his or her family unexpectedly.

A great number of the permanent life insurance policies also offer the advantage of increasing in value during the person's contract. This cash value can then be withdrawn when certain conditions are met by the policy holder. Generally, withdrawing these cash amounts closes out the policy. Beneficiaries of permanent life insurance products get the insurance policy face value but not the cash value upon the holder's death. Because of this, financial advisers will suggest that people purchase term life insurance for their insurance needs and then invest the money saved over permanent products in retirement accounts that provide tax deferred contributions and investment gains, like 401k's and IRA's.

Like with the majority of insurance policies, term life insurance pays out claims for the insured, assuming that the contract is current and the premiums are paid as due. Assuming that a claim is not filed, the premium is not given back to the policy holder. This makes term life insurance like home owners' insurance policies that pay claims if a home becomes destroyed or damaged as a result of fire, or like car insurance policies that pay drivers if they have a car accident. Premiums are not refunded when the product is no longer required. Because of this, term life insurance like these other products only provides risk protection.

Thrift Savings Plan

The Thrift Savings Plan represents a government created retirement savings vehicle. In 1986, Congress passed the Federal Employee Retirement System Act. This plan was established for the benefit of retired or present employees in the civil service of the federal government.

In 2001, Congress expanded the TSP so that it would include the members of the armed forces with the National Defense Authorization Act. This extended participation beyond the original civilian employees. Armed forces members were allowed to enroll beginning on October 9th of 2001.

The Thrift Savings Plan was set up to be a defined contribution plan. The goal behind its creation was to provide the federal government employees with similar retirement savings types of benefits as private sector workers had. Employees in the private sector already enjoyed these retirement savings opportunities via the available 401(k) plans. With every payroll check, plan contributions to both the 401(k) and TSP are deducted automatically.

These TSPs include a variety of different funds. Participants can choose from and invest in six different types. Among these are the government security fund, the common stock fund, the fixed income fund, the international stock fund, the small cap stock fund, and the life cycle fund.

The government security TSP fund is specifically managed by the Federal Retirement Thrift Investment Board itself. This fund's management purchases U.S. government guaranteed Treasury securities that are not marketable. Because of this conservative and safe strategy, the G Fund does not lose money. Its returns are also lower as a result of this low risk.

The common stock fund is one of the index funds that track a particular benchmark. In the case of this C fund, it invests in a stock index fund which mirrors the composition of the Standard and Poor 500 Index (S&P 500). This means it buys an index based on the various stocks of the 500 medium to larger sized American corporations. Its goal is to replicate the S&P 500s annual performance.

With the fixed income fund, it also tracks a benchmark index. This F fund's goal is to match the Barclays Capital US Aggregate Bond Index's performance. This broad based index was established to represent the bond market in the United States. As such it returns earnings commiserate with American corporate bond performances.

As the name implies, the international stock fund buys prominent stocks of international companies. It also follows a benchmark index. This particular I fund tracks the MSCI Europe, Australasia, Far East Index also known as the EAFE. Its returns are made up of gains or losses from the stock prices, income from dividends, and fluctuations in the comparative currency valuations. Regardless of what is happening in international markets, this fund and the fixed income, common stock, and small cap stock funds are always fully invested.

The small cap stock fund buys the index fund of stocks which follows the Dow Jones US Completion Total Stock Market Index. This S Fund earnings come from both dividend income received and any losses or gains in the prices of the underlying stock.

An interesting combination is the life cycle fund. These are managed to invest in the five different TSP funds. They professionally determine the allocations and percentages in each based on the retirement time frame set by the owner. There are L2020, 2030, 2040, and 2050 versions which assume that within a few years of those dates the owner will be looking to retire and be more conservatively invested.

TSP benefits are several. Government agencies are able to match employee contributions. They also have an agency automatic contribution option. Employees can make catch up contributions when they reach a certain age. These funds feature low, affordable expense ratios. All contributions made to these plans are not taxed until the point where the money is withdrawn at retirement.

Traditional IRA

The Traditional IRA is the most common type of the various individual retirement accounts available to savers for retirement. Besides this type of IRA, there are also SEP IRAs, Roth IRAs, and Self Directed IRAs. Each of these types of accounts has at least a few features in common with the original and still most popular plain IRA.

These accounts are all particularly designed to help save, grow, and fund individuals' retirements. They all permit investors to trade a variety of securities, such as stocks, mutual funds, ETFs, and bonds. Different from other kinds of brokerage and investment accounts, IRAs most importantly offer account holders tax benefits. The main difference between traditional IRAs and Roth IRAs centers on the way taxes are paid or deferred by the IRS rules.

With a Roth IRA, owners pay taxes on contributions now. All gains that account holders make in the account then accrue tax free for the entire life of the retirement savings vehicle. The traditional forms of IRAs give holders the advantage of tax deferred contributions. This means that they will not have to pay any taxes on money contributed until they withdraw them later on at retirement time. All gains that they earn in the account over the life of the IRA will be taxable at the time they withdraw them.

With all of these types of IRAs, the annual contribution limits remain the same. For tax year 2016, this amount is $5,500 for individual contributions or $11,000 for married individuals filing jointly. Catch up contributions are also the same in these various kinds of IRAs. When people reach age 50, they can make additional contributions amounting to $1,000 each year for an individual or $2,000 for married people filing jointly.

This means that instead of adding $5,500 individually to the IRA for the year, an individual could contribute $6,500 per year once he or she turns 50. Similarly married individuals would be allowed to add $13,000 per year instead of $11,000 annually once they both reach age 50.

Traditional IRAs do not feature any income limits while Roth IRAs do have these. People can be disqualified from making investments in their Roth

IRAs if they earn too much money any given tax year. Single filers are only allowed to make less than $110,000 each year. Above this income, the contribution amount which the IRS allows tapers down until the income reaches $125,000.

Once this income limit is reached, a Roth IRA contribution is disallowed for the tax year. With married filing jointly, the income maximum is higher. With under $173,000 earned for the year, the full $13,000 maximum contribution is permitted. This amount tapers off as the earnings rise to $183,000. Beyond these earnings, two individuals who are married are not allowed to utilize the Roth IRA in that particular tax year.

IRAs are different from 401(k)s, the other popular retirement savings vehicle, in several critical ways. Traditional and the other forms of IRAs can only be set up and maintained by an individual acting on his or her own behalf. 401(k)s are retirement accounts that employers set up on behalf of their employees. Many employers make partially matching contributions to their employees' 401(k) accounts.

IRAs also commonly offer superior choices in different investment possibilities than do the more limited 401(k) plans. Self directed IRAs are allowed to invest in most any type of investment that is not considered to be a collectible item. This means that Self Directed IRAs are allowed to invest in franchises, real estate, precious metals, mortgages, energy, and other alternative investment ideas.

Treasury Bills

Treasury Bills prove to be among the largest category of United States issued Treasuries. They are also called T-Bills for short. Treasury Bills have maturities of a year or less. They never pay investors interest before they mature, making them somewhat like zero coupon bonds. The government instead sells Treasury Bills at a face value discount, which causes there to be a positive yield to maturity. Numerous economists and ratings agency consider Treasury bills to be the lowest risk investments that American and foreign investors can purchase.

T-bills come issued with varying maturity dates. These typical forms of weekly Treasuries can have four week maturity dates, thirteen week maturity dates, twenty-six week maturity dates, and fifty-two week maturity dates. Every week, the government runs single price auctions for its Treasury bills. The quantity of thirteen week and twenty-six week Treasury bills available for purchase at auction are actually announced every Thursday. They are then offered on Monday and issued on the next Thursday.

Four week T-bill quantities get announced Mondays for next day auctions. The bills become issued on Thursday. Fifty-two week bills become announced only on the fourth Thursday, to be auctioned the following Tuesday and issued that Thursday. Associated purchase orders have to be received before 11 AM on Monday auctions at Treasury Direct. Minimum purchases for these T-bills are a reasonable $100, marked down from the former $1,000 minimum. The Treasury redeems T-bills that mature every Thursday. The biggest buyers of T-bills prove to be financial institutions such as banks, and primary dealers in particular. These Treasuries in their individual issue all get one of a kind CUSIP numbers.

Sometimes the Treasury cash balances are lower than usual. At these times, the Treasury often opts to sell CMB's, or cash management bills. They sell these in much the same way as T-bills, at auction with a discount. Their main difference lies in their irregular amounts and shorter terms of fewer than twenty-one days. They also possess different week days for auction, issue, and maturity. As these CMB's mature on the identical week day as typical T-bills, commonly Thursdays, they are termed on cycle.

When they instead reach maturity on another day, they are known as off cycle.

Treasury bills are regularly sold on the secondary market too. Here, they are both quoted and sold via annual discount percentages, known as a basis. The secondary market trades these T-bills heavily.

The Treasury has modernized its means of offering T-bills to investors recently. Treasury Direct is their means of selling T-bills over the Internet, so that funds can be taken out and then deposited straight to the individuals' bank accounts. This permits investors to make better rates of interest on their savings than with simple bank account interest.

Treasury Bonds

Treasury Bonds are also called T-Bonds. These financial instruments prove to be government debt issued by the United States federal government at a fixed rate of interest. Such debt securities come with maturity dates of longer than 10 years. The T-bonds offer interest payments twice per year. Because they are federal debt instruments, their earned income may only be taxed by the federal level authorities of the Internal Revenue Service. Though nothing is really risk free in the investing world, investors generally consider these bonds to be virtually without risk, since they are issued by the United States federal government. Investors perceive them to have a minimal amount of default risk.

Such Treasury Bonds turn out to be among the four kinds of Department of Treasury issued debt. They employ all of these to finance the runaway spending activities of the Federal Government. In these four debt types are the T-bills, Treasury notes, T-bonds, and TIPS Treasury Inflation Protected Securities. Each of these different debt securities is different according to both their coupon payments and their varying maturities.

Despite this, every one of them are the benchmarks for their particular fixed income categories. This is because they are American government backed, almost free of risk, and guaranteed by the revenues and tax base of the United States Treasury. In theory the Treasury can always levy higher taxes to make sure the interest and principles are repaid on these financial instruments. As they are all the lowest returns in their investment category, they are also deemed to be benchmarks for the various fixed income types of investments.

Such Treasury Bonds come standard issued with maturities which vary from 10 years to as long as 30 years. Their denominations start at $1,000 minimums. Each coupon interest payment pays out on a semi-annual basis. The bonds themselves sell via an auction system. The most of them that investors can purchase is $5 million when the bid proves to be non-competitive or as much as a full 35 percent of the entire issues when the bids turn out to be competitive.

It is important to understand what a competitive bid actually is. These types of bids declare that the bidder will accept a certain minimum interest rate bid. These become accepted according to the comparison versus the bond's set rate. With noncompetitive bids, bidders are guaranteed to receive the bonds so long as they will take them at the pre-set interest rate. Once the bonds have been auctioned off, the buyers may sell them off via the secondary market.

Investors call the active market for Treasury bonds re-sales the secondary market. Thanks to this enormous market, T-bonds and T-bills are extremely liquid. It means they can be easily resold on a constant continuous basis. It is this secondary market that causes the T-bonds' prices to gyrate considerably in the markets. This is why both yield rates and current auction rates for the T-bonds determine their prices via the secondary market.

As with all other kinds of standard bonds, these Treasury bonds will experience declining prices as the rates at auction increase. Conversely, the bonds will experience rising prices when the auction rates decrease. The reason for this inverse relationship is that the future cash flows of such bonds becomes discounted according to the higher rate.

T-bonds are also important because they are part of the yield curve for the fixed income markets. As one of the four principal investments which the American federal government offers, they make up this yield curve. The curve is critical because it pictorially displays the range of maturity yields. It is typically sloping upward since lower maturities provide lower rates than do the farther out maturity varieties. There are cases though when the farther out maturities experience peak demand. This causes the yield curve to become inverted. In such a scenario, the farther out maturities will have lower rates than the closer dated maturities.

Treasury Inflation Protected Securities (TIPS)

Treasury Inflation Protected Securities (TIPS) are a unique and useful form of Treasury issued securities. What makes them special is their expressed and close linkage to inflation levels in their coupon payments. They are set up this way to safeguard investors from the interest destroying impacts of inflation.

TIPS prove to be lower risk investments because they enjoy the expressed and unlimited backing of the U.S. government. Besides this, their par value increases at the same pace as the official rate of inflation as depicted by the CPI Consumer Price Index. The interest rate itself stays fixed with these investments.

The interest earned by these Treasury Inflation Protected Securities pays out twice a year on the same fixed dates. TIPS may be bought directly off of the U.S. government by utilizing the Treasury Direct system. This allows for simple $100 increment purchases of the TIPS in a minimum of only $100 order size. They can be obtained from the site with 30 year, 10 year, and 5 year maturity date options.

Unfortunately for the Treasury Inflation Protected Securities holders, the inflation adjustments of the TIPS bonds fall under the IRS definition of taxable income. This is the case despite the fact that investors do not realize any of those inflation adjusted gains until the point where the bonds mature or they sell out their holdings. Because of this, some investors opt to obtain their TIPS exposure by utilizing a TIPS mutual fund or ETF. Otherwise, they could simply buy and hold them within tax deferred retirement accounts like IRAs. This would save them the tax headaches of having to pay the IRS now on money they will not obtain for possibly years or even decades.

On the other hand, buying TIPS directly means that investors sidestep the costs and fees applied by mutual funds and even ETFs. TIPS bought directly also feature complete exemption from the double or even triple taxation of local income and state income taxes which some investors must pay, depending on where they reside. Residents of Puerto Rico do not have to pay any federal income taxes on these inflation adjusted gains or interest payments because of the Commonwealth's completely unique status which it enjoys within the U.S.

If investors purchased $1,000 worth of TIPS and held them through year end and received one percent coupon rates while there was no CPI measured inflation within the United States, the investors could count on obtaining $10 payments for the entire year in interest payments. Assuming inflation increases by two percent, the principal of the bond would increase by two percent or in this specific instance by $20, to reach a total value of $1,020. The coupon rate would remain locked at one percent, yet it would apply to the entire new principal amount of $1,020 to help the holder receive interest payments of $10.20.

In the extremely unlikely event that deflation reared itself, the bonds would similarly decline in total face value. Should the CPI decline by three percent, the principle would drop by three percent, or $30, resulting in a new par face value of $970 on the formerly $1,000 Treasury bond. This would reduce that next year's interest coupon payments total to $9.70.

When the bonds mature, investors would then get the principal equity which equated either to the $1,000 original par face value, or an applicably higher adjusted principal based on the CPI adjustments higher. Interest payments throughout the life of the bond will be calculated from the principal amount as it rises or falls. This does not apply to the downside if the investors hold their TIPS until they reach maturity. Investors who do not wish to hold their TIPS until this interval can choose to receive a lower amount of principal than the par face value by selling their investment via the secondary bonds market if they so desire.

Trust Account

A trust account refers to a type of account which a trustee holds on the behalf of the beneficiary. The trustee does not have the ability to utilize the funds in any personal capacity, but merely to safe keep, disburse, and invest them for the advantage of the beneficiary.

An example of this type of arrangement is when an attorney holds funds for the benefit of the client. The attorney will not be able to draw upon the funds until after a certain protocol takes place. As the attorney earns the lawyer fees, the client will have to first review and then actually approve the bill from the attorney before he or she can transfer the client funds from this trust account over to the general account of the attorney for settlement of bills.

There are a number of reasons and situations in which individuals may opt to establish a trust account. In some scenarios, people wish to disperse a pre-determined sum of money to their family or other loved ones over a number of years or throughout the remainder of their natural lives.

As a real world example, consider the following. Parents may wish to establish some trust accounts which will provide money to their dependents and/or children every month if and when they die. In such a scenario, it would normally be banking brokers who would manage such accounts. In fact these broker trustees would draw down the account values by the appropriate amount every month or year as they disbursed the either monthly or yearly funds to the beneficiaries for the individuals who originally formed the trust.

There are other common kinds of trusts as well. One of these is a property tax trust account. Such accounts will be established by entrepreneurs of real estate who own a variety of properties. Rather than have to be concerned about the property tax funds and disbursements to the appropriate taxing authorities themselves, they elect to form a trust account which will pay the taxes. This prevents the entrepreneurs from forfeiting their valuable properties because they forgot to pay the property taxes. There are a number of monetary benefits to having such an account. One of these is that estate taxes will not apply to properties contained in such a trust when the owner dies.

There are two different main types of trust accounts. These are revocable and irrevocable trusts. With revocable trusts, these represent deposit accounts whose owners chose to name one or several beneficiaries. These beneficiaries would then obtain the deposits in the account once the holder of the account died. As the name implies, such revocable trusts may be terminated, revoked, or altered on demand whenever the holder of said account wishes. In this particular case, the owner is the trustor, settlor, or grantor of the revocable trust in question. These types of trusts will be established as either informal or formal. While trustees are powerful and have a broad scope of authority over the assets of the beneficiary, they are not omnipotent, but must be bound by the laws and regulations of the jurisdiction which pertain to trust accounts.

Irrevocable trusts on the other hand are similarly deposit accounts but they are not titled in the name of the owner. Instead these become titled as an irrevocable trust for the name. The owner, trustor, settlor, or grantor also makes deposits of money or other valuable assets to the trust account. The principal difference is that the owners forfeit all ability to alter or cancel the trust once they have established it. These types of trusts also become created once an owner of a revocable type of trust dies. They can be set up through a judicial order as well, or even by a statute as appropriate.

Trust Fund

A trust fund proves to be a specific kind of legal entity. It contains property or cash which it holds to benefit another group, individual, or organization. Numerous different kinds of trusts exist. They are governed by almost as many provisions that determine how they work. Every trust fund involves three critical parties. These are the grantor, the beneficiary, and the trustee.

A grantor is the individual responsible for creating the trust fund. Grantors can do this with a variety of assets. They might give stocks, bonds, cash, mutual funds, real estate, private businesses, art, or other items of value to the fund. They also determine the terms by which the trustee will manage the fund.

Beneficiaries are the individuals who receive the benefit of the fund. The grantor sets it up on their behalf. The assets the grantor places inside of the trust fund are not the property of the beneficiary. The trustee oversees them so that the financial gain benefits this individual according to the rules laid out by the grantor at the time he or she establishes it.

Trustees are the managers of these funds. They could be an institution like a the trust department of a bank, an individual, or a number of trusted advisors. Their job is to make sure that the fund fulfills its duties spelled out by the governing law in the trust documents. Trustees typically receive small management fees. The trustee could manage the assets directly if the trust specifies this. In other cases, trustees have to pick out investment advisors who are qualified to manage money.

Trust funds come to life under the rules of the state legislature where the trust originates. Different states offer advantages to certain types of trusts. This depends on what the grantor wants to do by establishing the fund. This is why attorneys help to draft the trust documents to make sure they are correct and most advantageous. As an example, there are states which allow perpetual trusts that can continue forever. Other states make these illegal because they do now want to enfranchise a class of future generations who receive substantial wealth for which they did not work.

Special clauses may be inserted into these trusts. Among the most heavily used is the spendthrift provision. This keeps the beneficiary from accessing the fund assets to pay debts. It also allows parents to ensure that any irresponsible children they have do not find themselves destitute or homeless despite poor decisions they may make.

Trust funds provide a large number of benefits. They receive special protection from creditors. They ensure that family members follow wills after the grantor passes away. These trusts also help estates to avoid as many estate taxes as possible so that wealth can reach a greater number of generations.

Trusts can be an ideal way to ensure the continuity of a business. Sometimes business owners wish to protect a company and their employees after they die. They might still wish for the profits to benefit their heirs. In this case, the trustee would oversee the management of the business while the heirs reaped the financial rewards but could not break up or ruin the company through mismanagement.

Trusts can also be used with life insurance to transfer significant amounts of money which will benefit the heirs. A small trust could purchase a grantor life insurance. When the grantor dies, the insurance money funds the trust. The trustee will then buy investments and give the rents, interest, and dividends to the beneficiaries.

U.S. Treasury Bonds

U.S. Treasury bonds are bonds that the United States government issues so that it is capable of paying for Federal government projects. When a person or business purchases a Treasury bond, they are actually loaning the Federal government money. Like with all loans, the principal is paid back along with a set rate of interest.

Treasury bonds carry the full faith and credit guarantee of the United States government. This translates to them having very low risk, as the government is always able to print extra money to repay the loan. Another benefit to U.S. Treasury bonds lies in their being tax exempt from local and state taxes. You would still have to pay Federal taxes on all money that you make in interest.

The primary market is where the government markets its Treasury bonds through auctions. You might also buy them on the secondary market using a broker. While the government does not charge fees for partaking in their auctions, brokers likely will expect to receive fees for selling you a U.S. Treasury bond. The Treasury bonds are marketable securities since you are able to sell or buy them once you have obtained them initially. They are considered to be extremely liquid too, since the secondary market for them is very active. The prices for Treasury bonds both at auction and via the secondary market are set by their interest rates. Today's Treasury bonds can not be called back by the government before maturity, which means that you continue to receive interest until they mature.

Treasury bonds are not without their downsides. Should interest rates rise while you have a Treasury bond, then your money will be making lower interest than it might in another investment. If the interest rates were to increase, then the bond's resale price would also go down. Inflation that goes up also cuts into the Treasury bonds' interest that they pay. With practically no risk of the U.S. government defaulting on these bonds, Treasury bonds pay a low return on investment, so higher inflation rates will wipe out all or most of the interest profits as they lower the real worth of the principal and interest repayments.

If you are interested in becoming involved in government auctions to buy the Treasury bonds straight from the Federal Reserve Bank, then you can do so. Simply open a Treasury Direct Account. The government does not charge fees for such an account until it has in excess of $100,000. For these larger accounts, they collect tiny maintenance fees.

Besides Treasury bonds, the government also sells two other kinds of securities. These are Treasury bills and Treasury notes. Treasury bonds are distinguished from these other two types by their length of time till maturity. Treasury bonds do not mature until from twenty years to thirty years elapse. They do make coupon payments of principal and interest in every six month period, like with Treasury notes. Thirty years maturities prove to be more common than do the twenty year maturities with these Treasury bonds.

Unit Trust Fund

A Unit Trust Fund is effectively a vehicle in which individuals can invest their money. Investors can sink their funds into these investments using a range of financial service providers. These include an investment management company, a stock broker, and even sometimes a local or larger bank. These Unit Trust Funds are essentially a large pooled reserve of capital. They permit assortments of investors to combine their liquid assets to invest them. All of the investments together amount to the aggregate assets of a fund.

It is generally the case that such a Unit Trust Fund will have the legal structure like a mutual fund but which is unincorporated. They permit the funds to contain these shared assets and ensure that all profits become dispersed directly back to the individual unit share owners rather than reinvesting them. Such an investment fund becomes established under the auspices of a trust deed. Each investor is literally a member of the trust fund beneficiaries.

A Unit Trust Fund's success comes down to how experienced and professional a management company which runs it actually proves to be. The managers are allowed to invest in a wide range of investments. Some of the most typical of these include mortgages, securities such as stocks and bonds, real estate property, and cash equivalents such as CDs and money market funds.

The Unit Trust concept is widely utilized in Great Britain and a number of former British colonies and current day British territories. Among these are Jersey and Guernsey of the British Channel Islands, the Isle of Man, Ireland, Fiji, Australia, New Zealand, Singapore, Malaysia, South Africa, Kenya, and Namibia. Within the United Kingdom at least, unit trusts are interchangeable with the phrase mutual fund, though they are quite different from the American versions of mutual funds.

With regards to the assets of a Unit Trust Fund and their value, this can be expressed by taking the price per unit and multiplying it times the amount of units. Naturally there will be expenses taken off of this figure before it is considered final. Some of these expenses include management fees, trading transaction fees, and other relevant costs.

It is the unit trust fund managers who manage the trust in order to realize the greatest potential returns and profits. Trustees will be assigned in order to make certain the manager of the fund is properly pursuing the various objectives and goals of the Unit Trust Fund. Ultimately these managers work for the unit holders who have all rights to the assets of the trust in question. In between the stakeholders in the trust and the manager of the fund in question are the registrars. These middlemen are merely a type of liaison standing in between the two parties. They carry out a number of administrative duties.

These unit trust funds turn out to be open-ended in nature. This means that as new or existing investors add additional money to the trust, then more units will be created at the unit buying price that is current. Similarly, as holders sell their units for cash, an equivalent amount of the fund assets will be sold off at the present selling price per unit.

The income of the fund managers is realized by the bid and offer spread. This represents the difference between the price of buying the units and the price of selling them. This spread will vary from one moment to another and be based on the types of assets the fund manages. It might be merely a couple of basis points for those assets which can be liquidated expeditiously and simply, as with government sovereign bonds. The spread could be even five percent or still higher for assets which are more difficult to buy or sell. Real estate properties are examples of less liquid assets that take longer to transact.

Value Investing

Value investing is the strategy that Benjamin Graham developed for investing in stocks. Warren Buffet later made it famous after he left Graham's company and went on to found Berkshire Hathaway. Buying stocks this way involved a level of discipline practiced by insurance underwriters. The method focuses on several key ideas. Investors have to consider risks involved carefully, avoid stocks which show a high amount of uncertainty, and allow a margin of safety.

Graham developed his different investing techniques while managing money as President of his Graham-Newman Corporation. He focused on net working capital investments, arbitrage, diversification, and tangible assets. Investors continue to use all of these but the first one over seventy years later.

Net working capital originally functioned as a cornerstone of value investing until changes in transparency rules and market technology made it obsolete. Net working capital investments were those where the stock's shares traded at a large 30% or higher discount to their amount of working capital.

The idea was that a value investor could buy dollar investments for effectively 70 cents or less. Some of these companies failed. This was mitigated by diversifying into many different stocks. On a combined basis, these companies brought Graham and his investors good returns. Warren Buffet utilized this category of investments heavily in his early years running the Buffet Partnership that eventually became Berkshire Hathaway.

Arbitrage proved to be the value investors' secret weapon. Graham passionately believed arbitrage would routinely provide 20% annual returns. This boosted the total return on the overall value investing portfolio. Arbitrage seeks to make money on discrepancies in price with little or even no risk.

If a company makes an offer for a rival at $60 per share, but the shares trade at $57, there is a $3 price discrepancy between that point and when the deal closes. This amounts to possibly 5% that investors can acquire in a matter of a few months. Assuming the deal closes, there is no risk in this trade. Value investors simply use arbitrage as a way to profit from a security and the money time value that is literally undervalued.

Diversification remains a critical component of Graham's investing strategy. He believed in diversifying into as many individual investments as made sense. He also practiced diversification into different kinds of asset classes. Value investing puts a certain percentage into common stocks, preferred stocks, mutual funds (which did not yet exist when Graham created the strategy), and bonds. This went along with the main premise that first investors must avoid losing their money. Receiving a good return on investment money is secondary to this idea.

Tangible assets is another value investing principle that still holds today. Graham was interested in the actual physical assets that lay behind his common or preferred stocks and bonds. This might include factories, office buildings, equipment, real estate, or rail cars. He would only buy into companies whose assets were great enough to fully back up the principle and dividend or interest payments. They would have to liquidate these assets to get back their investment money. Graham told those who valued invested to constantly look at the bonds they held and be prepared to change to other bonds if they had stronger assets.

Benjamin Graham and value investing also proved to be among the earliest groups to practice tactical asset allocation. If investors studied and determined stocks were overvalued, they should sell stocks and move money into bonds. When stocks were undervalued, he counseled investors to sell bonds and go heavier into stocks. This is still a cornerstone idea of investing today.

Weighted Average Cost of Capital (WACC)

Weighted average cost of capital (WACC) refers to a calculation of the cost of a capital for a company. It involves every category of the company's capital being weighed proportionately. Each source of capital for the relevant corporation will be considered by this designation. This means that preferred and common stock, bonds and all types of longer-term debt will all be included in the WACC calculation. It will go up with the rate of return on equity and beta increases. When the WACC increases, this means that the risk has increased while the valuation for a firm has decreased.

Calculating weighted average cost of capital requires taking each part of the capital components and multiplying them by their appropriate proportional weight. These individual calculations are then added together to come up with the WACC.

Companies can finance their needs through one of two main types of funding. This is either via equity issuing in the form of primarily stock shares or through debt issuance as with bonds. This measurement actually weights appropriately the two main forms of corporate financing, with each weighted according to its relevant utilization in a particular situation. It allows companies and analysts to decide how much every dollar they are financing will cost them in interest, making it imminently practical.

The reasons this is important are evident. The holders of equity and lenders of a corporation will demand specific minimal returns on their capital or lent money they have delivered. This is why WACC proves to be so useful. It shows the cost of capital for both the stake holders (as equity owners) and the lenders (as the debt holders). This means that both groups will be able to understand the levels and amounts in returns they can anticipate receiving. Another way of looking at the weighted average cost of capital is that this is the opportunity cost of any investor for assuming the risk which investing in the corporation entails.

A firm's WACC represents the all around return on capital for the company. This means that the directors of the corporation will commonly utilize the numbers internally to make appropriate decisions for the organization. Such decisions might include evaluating opportunities for expanding the business or the financial practicality of engaging in an acquisition or a merger.

It is helpful to consider examples to best understand this complex concept of weighted average cost of capital. Assume that a corporation is a money pond. Money comes into this pond out of two separate streams which are the sources. These streams represent the equity and the debt of the company. Money which the daily business operations bring in does not count as another source. The reason for this logic is that once a firm pays down its debt, any remaining money that they do not pay out as dividends or for share buybacks becomes what analysts call retained earnings held in trust for the shareholders.

Consider lenders that want eight percent return for their funds they loaned to a given company. At the same time, the stakeholders possessing the stock share may want a minimum 16 percent return on their investments or they will not hold onto the shares of the company. This means that the projects which the corporation funds using its money pond will need to provide an annual recurring return of 12 percent so that both their lenders and equity holders will remain happy. This 12 percent represents the weighted average cost of capital.

Going back to our original example of the money pond, if it contained $100 in debt holder money and $100 in investments from shareholders, the company might invest $200 in one of its projects. They would then require an annual return of 12 percent total, or $24 from the project funded by the pond. This would mean that $16 of this return was for the share holders while $8 of the total return was for the debt holders.

Working Capital

Working Capital is a company metric. This proves to be a useful corporate measurement for two significant purposes. On the one hand it is a metric for discerning shorter-term financial health. On the other hand, it is also a means of ascertaining the firm's efficiency. The equation for working capital is current assets minus current liabilities. The working capital ratio is defined as current assets divided by current liabilities. This reveals if a corporation possesses sufficient shorter term assets to cover its shorter term time frame debt liabilities. Sometimes this concept is also referred to as net working capital.

When the number comes in at less than one, this reveals a negative working capital (also known sometimes as W/C). Any number which proves to be higher than two means that the company does not sufficiently invest its excessive assets. The most highly desired ratio proves to be a figure between 1.2 and 2.0.

The sobering facts are that when the firm's current assets are not greater than its current liabilities, it can run afoul of its creditors and the ability to repay them over the shorter term. In the worst case, bankruptcy can ultimately result. Decreasing working capital ratios throughout an extended time frame serve as a prescient warning that should be carefully and thoroughly investigated by analysts and would-be investors alike. It might be that the critical company metrics of sales volumes are steadily declining over time. This would mean that the account receivables amounts would go down and continuously deteriorate little by little.

This figure also reveals to investors and analysts alike the underlying operational efficiency of the firm. Money which is tied down in the form of inventory or which other clients still have not paid to the firm in due receivables will not be available to pay down company bills and other obligations. This means that if a company has consistently slow collections, it will be revealed as a rising number in the working capital figure. The best way to understand this is through contrasting the figure from one time period through to another one or even several like time periods. Slower collections can mean that the company and its operations have potentially fatal flaws.

It is important for investors to remember that high working capital ratios do not signal good things for the company in question. Instead, it means either that they are not sufficiently investing their excess reserves, or that they possess too large an inventory. Investors know all too well that they can quickly ascertain the company balance sheet strength by considering three important categories of quality. These include asset performance, working capital adequacy, and capitalization structure.

This means that analysts can discern the real liquidity of the firm and its efficiency with regards to the current position of the firm. Companies utilize an analytical tool to successfully accomplish this. It is called the firm's cash conversion cycle. Still, while companies like to bandy about this number in such important arenas as their annual reports, the quantity of working capital does not provide much insight on the quality of the liquidity position of the firm in question.

The cash conversion cycle proves to be the gold standard analytical tool for assessing the investment grade quality for the two crucial assets of the firm, the accounts receivable and the inventory. This CCC cycle is made up of three standards. These include the trade receivables category, the trade payables category, and the associated ratios pertaining to the inventory turnover. The three parts may be detailed in a number of days or a number of times each year.

Xetra

The Xetra is a Frankfurt, Germany based trading system. What makes it so significant is that it is a completely electronic platform for trading German stocks. The Deutsche Borse first launched this platform for handling the stock trades back in 1997. This system provides broad order depth and greater flexibility for viewing the German markets. Traders can watch and access trading in German stocks, bonds, funds, commodities contracts, and warrants on the Xetra system.

The system has proven itself well enough to be adapted by other stock exchanges throughout Europe and the world since it began operating. The creators of Xetra originated it for the Frankfurt stock exchange. Since then, it has spread to other national stock exchanges in Vienna, Austria; Dublin, Ireland; and Shanghai, China.

Part of the success of Xetra lay in its relatively early launch. As such, it became among the first of the great electronic and global trading systems. Making German capital markets more accessible for foreigners and their investment proved to be one of its key benefits. Xetra has expanded to handle over 90% of all of the stock trades for the Frankfurt Stock Exchange.

The Frankfurt Stock Exchange represents Germany's largest trading exchange. Also known as the FRA, it is based in Frankfurt. Deutsche Borse owns and operates Xetra and the Frankfort Stock Exchange along with all of Germany's other trading exchanges. Thanks in part to the success of the Xetra, this exchange represents one of the most efficient and biggest facilities for trading markets on earth. It is also among the oldest stock exchanges around the globe.

The Frankfurt Exchange handles practically all of Germany's trading. It also manages a significant portion of all trading in the whole of Europe. The FRA makes a large portion of its profits from the Xetra trading system. The many foreign investors flowing in because of Xetra are responsible for a significant share of the profits. FRA is open each day of the week from 9:30am till 5:30pm.

There are a number of important stock indices based on the Frankfurt Stock

Exchange and run by Xetra. Among these are the DAX, the Eurostoxx 50 and the VDAX. Xetra DAX is Germany's equivalent of the Dow Jones Industrial Average in America and the Financial Times Stock Exchange 100 in London. This blue chip index of their stock market exchange contains the 30 most important German companies that are traded on the FRA.

Deutsche Borse states that the performance of these companies is measured according to market capitalization and order book volume. All of the prices from the DAX are taken off of the Xetra trading system. While the DAX is an important index with its 30 Prime Standard companies represented, this does not equate to the strength of the whole German economy.

Prime Standard companies listed on the Xetra DAX and other important Frankfurt exchanges such as SDAX, MDAX, and TecDAX have to attain international transparency standards. This means they have to use international accounting standards as with US-GAAP or IAS. Their quarterly reports and ad hoc disclosure must be in German as well as in English. They must hold minimally one analyst conference every year. Finally, these companies must publish a financial calendar.

Xetra computes the DAX index values once every second. It has done this since the technology began managing all electronic functions for the DAX on January 1, 2006. After the Xetra closes each weekday, the DAX index keeps trading under the name L-DAX. These prices are based on the FRA trading venue floor trades and continue until 5:45pm. At this point, the L/E-DAX Index picks up trading until 8pm.

Yield

In business and finance, yield is the word that states the quantity of cash that comes back to a security's owners. It is measured independently of variations in price. It proves to be a percentage of total return. It is used for measuring the return rates of fixed income investments, such as bonds, bills, strips, notes, and zero coupons; stocks, including common, convertible, and preferred; and various other insurance and investment hybrid products like annuities.

Yield can mean different things in varying situations. It is sometimes figured up as an IRR, or Internal Rate of Return, or alternatively as a ratio. Yield describes an investment owner's entire return or a part of the income.

The end result of the many differences in yield is that they can not be compared one against the other. This is because they are not all the same from one branch of finance and investments to another. You could see numerous different formulas for figuring up yield used by different investments and groups.

Bonds are a classic example of this. Nominal yield is also known as coupon yield. This proves to be the face value of a bond divided into the annual interest total. Current yield instead is those interest payments over the bond's price on the spot market.

A yield to maturity is the internal rate of return on the bond cash flow, including the bond principal when maturity arrives plus the interest received, and the purchase price. Finally, a bond's yield to call is the bond's cash flow internal rate of return if it is called in by the company at their earliest opportunity.

Bonds yields are unusual in that they vary inversely to the price of the bond. Should a bond price decline, then the yield will rise. If instead the rates of interest drop, then the bond's price will go up in general.

Some securities come with real yields. TIPS are a primary example of this. A real yield means that the face value of the instrument will be adjusted upwards compared to the CPI inflation index. It would then be set against this principal that is adjusted to make certain that an investor makes a better return than the rate of inflation.

This ensures that his or her purchasing power is protected. TIPS are one rare investment that will not allow investors to lose money if they purchased them in the auction and keep them until they mature, either as a result of deflation, meaning falling prices, or inflation, signifying rising prices over time.

Yield to Maturity (YTM)

Yield to Maturity is also widely known in investment and analyst circles by its acronym YTM, as well as by the phrases book yield and redemption yield. This represents the aggregate return which investors can expect to receive for a bond if they keep the security until the end of its actual life. This is why YTM is generally called a longer term bond yield even though it is still expressed as a rate per year. Another way of saying this is that this proves to be the investment's internal rate of return for the bond if the owner keeps it all the way through maturity. This assumes of course that the bond issuer makes all of its payments both on time and in the full amounts contracted.

In order to understand the Yield to Maturity calculations, it is critical to realize that the formula assumes all coupon payments the issuer makes will be exactly reinvested for the rate of the current yield of the bond. The formula similarly considers the bond's par value, current price on the market, term to maturity, and coupon interest rate. All of this makes the YTM a complicated yet good formula for determining the return of a bond. It allows investors to effectively compare and contrast those bonds which possess varying coupon rates and maturity dates.

There are several different ways to figure out the Yield to Maturity. It is a complicated formula so many investors simply fall back on pre-printed and -figured bond yield tables. Determining the exact YTM requires either a software program or the use of a financial or business calculator. This is because the value for a basis point drops as the price for a bond increases in an inverse manner. Many firms actually calculate YTM for six month time frames as well as on an annual basis. They do this because most coupon payments take place twice per year.

A significant difference between Yield to Maturity and the current yield lies in the fact that the YTM takes into account money's time value, while the simplified current yield computations will not. This is why investors often prefer to utilize the YTM instead of the current yield when they are crunching number on bond returns to compare and contrast with other bond issues and different types of investments.

There are a number of similar yet still variations on the classical Yield to Maturity figure. These should never be confused with the true YTM. Among these are the Yield to call (YTC), Yield to put (YTP), and the Yield to worst (YTW). Yields to call go with the assumption that the bond issuer will recall the bond by repurchasing it in advance of it reaching maturity. This assumes that the resulting cash flow period will be shortened. Yield to put is much like the YTC, only the seller is allowed to and may sell the bond back to its issuer on a specific date for a pre-determined price. Finally, Yield to worst means that the bonds in question can be put, called, or even exchanged. This is why YTW bonds usually have the smallest yields from the three variations on YTM and the YTM rate itself.

There are some important limitations to the utility of Yield to Maturity as a measurement for comparing and contrasting various bonds against other bonds and other forms of investment classes as well. With YTM, these calculations never take into account the actual taxes which investors will have to pay on the bonds. This is why YTM is sometimes called the gross redemption yield. These calculations for yield also do not factor in either selling or buying costs for the bonds themselves.

It is also important to keep in mind that YTM is limited by the fact that both it and current yields are estimate calculations. They can not ever be 100 percent accurate or reliable. The true returns will vary with the realized price of a bond when a holder sells it. The prices of such bonds can vary significantly as the market actually determines them (and not the issuer). Such variations in the value of a bond and the price for which it is sold may impact the YTM substantially. They more drastically impact the current yield calculations and measurement in the end.

Other Financial Books by Thomas Herold

The Money Deception - What Banks & Governments Don't Want You to Know

High Credit Score Secrets - The Smart Raise And Repair Guide to Excellent Credit

Other Books in the Herold Financial IQ Series

99 Financial Terms Every Beginner, Entrepreneur & Business Should Know

Personal Finance Terms

Real Estate Terms

Bank & Banking Terms

Corporate Finance Terms

Investment Terms

Economics Terms

Retirement Terms

Stock Trading Terms

Accounting Terms

Debt & Bankruptcy Terms

Mortgage Terms

Small Business Terms

Wall Street Terms

Laws & Regulations

Financial Acronyms

www.ingramcontent.com/pod-product-compliance
Lightning Source LLC
Chambersburg PA
CBHW071543210326
41597CB00019B/3105